L.A. City Limits

G

THE GEORGE GUND FOUNDATION
IMPRINT IN AFRICAN AMERICAN STUDIES

The George Gund Foundation has endowed
this imprint to advance understanding of
the history, culture, and current issues
of African Americans.

L.A. City Limits

African American Los Angeles from
the Great Depression to the Present

Josh Sides

UNIVERSITY OF CALIFORNIA PRESS

Berkeley / Los Angeles / London

University of California Press
Berkeley and Los Angeles, California

University of California Press, Ltd.
London, England

Portions of chapter 5 appeared in " 'You Understand My Condition':
The Civil Rights Congress in the Los Angeles African-American Commu-
nity, 1946–1952," *Pacific Historical Review* 67, no. 2 (May 1998): 233–257.
© American Historical Association, Pacific Coast Branch.

Portions of chapter 3 appeared in "Battle on the Home Front: African
American Shipyard Workers in World War II Los Angeles," *California
History* 75, no. 3 (fall 1996): 250–263. © California Historical Society.

Library of Congress Cataloging-in-Publication Data

Sides, Josh, 1972–.
    L.A. city limits : African American Los Angeles from the Great Depres-
sion to the present / Josh Sides.
        p.   cm.
Includes bibliographical references and index.
    ISBN 0–520–24830–9 (pbk : alk. paper)
    1. African Americans—California—Los Angeles—Social conditions—
20th century.   2. African Americans—California—Los Angeles—
Economic conditions—20th century. 3. Los Angeles (Calif.)—Race
relations. 4. Los Angeles (Calif.)—Social conditions—20th century.
5. Los Angeles (Calif.)—Economic conditions—20th century. I. Title:
LA city limits. II. Title: Los Angeles city limits. III. Title.
    F869.L89 N4 2003
    979.4'9400496073—dc21

                                                    2003003888
                                                        CIP

Manufactured in the United States of America
13   12   11   10   09   08   07   06
10   9   8   7   6   5   4   3   2   1

The paper used in this publication is both acid-free and totally
chlorine-free (TCF). It meets the minimum requirements of ANSI/NISO
Z39.48–1992 (R 1997) (*Permanence of Paper*). ⊗

To Henry and Sudie Sides, my first and best teachers

Contents

Illustrations

Acknowledgments

Like most historians, I have accrued a number of debts while writing this book, and it gives me great pleasure to thank a few of the people who have helped me along the way. As a graduate student at the University of California, Los Angeles, I was fortunate to be surrounded by outstanding colleagues and mentors. It would be difficult to overstate my gratitude to Janice Reiff, my graduate advisor, who always took time to ask tough questions and point me in new directions, despite her tremendous workload. She has been an impeccable mentor, gently guiding me toward greater sophistication without a shred of condescension, even when it was warranted. Additional graduate committee members John Laslett, Eric Sundquist, and Brenda Stevenson all provided invaluable advice at the early stages of research and writing. John Laslett was particularly generous with his time, closely reading early drafts of several chapters and sharing his immense knowledge of labor history. From San Francisco, Bob Cherny offered vital support and encouragement through every stage of the book, for which I am grateful. I am also indebted to the UCLA History Department for the generous financial support I received during the last two years of graduate school. The Historical Society of Southern California complemented that support by awarding me a travel grant to wrap up my East Coast research. Fellow graduate students Lisa Marovich, Jen Koslow, Allison Varzally, and Jane Dabel were amazingly supportive intellectual companions through my time at UCLA and beyond.

I had the great fortune of spending the 2000–2001 academic year at the Humanities Research Institute (HRI) at the University of California, Irvine, as a Kevin Starr Fellow in California Studies. The fellowship allowed me to devote an entire year to full-time research and writing without teaching responsibilities, an uncommonly generous postdoctoral appointment. In addition to giving me the time and space to work, HRI provided a rigorous and very exciting intellectual environment in which I learned a great deal. I am very grateful to Kevin Starr, Dante Noto, David Goldberg, Debra Massey Sanchez, Susan Feign, Rosemarie Neumann, Natalie Baquerizo, Brian Rowatt, and the entire HRI staff for making it such a wonderful year.

Some of the best feedback on this project has come from my colleagues in the Huntington Library's Los Angeles History Research Group. Ralph Shaffer, Tom Sitton, and Michael Engh all provided helpful comments on my fourth chapter. Becky Nicolaides read several chapters closely and asked particularly tough questions that have made this book much better. Mark Wild has been a model of collegiality and a great friend. Douglas Flamming generously read an early draft of the entire manuscript and challenged me to push in new directions that I had not considered. William Deverell has consistently helped guide me through the slow points, reminding me that the book mattered. In addition to the Research Group, the Huntington Library itself played an important role in the genesis of this book. Susi Krasnoo, Christopher Adde, and the entire staff gave me space to work, allowing me to immerse myself in the library's remarkable collections. Curator William P. Frank directed me to pertinent resources in the Huntington's vast holdings. And I benefited immensely from conversations with Lisbeth Haas, Michael Engh, and other scholars who were also working at the Huntington while I was there. I am most grateful for the time I got to spend with Clark Davis, whose sudden death has saddened me, and his countless friends and colleagues, deeply.

As a rule, historians owe a great debt to librarians, and I am certainly no exception. Archivists and librarians at the Schomburg Center for Research in Black Culture in Harlem and at the National Archives and Library of Congress in Washington, D.C., were extremely helpful, often working under time constraints imposed by my tight travel schedules. Sarah Cooper and Mary Tyler at the Southern California Library for Social Studies and Research helped me identify relevant resources on South Central and directed me toward my first oral history interviews. At UCLA's Young Research Library, Valerie Rom-Hawkins cheerfully made sure that what I needed was there; and at Special Collections, Octavio Olvera and Jeff Rankin helped me navigate their tremendous collection. Robert Marshall, at the Urban Archives Center of California State University, Northridge, pointed me toward excellent resources and shared his knowledge of Los Angeles labor history. Carolyn Cole at the Los Angeles Public Library's Photo Collection directed me through the collection that contained most of the photographs in this book.

I have also benefited greatly from the personal memories of African American migrants. Though they represent just a fragment of the research completed for this book, the interviews I conducted were immensely rewarding, both intellectually and emotionally. The late Barbara Hampton, of the vibrant Watts Senior Citizens Center, graciously allowed me to conduct oral history interviews at the center. I am sad that she will not get to see the final book. I owe a huge debt of gratitude to those interviewees who patiently shared their memories with me, including O'Neil Cannon, Mary Cuthbertson, Sylvester Gibbs, Arvella Grigsby, Dorothy Healey, Evelyn Hendrix, Andrew Murray, Chester Murray, Ersey O'Brien, and the late Donald Wheeldin. Mr. Wheeldin and Mr. O'Brien graciously opened their homes and hearts to me, and I will be forever grateful.

At Cal Poly Pomona, Barbara Way gave me much-needed release time to complete this book, and my colleagues in the History Department have been immensely supportive. Michael Bufalino, project coordinator at the Center for Geographic Information Science Research, made the maps for this book based on a census data set created by Philip J. Ethington, Anne Marie Kooistra, and Edward De Young at the University of Southern California *(Los Angeles County Union Census Tract Data Series, 1940–1990)*. I owe special thanks as well to the Minnesota Population Center at the University of Minnesota, which created the Integrated Public Use Microdata Series (IPUMS), an important source of demographic data in my research. Student assistant Jessica Durkin patiently helped me compile the bibliography for the book.

The University of California Press has been a great partner in this undertaking. Monica McCormick's enthusiasm for the project kept me motivated. Superb close readings by readers Laura Pulido and Lawrence B. de Graaf pushed me to sharpen my arguments and rethink my assumptions. Mary Renaud greatly improved this book at the copyediting stage, and Rachel Berchten pulled it all together. Randy Heyman faithfully kept me up to date on the press's progress and guided this first-time author quite patiently.

Close friends and family have been indispensable for my happiness and sanity while completing this book. Patrick Byrne, Scott Herndon,

Introduction

Mary Trimble stood on the porch of her Los Angeles home in 1950 and spoke openly with a local newspaper reporter about her decision to migrate to the city seven years earlier. Born in 1898 in Keithville, Louisiana—a heavily segregated rural town in the heart of America's infamous "black belt"—Trimble understood that her educational and occupational opportunities there had been hopelessly limited. Educated in separate and patently unequal schools, confined to the most menial and degrading jobs, and always fearful of wanton racial violence, African Americans in Keithville and other small towns throughout the American South had to wear what black poet Paul Laurence Dunbar once called "the mask": that veil of racial inferiority and servility mandated by Jim Crow society. Trimble may have worn the mask, but it never became part of her: "I knew my place and kept it. Of course I knew better but I never let on."[1] Trimble's family later moved to Texas in search of better opportunities, but Mary, like virtually all black women across the country, still found that domestic service was the only field open to her.

Yet, during World War II, Trimble had a revelation that changed her life forever. "I remember the day in '43," she recounted, "when I decided to come here." Shortly after beginning her shift cleaning house for another "rich family,"

the woman of the house told me, "Now, you can draw Mr. Harry's bath. He'll be home right away." Suddenly it struck me. "Mr." Harry was 18. The family had lots of money, but they were afraid that he'd be drafted so they put him to work in a war plant. I just decided, sudden-like, I was through "Missing" and "Mistering"— that I'd go where I could get a job in a war plant myself.

With little hesitation, Trimble bade farewell to the South and migrated to Los Angeles, where she quickly found work at the booming California Shipbuilding Company (Calship) yard on Terminal Island, in the bustling port of Los Angeles at the southernmost tip of the city. No longer forced to clean house for a living, Trimble had joined the thousands of other black and white migrants entrusted with the awesome responsibility of building the "arsenal of democracy"—and, as she remembered, "I liked it."

This is a book about people like Mary Trimble and the cities that were transformed by their migration. Bitterly resentful of southern racial bigotry and brutality, enticed by well-advertised job opportunities in the nation's booming defense industries, and cautiously optimistic about the potential for racial equality in America's big cities, African Americans launched an exodus from the South that would continue uninterrupted for twenty-five years. During the 1950s and 1960s, the violent white backlash that accompanied the civil rights movement in the South stimulated further black out-migration. Ultimately, almost five million black people left the South between 1940 and 1970.[2] Not until the 1970s, as opportunities dwindled in the urban North and West, and racial violence waned in the South, did the exodus finally abate.[3]

In their migrations, African Americans not only radically altered their own lives and opportunities but also permanently transformed urban America. From Charleston and Mobile in the South, to Chicago, Cleveland, and Detroit in the North, to Seattle, Portland, San Francisco, San Diego, and Los Angeles in the West, America's cities became increasingly black, a trend with far-reaching social, political, and economic implications.[4] Between 1940 and 1970, the black population in Los Angeles grew faster than in any other large northern or western city, climbing from 63,744 to almost 763,000. Although this phenomenal growth has slowed considerably since the 1970s, Los Angeles now has the seventh largest black population in the country.[5]

World War II was a critical turning point for blacks in America.[6] The deepening labor shortage, coupled with the vast new demand for industrial output, forced the nation's defense manufacturers to look beyond their traditionally white, male, and often skilled labor pool. Shipbuilding, aircraft, steel, and automobile plants retooled for war production; and a host of other large industrial manufacturers were reorganized to speed production by "deskilling" the production process.[7] Lower skill requirements and greater labor demand opened the door of industrial employment to women and African Americans, who had long been denied both the training and the experience necessary for such work.

African Americans also benefited from President Franklin Delano Roosevelt's Executive Order 8802, issued in 1941, which forbade discrimination in wartime defense industries and created the Fair Employment Practice Committee (FEPC) to investigate charges of racial discrimination. Issued as a direct response to black labor leader A. Philip Randolph's call for a fifty-thousand-person march on Washington unless blacks were given wartime job opportunities, Executive Order 8802 was hailed as a clear victory for racial equality. Although the FEPC finally proved a highly contentious and sometimes ineffective tool for resolving discrimination issues, its symbolic importance for African Americans is difficult to overstate. Not since Congress passed the Thirteenth, Fourteenth, and Fifteenth Amendments during Reconstruction had the federal government significantly intervened on behalf of African Americans. The U.S. Supreme Court, in fact, had consistently reaffirmed the constitutional foundations of racial discrimination in several landmark decisions. Thus, FDR's executive order, despite its shortcomings, was emboldening for African Americans throughout the nation because it demonstrated that the federal government, when compelled, could be a potent force for desegregation. This notion, combined with the actual opening of thousands of well-paid industrial jobs to blacks, proved to be a heady mix for those concerned about racial equality in the United States.

Throughout the country, black leaders, black workers, and both black and white scholars expressed guarded optimism about the future of black America. In his exhaustive *An American Dilemma*, published in 1944, Gunnar Myrdal predicted that "there is bound to be a redefinition of the Negro's status in America as a result of this war." St. Clair Drake and Horace Cayton's famous study of black Chicago—which explored the myriad and truly crippling effects of racial discrimination in urban America—ended on an optimistic note: "Important changes are on their way and the present system may reform into something quite different which will give Negroes many—if not all—the opportunities now denied them."[8] The potential for phenomenal change was even more pronounced in Los Angeles than it was in Chicago or other northern cities where blacks had long been an important part of the industrial labor force. In Los Angeles, employers' preference for Mexican labor in manual occupations had traditionally circumscribed job opportunities for blacks, relegating most African Americans to poorly paid and sometimes degrading positions in the city's robust service sector. It was little wonder, then, that Los Angeles Urban League director Floyd Covington referred to Executive Order 8802 as the "Second Emancipation for the American Negro" in his 1943 address to the National Urban League.[9]

The optimism with which blacks viewed the future was actually borne out in many concrete ways in the two decades after World War II. In absolute and relative terms, black employment increased in several sectors of the economy, particularly in manufacturing industries. Across the country, and particularly in Los Angeles, blacks purchased homes in rising numbers. And postwar executive, judicial, and legislative assaults on Jim Crow crippled the legal basis of segregation in schools, in neighborhoods, and at work. These postwar advances culminated in the passage of the Civil Rights Act of 1964, which promised to finally stamp out workplace discrimination, the greatest remaining barrier to economic equality for African Americans. As historians have increasingly recognized, the World War II and postwar years represented a window of opportunity to end or, at the very least, dramatically reduce racial inequality in America.[10] This certainly seemed the case in Los Angeles, ranked in a 1964 National Urban League survey as the most desirable city in America for black people.[11]

But the violent race riots that engulfed urban America in the 1960s shattered the notion that racial equality was imminent. And perhaps none was more shattering than the Watts riot of 1965, not only because it was the most destructive racial clash since the Detroit riot of 1943 but also because it happened in Los Angeles, a city long considered uniquely hospitable to blacks. It was also the first in a new wave of race riots that spread to Chicago, Tampa, Cincinnati, Atlanta, Newark, Detroit, and numerous smaller cities and communities in the late 1960s. As images of young black men burning and looting urban America continued to flash across television screens, few could doubt the Kerner Commission's famous 1968 assertion that "the nation is rapidly moving toward two increasingly separate Americas," one white, one black. The Kerner Commission, Los Angeles's McCone Commission, and the Department of Labor's Office of Policy Planning and Research, which published the controversial "Moynihan report" on the black family in 1965, all offered explanations for racial unrest in America, including a severely compromised black family structure, poor educational and job opportunities, and an increased disaffectedness among black youth.[12] By the 1970s, social scientists had identified an urban "underclass," a permanently poor and predominantly black stratum of American society; in the 1980s, they debated the relative importance of behavior, public policy, culture, family, and ecology in creating and shaping that underclass.[13]

Although these debates produced important insights, they too often buried the critical historical dimensions of their subject. Indeed, from the viewpoint of these studies of the underclass, the era of black optimism and advance was not only absent but also scarcely imaginable. Fundamental questions were left unanswered: Why did the end of de jure racial inequality not produce de facto racial equality in urban America? And, more specifically, why did the wartime predictions of imminent economic parity with whites not come true for the majority of African Americans?

In the past decade, scholars, and particularly historians, have made great strides toward answering these questions. For example, in their investigations of racial politics in Boston, in New York, and at the national level, Ronald Formisano, Jonathan Rieder, Jim Sleeper, Thomas Byrne Edsall, and Mary D. Edsall have emphasized the retreat of liberalism among working-class whites, a group disproportionately affected by court-mandated desegregation in schools and in the workplace.[14] Others, such as Douglas Massey, Nancy Denton, Arnold Hirsch, and William Julius Wilson, have explored the willful re-creation of the ghetto in postwar Chicago, emphasizing the role of real estate agents, civic leaders, and white homeowners in perpetuating residential segregation.[15] Perhaps the most comprehensive explanation is Thomas J. Sugrue's study of postwar Detroit, which attributes persistent racial inequality to deindustrialization, grassroots conservatism, and impoverished public policy.[16]

Although these narratives of the urban crisis present disparate viewpoints about the persistence of postwar racial inequality, they share one constant: they all unfold in the northern and northeastern United States. Their near-exclusive focus on northern cities has had the effect of obscuring the critical role that place has played in shaping postwar opportunities for urban blacks. Chicago and Detroit are not, as it turns out, synonymous with urban America.[17] In fact, the modern history of Los Angeles has unfolded in ways that diverge, sharply at times, from the histories of America's "rust belt" cities. African Americans' pursuit of equality and opportunity in Los Angeles has been shaped by at least three distinctive features of the city's history: its diverse racial composition, its dynamic economic growth, and its dispersive spatial arrangement.

First, Los Angeles's magnetic appeal to successive waves of Latin American, Asian, and European immigrants ensured that the black freedom struggle would develop in a strikingly multiracial context. Thanks to a growing body of rich scholarship by Kevin Leonard, Douglas Monroy, George Sánchez, Mark Wild, and others, we have a much clearer understanding of the contours of Los Angeles's diverse population, including its largest minority group, Mexicans.[18] Yet the extent to which the multiracial character of the city affected opportunity for African Americans is generally less understood.

The effect of this racial diversity on blacks in Los Angeles has not been static; rather, it has changed through both time and space. Before World War II, most African Americans in Los Angeles lived among and interacted with Mexicans, Japanese, Italians, Jews, and the city's small Chinese population. This arrangement, coupled with the vast size and low population density of the city, mitigated the harshest social and psychological effects of racial segregation by diffusing the racial animosity usually reserved exclusively for blacks in other cities. Economically, however, the multiracial character of the city worked against blacks by generating increased competition for the menial labor and manufacturing jobs that would have gone to them easily in a city like Chicago or Detroit. After World War II, the vast influx of blacks and the changing social status of other racial and ethnic groups in Los Angeles created a situation where black isolation, rather than the multiracial integration of the prewar era, became more common. As industrial employment opportunities for nonwhites expanded in the two decades after the war, African Americans increasingly understood Mexicans to be competitors for coveted jobs. Between the 1920s and the 1970s, the multiracial character of Los Angeles moved from being a qualified blessing to a qualified curse for blacks, particularly those in blue-collar occupations.

Second, while histories of the rust belt north emphasize the crucial role of deindustrialization and overall urban economic decline in perpetuating racial inequality, the story in Los Angeles is far more complex. In striking contrast to the steady decline in manufacturing jobs that began in the 1950s in Chicago and Detroit, Los Angeles gained thousands of new manufacturing jobs through the 1970s, thanks in large part to the crucial aerospace industry. Like its northern counterparts, however, Los Angeles did lose many of its automobile, steel, and rubber tire plants during and shortly after the recession of the mid-1970s. Beginning during World War II, African Americans in Los Angeles had fought for complete integration into these jobs, and by the 1970s they had achieved a measure of success. More important, these jobs had created the economic foundations for a rising class of homeowning, blue-collar black workers. Thus, the swift disappearance of those jobs was traumatic for an important element of black Los Angeles.

But the decline in these older smokestack industries cannot alone sufficiently explain persistent racial inequality; in fact, even as Los Angeles was suffering this selective deindustrialization, it was also experiencing a dynamic wave of reindustrialization.[19] Starting in the 1960s, a new wave of both very high-skill and very low-skill manufacturing industries, along with the expansion of retail and service industries, created thousands of new jobs in Los Angeles and Southern California in general, allowing both the city and the region to weather the recession better than most American cities. But, again, blacks found that they did not share equally in Southern California's continuing economic boom. That such inequality persisted despite the creation of new jobs suggests that just as African Americans were challenging and conquering relics of historic discrimination, new barriers emerged. Although race "declined in significance," to use William Julius Wilson's oft-quoted phrase, blackness continued to be a significant handicap long after legal segregation ended.[20]

Finally, the dispersive spatiality of Los Angeles greatly influenced the opportunities available to African Americans, sometimes concretely and other times perceptually. Before World War II, the vast geographic size and relatively low population density of Los Angeles distinguished it from other major American metropolises. This dispersion, combined with the proportionally small size of the black population, the rigid racial segregation of the workplace, and the city's heavy dependence on private rather than public transportation, created an atmosphere in which compulsory social interaction between blacks and whites was minimized, thereby allowing black residents in prewar Los Angeles to avert many of the racially degrading or violent encounters typical in other cities. For blacks in Los Angeles, and their friends and families who visited, this distinction was palpable and lent some credence to their glowing characterizations of opportunity in the city.

Paradoxically, however, it also allowed civic leaders and whites in general to completely ignore the rising cost of racial segregation. African Americans remained essentially out of sight and out of mind until World War II, when the sheer volume of black migration finally forced white Los Angeles to recognize the consequences of housing segregation in the overcrowded slums of Little Tokyo. But even as civic leaders grappled with the problems of segregation, many white residents and homeowners responded to the flood of black migrants by more aggressively defending racial segregation in both public and private spaces. Thus, whatever benefits blacks accrued from the city's special arrangement prior to World War II quickly disappeared in the postwar years.

In the process of writing this book, I have read countless other books, articles, dissertations, and theses. I have consulted the records of more than thirty federal agencies, civil rights groups, labor organizations, and individuals; and I have analyzed and interpreted eight decades of census data and labor statistics. I have read hundreds of issues of the two largest black newspapers of the era, the *California Eagle* and the *Los Angeles Sentinel,* as well as the *Los Angeles Times* and a handful of smaller newspapers. I have consulted numerous oral histories and conducted some of my own interviews with longtime residents of South Central Los Angeles, the heart of black Southern California. I have studied hundreds of photographs, maps, pamphlets, and letters from the era. And I have spent time in South Central, walking the streets, looking and listening for history's fading cues. All of this research has pointed to one central idea: the history of urban America is inseparable from the history of race in America.

Race is not simply a category of analyses that can be applied or removed from a map of the "real" urban landscape like a thematic overlay. Rather, it is a concept that has been integral to the way American cities have developed and the way urbanites of all backgrounds have made decisions. In Los Angeles, the Great Migration of African Americans during and after World War II profoundly influenced decisions about politics, law enforcement, housing, and education. Before the war, policy decisions on such issues had been made almost exclusively by whites, who certainly continued to dominate the urban decision-making process long after the war. But beginning during the war years, African Americans increasingly influenced that process in several ways.

Blacks most often affected the evolution of the city simply by making everyday choices about where to work, where to live, where to send their children to school, and where to relax at the end of the day. Although pervasive racial discrimination continued to limit their options, by making those choices, black residents thrust themselves into the public spaces and civic consciousness of the city of Los Angeles in ways that forced civic leaders to react. Blacks also affected the urban decision-making process by explicitly challenging discriminatory employers, racist police, insensitive city councils and mayors, and obstinate white co-workers and neighbors through pickets, boycotts, protests, and organized electoral political activity. Ultimately, African Americans were not peripheral to the history of Los Angeles or other large American cities but were, rather, important shapers of urban destiny in ways that have yet to be fully appreciated.

By locating my study of postwar African American history in Los Angeles, I hope to offer more than simply a corrective to our near-exclusive reliance on the northern rust belt story. Understanding the history of modern black Los Angeles may give us an opportunity—to borrow a phrase from Mike Davis—to "excavate the future." In addition to inspiring greater investigation into the rich history of Los Angeles, Davis's popular *City of Quartz* reinvigorated the longstanding notion that postwar Los Angeles has been a bellwether of urban America.[21] Often exaggerated by the city's boosters, this idea nonetheless has history on its side, at least as it applies to the "sunbelt" cities. Indeed, over the past forty or so years, many of America's sunbelt cities have come to resemble Los Angeles in their rapid growth, their sprawling landscapes, their new immigration, and their diversified economies, often bolstered by heavy federal investment.[22] Meanwhile, rust belt cities such as Cleveland, Pittsburgh, Baltimore, and Detroit continue to experience steady population loss and economic decline.[23] Joel Garreau's assertion that "every single American city that *is* growing, is growing in the fashion of Los Angeles" may be overstated, but if recent history is any guide to the future, it seems likely that much of urban America will soon resemble Los Angeles more than it will Detroit or Pittsburgh.[24] Thus, there is a special urgency to understanding the city's recent racial past because it has a direct bearing on urban America's racial future, especially in an era in which de jure segregation no longer exists. Because de facto racial inequality still plagues our nation, we would be well served by a comprehensive understanding of how our most modern cities have incubated it.

Finally, I must acknowledge the limitations of this study. In my investigation of the Los Angeles African American community, I have focused chiefly on those aspects of life that have historically been at the center of black struggles for equality: jobs, housing, education, and political representation. Readers seeking greater insight into the many rich spiritual, artistic, and cultural traditions and contributions of Los Angeles's black community may find this book lacking. Happily, such readers will benefit from the recent publication of *Central Avenue Sounds, California Soul,* and *Central Avenue: Its Rise and Fall,* three comprehensive works on the history of black music in the city and state. Far less documented is the fascinating history of the city's many black churches and influential pastors, as well as the story of its visual artists and writers.[25] Much work remains to be done on these and other aspects of black Los Angeles, and it is my hope that this book might serve as a foundation upon which future studies of these topics can build.

CHAPTER I

African Americans in Prewar Los Angeles

Los Angeles was wonderful. The air was scented with orange blossoms and the beautiful homes lay low crouching on the earth as though they loved its scents and flowers. Nowhere in the United States is the Negro so well and beautifully housed, nor the average efficiency and intelligence in the colored population so high. Here is an aggressive, hopeful group—with some wealth, large industrial opportunity and a buoyant spirit.

> W. E. B. Du Bois, *The Crisis,* July 1913

W. E. B. Du Bois's statement, penned in New York shortly after a visit to Los Angeles, exemplified a common perception among many black Angelenos that Los Angeles was a kind of racial paradise for African Americans. Jefferson L. Edmonds, editor of the black Los Angeles newspaper the *Liberator,* also expressed this sentiment in 1902 when he declared, "California is the greatest state for the Negro," and in 1911 when he elaborated:

Only a few years ago, the bulk of our present colored population came here from the South without any money, in search of better things and were not disappointed. The hospitable white people received them kindly, employed them at good wages, treated them as men and women, furnished their children with the best educational advantages offered anywhere. . . . They were treated absolutely fair in courts. . . . Feeling perfectly safe, the colored population planted themselves.[1]

Caleb Holden, however, would likely have been astounded by the re-marks of Edmonds and Du Bois. In 1912, Holden and a white associate entered a bar for an afternoon beer, but when they ordered, Holden was charged one dollar while his white companion was charged only a nickel. When a delegation of concerned black citizens protested to the mayor, city attorney John Shenk issued the much-despised "Shenk Rule," supporting the right of business owners to discriminate. Nor would the words of Du Bois and Edmonds have made much sense to black children in Los Angeles in the middle of a hot summer, when the children were restricted to segregated beaches and allowed to swim in public pools only on the night before the pools were cleaned.

How does one reconcile the stunning inconsistency between Du Bois's and Edmonds's sanguine assessments of the opportunities avail-able to African Americans in Los Angeles and the experiences of Caleb Holden and those black children seeking relief from the summer heat? First, one must recognize that Du Bois, Edmonds, and others did not view opportunity in absolute terms, but rather in relative terms. Mi-grating from areas in the South where a black man was lynched, on av-erage, every four days deeply influenced views about what constituted paradise.[2] In Los Angeles, black residents could usually avoid the most debilitating effects of racism endemic to the South, including ceaseless humiliation, gratuitous racial violence, poverty and spiraling debt, po-litical powerlessness, and patently unequal educational opportunities.

Less obvious, however, is that in their praise of Los Angeles's bounty, Edmonds, Du Bois, and others were implicitly comparing Los Angeles and the more famous "promised lands" of the urban North. These northern cities provided unprecedented opportunities for southern black migrants in the first decades of the twentieth century, as numer-ous thoughtful studies have demonstrated.[3] But black people in these cities also experienced increased social and spatial isolation as well as a wave of racial violence, as race riots in New York (1900), Springfield, Ohio (1904), Greensburg, Indiana (1906), Springfield, Illinois (1908), East St. Louis (1917), and Chicago (1919) made painfully clear. Many Af-rican Americans had come to see life as a choice between—as one mor-bid satirist put it—being "gently lynched in Mississippi [or] beaten to death in New York."[4]

Second, this contradictory picture reflected the fact that, for blacks, pre–World War II Los Angeles was a city of paradoxes. It was a city where white supremacy was as central to white self-perception as it was in southern Mississippi but where anti-black violence was quite limited.

It had one of the highest proportions of black homeowners of any major American city as well as an extensive network of racially restrictive housing covenants designed to minimize black residential mobility. It was a city where the presence of an extraordinarily diverse multiracial and multiethnic population mitigated the harshest effects of racial segregation in neighborhoods and in schools but exacerbated those effects in the workplace. Finally, it was a city in which the black community delicately balanced competing desires for both activism and accommodation. These paradoxes, of course, were the products of the city's early history.

Tracking the Multiracial Metropolis

In the mid-nineteenth century, shortly after California was admitted to the Union, most Americans rightly considered Los Angeles a remote, violent, lawless, unprofitable, and almost wholly undesirable frontier village.[5] That accurate perception might have permanently doomed Los Angeles had the Southern Pacific railroad not connected the city to the rest of the country in the late nineteenth century. Several years after the transcontinental railroad reached the thriving, cosmopolitan city of San Francisco in 1869, the Southern Pacific and Santa Fe railroads connected Los Angeles to San Francisco and to their southern transcontinental routes. In the late nineteenth century, Henry Huntington, nephew of railroad magnate Collis P. Huntington, almost single-handedly defined Southern California's dispersive geography by developing radiating rings of distant suburbs connected by his Pacific Electric railway, a remarkably extensive interurban rail system.[6] It is well recognized that both the transcontinental and the interurban railway systems greatly affected the growth and economy of Los Angeles, but it is less understood that they also steered the ethnic history of the city, particularly the history of its three largest migrant groups: whites, Mexicans, and blacks.

Because tracks alone did not guarantee migration, Los Angeles city boosters and the owners of the Southern Pacific railroad embarked on a now-famous advertising crusade touting the region's congenial climate and the city's spaciousness. The bucolic image of Los Angeles proved most alluring to white, rural, and relatively prosperous midwesterners, eager to trade the drudgery of agriculture for the comfort of paradise for the mere price of a train ticket.[7] Like most Americans, Los Angeles's white migrants tacitly believed in the racial superiority of white people of European descent. As the city's economy developed in the early twentieth century, its white population became fragmented along class lines, but few whites of any social class doubted their innate racial superiority. Blue-collar whites joined all-white craft unions and lived in working-class suburbs that were thoroughly race restricted. Among white-collar workers, as Clark Davis has recently described, there was even a strong "cult of Anglo-Saxonness," which further sharpened the already restrictive taxonomy of racial classification.[8] The very need to articulate this "Anglo-Saxonness," of course, reflected the presence of nonwhite people in Los Angeles.

While Chinese immigrants performed most of the labor necessary for connecting Northern California to the transcontinental railroad, in Southern California the extension of the Southern Pacific and the expansion and maintenance of Huntington's vast interurban railway depended heavily on Mexican labor. Beginning in the eighteenth century, continuing through California's admission to the Union, and peaking in the 1920s, Mexican immigration was indispensable to the growth of Los Angeles. During the early twentieth century, thousands of Mexicans fled the devastation and dislocation of the Mexican Revolution to work throughout the Southwest on the railroads and in the fields.[9] The railroad served not only as a source of employment for Mexicans but also as a vehicle for immigration. From 1884, when the Mexican Central railroad was completed, until 1920, when it became prohibitively expensive, many Mexican immigrants came to the United States via the train.[10]

As it is even now, the relationship between Mexicans and whites in Los Angeles was often ambiguous. White Angelenos who believed in the innate racial superiority of whites also found themselves unusually dependent on the labor of dark-skinned immigrant workers. The all-white Los Angeles Chamber of Commerce, for example, used the presence of Mexicans as a selling point in its bid to lure manufacturers to the city.[11] Mexican immigrants themselves viewed Los Angeles, and "El Norte" in general, with similar ambivalence. The availability of steady work, even if it was grueling and poorly paid, was a clear improvement over the poverty and unemployment plaguing Mexico. Yet Mexican immigrants and Mexican Americans in Los Angeles were confronted every day with harsh reminders that they were not regarded as equals. In addition to harassment from the police, Mexicans endured persistent discrimination in employment, in housing, and in schools, where the chil-

dren of recent immigrants were routinely diverted into separate classrooms and labeled "retarded" by educators.[12]

While whites rode the railroads and Mexicans maintained the tracks,
blacks served as porters and waiters on the trains and at the station
stops. The first identifiable black settlement in Los Angeles, which coincided with the great land boom of 1887–1888, was on First and Los
Angeles Streets adjacent to the downtown rail yards. In addition to establishing a black settlement, Pullman porters likely played a central role
in disseminating information about Los Angeles to their families and
friends in the South.[13] In a pattern that would continue throughout the
century, most black migrants came to the city from Texas and Louisiana, states served by the Southern Pacific's Sunset Route between New
Orleans and Los Angeles.[14]

Black migrant Augustus Hawkins, later to become a member of the
state assembly and a Congressional representative, arrived in Los Angeles in the 1920s. Later he recalled that "when people from Texas or
Louisiana came out and wrote back South it made people in the South
believe that this was heaven. . . . It was a land of golden opportunities—
orange groves and beautiful beaches—and life was all a matter of milk
and honey."[15] While some southern blacks were probably enticed by
this mythical portrait, they were also drawn to California's real freedoms. Admitted as a free state in 1850, California repealed testimony
restrictions in 1863, outlawed de jure racial segregation in California
schools, and passed a state anti-discrimination law in 1893.[16] These advantages, coupled with the city's history of minimal anti-black violence,
convinced a growing number of African Americans to head west. The
black population of Los Angeles climbed steadily, from 2,131 in 1900, to
15,579 in 1920, to 38,898 in 1930. Blacks never constituted more than
3.14 percent of the total population, however, a testament to the rapid
parallel growth of the city overall.[17]

As the black settlement of early twentieth-century Los Angeles grew,
so too did its renown. The historical record of prewar black Los Angeles is replete with effusive descriptions of the city's promising racial climate. When Joseph Bass, future editor of the *California Eagle,* arrived
in Los Angeles in 1911, he felt that the city was a "Beulah Land and just
what I had been looking for."[18] Perhaps the most often cited benefit to
living in Los Angeles was that African Americans could easily purchase
homes. The same year that Bass arrived, black newspaper editor and Los
Angeles propagandist Jefferson L. Edmonds wrote: "We are here like
other people, to share these splendid conditions found in California,

buying houses and contributing our efforts to the common cause, building up this great state."[19] Indeed, in 1910, almost 40 percent of African Americans in Los Angeles County owned their homes, compared to only 2.4 percent in New York and 8 percent in Chicago.[20]

More important, between their initial settlement and the 1920s, blacks were not rigidly confined to one geographic area, as they were in other cities. As the black community grew, the original settlement expanded south on San Pedro and east on Fifth and Sixth to Central Avenue. Four noncontiguous pockets of black settlement emerged as well.[21] African American residents viewed this development hopefully, as one black real estate agent observed in 1904:

The Negroes of this city have prudently refused to segregate themselves into any locality but have scattered and purchased homes in sections occupied by wealthy, cultured White people, thus not only securing the best fire, water, and police protection, but also the more important benefits that accrue from refined and cultured surroundings.[22]

But the high proportion of black homeowners and the relative dispersal of the black population were not, as this real estate agent suggested, the result of blacks' "prudent refusal to segregate themselves," nor were they the result of greater racial tolerance among whites. Rather, these tandem developments were the product of the city's greatest asset, space, which created an illusion of tolerance that would influence thinking about race in Los Angeles until the 1960s.

The vast size of the city kept the price of property relatively low, within the reach of even poorly paid African Americans; and the low population density of the city, combined with the relatively small size of the black population, minimized white hostility to black dispersion. This allowed the city's black community to flourish during the first three decades of settlement. In 1872, Los Angeles's first black church, the First African Methodist Episcopal (AME), was founded; and by 1910, there were ten black churches in the city.[23] Black Angelenos founded numerous self-help organizations such as the Forum and the Sojourner Truth Industrial Club. By World War I, chapters of the Urban League and the National Association for the Advancement of Colored People (NAACP) had appeared, the latter of which scored an early victory by forcing the county to desegregate its nursing school. Most of these organizations were located on South Central Avenue, which by World War I had become the bustling economic and cultural center of black Los Angeles. Known as "Central Avenue," "the Avenue," or

"South Central," this community, which straddled Central Avenue south of downtown, was home to numerous small black professional practices as well as larger businesses such as the Hotel Somerville (later the Dunbar Hotel) and the Golden State Mutual Life Insurance Company, the largest black-owned insurance company in the western United States. Furthermore, black Los Angeles boasted three newspapers, the *Los Angeles New Age,* the *Liberator,* and the *California Eagle.* Finally, African Americans in Los Angeles availed themselves of their right to vote, free from fear, and elected black attorney Frederick M. Roberts to the California State Assembly in 1918.[24]

Remarkably, this cultural and political flourishing captured the attention of the *Los Angeles Times,* then very much the voice of the city's white financial leadership. In a special issue on the anniversary of Abraham Lincoln's birthday in 1909, the *Times* lavished praise on its "brothers in black":

If the Negroes of Los Angeles and Southern California can be taken as examples of the race, it would seem from their own showing of indisputable facts that the "Negro problem" is a thing that has no existence. . . . They are engaged in business—some of them on a large scale; they are practicing in the professions; they maintain highly organized bodies of Christian worshipers; they have hundreds of good, comfortable homes and not a few that rival in elegance and luxury the best in the whole city; they buy and read books; their children attend the schools and often outstrip their white companions in ability; music and art appeal to them and are fostered and advanced by them; they are good, God-fearing, law-abiding men and women.[25]

The Strange Career of Jim Crow in Los Angeles

But glowing descriptions of black Los Angeles could not conceal the hardening racial segregation of the late 1910s and 1920s. As it was elsewhere, residential segregation in Los Angeles was maintained through a web of racially restrictive housing covenants. One black Angeleno in 1917 described the covenants as "invisible walls of steel. The whites surrounded us and made it impossible for us to go beyond these walls."[26] First appearing in California as early as the 1890s, covenants had become a widespread phenomenon on the urban landscape by the 1920s. The California Real Estate Association—which would continue to encourage racially restrictive housing covenants well into the 1960s—regularly endorsed the use of covenants for keeping out African Americans as well as Japanese and Mexican residents. Provisions against "alien races" and "non Caucasians" also sometimes applied to Los Angeles's Jewish population, already the nation's second largest by the 1920s. Thus, politically active blacks, Mexicans, Japanese, Chinese, and Jews shared a common interest in eradicating covenants, a fact reflected in the dozens of lawsuits brought against the institution between 1917 and 1945.

One of the nation's first legal challenges to racially restrictive covenants, in fact, came from Los Angeles. In 1919, the California Supreme Court ruled in *Los Angeles Investment Co. v. Gary* that it was not legal to restrict sales of property based on race.[27] At the same time, however, the court upheld the covenanters' right to keep out nonwhites. Thus, African Americans could buy property in a racially restricted tract, but they could not live there. In 1926, in *Corrigan v. Buckley,* the U.S. Supreme Court upheld judicial enforcement of racially restrictive housing covenants and for the next twenty years refused all requests to review cases challenging that decision. Not until 1948, when the U.S. Supreme Court finally ruled against housing covenants in *Shelley v. Kraemer,* was the city's nonwhite population freed from the odious restrictions. Moreover, in communities where restrictive covenants had failed to restrict minorities, the Ku Klux Klan, which surfaced in Los Angeles during the 1920s, served a similar function, intimidating, threatening, and sometimes attacking blacks who moved into white neighborhoods.[28]

In Los Angeles, however, residential segregation produced qualitatively different results than it did in other American cities. Shortly before World War I, cities such as Detroit, Cleveland, Harlem, Chicago, and Milwaukee developed black ghettos, neighborhoods where most people were black and where most black people in the city lived.[29] But in Los Angeles, the use of covenants to protect and maintain white neighborhoods had the effect of creating some of the most racially and ethnically diverse neighborhoods in the country. Like other cities, Los Angeles was clearly divided by a color line, but on one side of that line was a white (and largely Protestant) population while on the other was a large and vibrant patchwork of races and ethnicities. Many African Americans lived in the ethnically diverse communities of Boyle Heights and East Los Angeles, and large number of Mexicans and Italians lived along Central Avenue, the heart of the African American community.[30] As the city's black population grew in the 1920s and 1930s, blacks became increasingly concentrated in South Central, but even then they shared "the Avenue" with other groups. A 1940 report commissioned by the Los Angeles Urban League reported that approximately twenty-two thousand Mexicans lived in the "black neighborhood" of Central Avenue.[31]

The community of Watts, about seven miles south of downtown Los Angeles and five miles south of the heart of South Central, was similarly diverse. Nicknamed "Mudtown" for its marshy terrain, Watts was located in a low basin close to the water table. One longtime Watts resident remembered that, in the 1920s, "Watts was all-but-barren land. Houses were few and far between. . . . In those days, the people of Watts fished for crawfish and catfish in mud and slime."[32] These circumstances meant that land was cheap. After 1902, when the Pacific Electric completed a depot in Watts, several developers built housing tracts, "where the price is within reach of all."[33]

In addition to its white majority population, the Mexican and black populations of Watts grew quickly in the 1920s. In 1925, whites in the community successfully petitioned the Los Angeles City Council to annex the city of Watts, allegedly to avoid the real possibility that a black mayor would be elected and the political power of African Americans would be expanded.[34] Jazz musician and Watts native Buddy Collette remembered: "In the thirties in the Watts area where I grew up, we had whites, Japanese, Mexicans, and Blacks living in the neighborhoods, and it worked. We got along fine."[35] In his 1931 *God Sends Sunday,* Arna Bontemps, a leading author in the New Negro Renaissance, captured a bucolic scene in a Watts park, "where Negro and Mexican children flocked there in Sunday school clothes."[36] In the 1930s, the area became decisively more black, but as late as 1940, the population of Watts was 50 percent white or Mexican American, 35 percent black, 13 percent Mexican immigrants, and 1.5 percent Asian.[37]

Multiracial neighborhoods brought blacks and other groups into contact with one another not just as neighbors but also, at times, as fellow parishioners, club members, consumers, friends, and even spouses. Perhaps the most meaningful and memorable interactions were as classmates in Los Angeles public schools. Though the Los Angeles Board of Education never fully committed itself to racial segregation, pressure from neighborhood groups, students, and parents led to an unusually liberal transfer policy that encouraged de facto racial segregation. By the late 1920s, white parents and students, unsettled by the fact that nonwhite students (including Mexicans and Asians) made up one-quarter of the city's student population, increasingly sought refuge in white-only schools.[38] This did not cause blacks to be isolated, however; rather, as had been the case with housing, it fostered increased integration with other nonwhite racial groups.

By the early 1930s, most black high school students in Los Angeles attended Jefferson and Jordan High Schools, adjacent to Central Avenue and Watts, respectively. While Chicago's "black" high schools were more than 90 percent black by the 1920s, most black high school students in Los Angeles found themselves in thoroughly multiracial classrooms.[39] For Ersey O'Brien, who attended Jefferson High during the Great Depression, interracial relations were quite harmonious: "Believe it or not, [blacks] were just about the minority there. . . . Jeff was not an all black school. . . . [W]e were close, the Japanese, the Asians . . . going to school brought everyone together. We never thought about it like 'you're Japanese' or 'you're Chinese' or 'you're a white kid' or 'I'm a black kid.'"[40] Legendary jazz bassist and composer Charles Mingus grew up in prewar Watts and remembered (in the third person) his days at Jordan High School: "So finally Charles gassed his hair straight and ran around with the other mongrels, the few Japanese, Mexicans, Jews and Greeks at Jordan High. The light Mexicans called themselves Spanish, the light Chinese said they were white."[41]

Certainly, multiracial interaction was not always harmonious. Mingus, whose mother was light skinned, also remembered the animosity toward Mexicans his father instilled in him: "During these discussions Mama would look in the mirror and say how often she was taken for a Mexican because of her freckles, her thin chiseled nose and tiny feet. She believed she was part Indian. But the kids remembered that Daddy said Mexicans and Indians were dirty greasers with lice in their hair. It was confusing." The animosity Mingus learned to feel was apparently reciprocated. Once when he inquired about a young girl who was one of his schoolmates, "two Mexican boys, not much older than he but far larger, opened the door. 'Get out of here NIGGER! Betty's our girl and we don't want any NIGGERS hanging around.'"[42]

Yet despite these incidents of friction, the multiracial character of black neighborhoods and schools in Los Angeles probably provided African Americans a greater degree of social comfort than they found in the more rigidly segregated communities of the South and the urban North. As one researcher for the Los Angeles Urban League observed in 1933: "The presence of other dark skinned people, Mexicans and Japanese, tends to cause the color line to be drawn more finely."[43] The fineness of this line, many blacks believed, diffused anti-black hostility in Los Angeles. In 1928, black sociologist Charles Johnson observed that "the focusing of racial interest upon the Oriental has in large measure overlooked the Negro, and the city, accordingly, has been regarded by them, from a distance, as desirable."[44] Put another way, as the editor of the *Liberator* wrote in 1911, blacks in Los Angeles "have no monopoly of the embarrassing attention and prejudice so often directed mainly at them."[45]

Beyond neighborhoods and schools, racial minorities in general—and blacks in particular—understood that the city's public space was tacitly racialized. Though never codified in law, there were many real racial barriers to the alluring amenities of public life in Los Angeles. African American youths, eager to escape the heat of central city summers, seldom found refuge in city swimming pools. In many parks, such as Centinella Park in the all-white suburb of Inglewood, blacks were simply not allowed in the pool. In other parks, blacks were allowed to swim only on the day before the pool was cleaned. In 1932, the California Superior Court ruled that the Los Angeles Department of Playgrounds and Recreation could no longer segregate its pools, but the practice continued well into the 1940s nonetheless.[46] At the wildly popular Santa Monica Pier amusement park, then a private enterprise, African Americans were welcomed as patrons; but on the public beach below, they were restricted to a small patch of sand away from white beachgoers. At dusk, police officers ushered blacks off the beach, while whites were allowed to stay well after dark. Sometimes blacks defiantly transgressed these racial boundaries, as in the remarkable case of "Bruce's Beach," a small black-owned patch of beach reserved exclusively for African Americans in the otherwise lily-white community of Manhattan Beach.[47]

But more often black residents found comfort in public places where they were not feared and despised. For example, at Central Playgrounds, right off Central Avenue, blacks could swim and play sports without interference from white authorities. One of the most popular destinations for black and Mexican youths was Lincoln Park in East Los Angeles. In addition to drawing the large Mexican and substantial black populations of East Los Angeles, Lincoln Park also drew black children from South Central, who rode the inexpensive Pacific Electric railway to the park. On Sundays and holidays, the mixed racial makeup of Lincoln Park's teeming crowds closely resembled that of the neighborhoods in which many blacks were raised (see figure 1).[48]

Work and the Narrowing of Opportunity

Although housing and educational opportunities for African Americans in Los Angeles were superior to those available to blacks in other major

FIGURE 1. African American and Mexican children at Lincoln Park in East Los Angeles, ca. 1930. Lincoln Park was one of the few public spaces open to blacks before World War II. Courtesy of the Los Angeles Public Library.

American cities, employment opportunities were not. Before World War II, the greatest barrier to economic prosperity for black men and women in the United States was racial discrimination in employment. Across the country, even the most well educated African Americans found their job options severely restricted. In the rural South, black men and women struggled as sharecroppers and farm tenants, jobs that virtually guaranteed them lives of misery and bitter poverty. In the North, blacks enjoyed greater opportunity, although most men worked as unskilled laborers in the lowest-paid, most unstable, and most dangerous industrial jobs and as service workers in restaurants, hotels, hospitals, and train stations. Black women's opportunities were even more limited: virtually all employed black women in urban America worked as housekeepers.[49] It was well understood throughout the United States that no white employer would ever hire an African American to do a job that a white man wanted and that, even where whites and blacks worked side by side, blacks would never earn the same wages as whites. In Los Angeles, this tradition of discrimination was compounded by the re-

gion's heavy dependence on Mexican labor. In one of the great pa
doxes of prewar Los Angeles, the multiracial character of the city, which
mitigated the harshest effects of residential segregation, actually exacerbated the effects of employment discrimination by increasing competition at the lower end of the labor market.

By the 1920s, most Americans associated Los Angeles principally
with its film and tourist industries, but the local economy was in fact anchored by a heavy manufacturing base. The completion of the Los Angeles harbor (1912) and aqueduct (1913) provided a solid foundation for
the city's swift, albeit belated, economic and commercial growth. The
aqueduct provided not only abundant water but also affordable hydro-
electric power, which, along with the region's spectacular petroleum
output and the affordability and availability of land, enhanced the desirability of the city for prospective manufacturers. In addition to the
hundreds of local manufacturers, many national manufacturing firms
established branch plants in Los Angeles in the 1920s, including Goodyear, Goodrich, Firestone, Ford, Swift and Company, Phelps-Dodge,
U.S. Steel, and Willys-Overland. In 1929, Bethlehem Steel bought the
California Iron and Steel Company; and in 1936, General Motors
opened a large plant in South Gate. During the 1920s, Los Angeles became the country's eighth largest manufacturing center. Unlike its geographically dispersed film and oil industries, Los Angeles's manufacturing firms were heavily concentrated in the Eastside industrial district
and the central manufacturing district, both east of South Central,
across Alameda Boulevard. Also east of Alameda Boulevard were the
thoroughly race-restricted white working-class suburbs of Huntington
Park, South Gate, Bell Gardens, Lynwood, Maywood, and Bell, "an island of homes in a sea of industry." [50]

In its campaign to lure manufacturers west, the Chamber of Commerce benefited from Los Angeles's well-known reputation as an open-
shop town, "the cradle of industrial freedom." The chamber ranked the
"large supply of open shop labor" as the city's greatest attribute in its
promotional literature, widely distributed to manufacturing firms in the
North and East. [51] Well-organized employer groups such as the Merchants and Manufacturers Association (M&M), led by the domineering
Harrison Gray Otis, were remarkably successful at reducing the threat
of organized labor. Otis and the M&M enjoyed the tacit and often explicit support of the Los Angeles Police Department (LAPD) and its infamous "red squad." Under the leadership of Chief James E. Davis and
Captain William Hynes, the LAPD's red squad engaged in sophisti-

id outright physical violence against labor unions,
os, and civil rights organizations. Through the 1930s,
ncreasingly autonomous unit until 1938, when reform
ier Bowron won the mayoral recall election with a
ish the red squad.[52]

to Los Angeles's abundant natural resources and its large
skilled ⸺ miskilled, nonunion workforce, the Chamber of Commerce touted the city's growing Mexican labor supply. One pamphlet published by the chamber in 1927 read:

We have a Mexican population in this section in excess of 50,000 people and these people make excellent workers, the men as common laborers in different crafts and the women make splendid workers in textile plants, wearing apparel plants and in other plants where skilled female labor is desired. . . . [T]hese women come from a race who have been workers in textiles, laces and embroideries for centuries and are naturally adept with their fingers.[53]

The chamber's failure to mention the city's growing black population, then only slightly smaller than the Mexican population, reflected the general preference among industrial employers in prewar Los Angeles for Mexican over black workers. This preference did not go unnoticed in black Los Angeles. In 1931, a black spokesman for the California State Employment Bureau reminded members of the Los Angeles Industrial Council, an organization devoted to improving employment opportunities for blacks, that "we are not regarded as laborers in this section of the country." "No other part of the country," he told the crowd, "would stand to have the labor done by persons other than citizens, [but] the Mexicans are regarded as the labor here."[54] In the prewar years, this preference for Mexican labor further narrowed the range of opportunities available to African Americans in an already racially discriminatory labor market.

In contrast to their counterparts who had migrated to northern cities, black migrants to 1920s Los Angeles found far fewer opportunities for industrial work. In the mid-1920s, Charles S. Johnson, a sociologist trained at the University of Chicago and director of the National Urban League's Department of Research and Investigations, conducted a survey of 456 manufacturing firms in Los Angeles County to determine the extent of employment possibilities for African Americans. Johnson found that many firms refused to hire blacks on the grounds that they simply had never done so before; Los Angeles manufacturing had emerged during an era of labor surplus, and the need to hire blacks had never arisen. With a labor surplus and no federal laws prohibiting discrimination based on race, employers were free to be capricious. One furniture manufacturer reported: "A [black] night watchman was employed for five years and was always satisfactory and reliable; the only reason we made any change was that we want a white man to have the job." Automobile manufacturers, though major employers of blacks in Detroit, unabashedly declared that "we prefer white labor in our line" in Los Angeles. Of the 104 plants Johnson personally visited, only 54 hired blacks in any position, most commonly as janitors, porters, and laborers. And where blacks worked in large plants with work crews, the majority worked in segregated crews. Compounding segregation was the intense competition for work in manufacturing. Johnson observed that "the outstanding competitors of Negroes in industry at present are Mexicans," who "hold down [the] numbers" of blacks. Johnson discovered numerous plants where Mexican labor was used and black labor was prohibited, particularly in the iron and steel, brick and clay, and oil industries.[55]

Perhaps the most discouraging aspect of the study was the response of employers to this question: "If competent Negro workers were available, would you employ them?" Of the 104 employers interviewed, 30 flatly stated that they would not do so under any conditions. Most opposed to hiring blacks were employers in wearing apparel, machinery, oil wells, paints and varnishes, and furniture; door manufacturers; manufacturers of electrical goods; and construction companies.[56] In the region's aircraft industry, largely located in outlying suburbs away from the central manufacturing district, blacks were entirely excluded. A 1941 survey of aircraft employers conducted by *Fortune* magazine found "an almost universal prejudice against Negroes" in the industry.[57]

Hollywood, Los Angeles's top-grossing industry, also restricted opportunities for blacks through the 1930s. Johnson observed that African Americans' "closest consistent connection with the industry is in the capacity of servants of the principals: chauffeurs, maids and porters."[58] Los Angeles studios frequently hired black representatives to recruit blacks from Central Avenue, but only for bit parts or as extras. For example, Universal Pictures hired six hundred black extras for the production of *Uncle Tom's Cabin* (1927). The late 1930s were better for black actors in Los Angeles, with the production of *Slaveship* (1937), *Safari* (1939), *Gone with the Wind* (1939), and *Tarzan* (1939), but these films were exceptions to the rule. By the end of the 1930s, African Americans held no writing jobs (with the exception of Langston

Hughes), and no technical jobs were available for blacks. Only Paramount Studios had two African Americans on a regular payroll; both men were janitors.[59]

Before World War II, there were only a few fields of employment in Los Angeles for which race was not a significant handicap for blacks. The first and most significant was domestic service. According to the 1930 census, 87 percent of employed black women and 40 percent of employed black men in the city worked as household servants. A significant proportion of employed men (17 percent) worked in the transportation industry, almost exclusively as porters and waiters. Another 22 percent of male workers were employed in manufacturing industries, usually as janitors and laborers. Outside the manufacturing industries, the City Engineers Office hired blacks in large numbers as garbage collectors, streetsweepers, and asphalt truck drivers. Public employment was perhaps the one area where black laborers were shielded from competition with Mexican immigrants, whose citizenship status made them ineligible to work for the city. A small number of blacks appear to have made inroads in the building trades, and the American Federation of Labor (AFL) Bricklayers Local 2 had a substantial black membership.[60]

Finally, black musicians found ample employment in Central Avenue's many thriving nightclubs and theaters, particularly during the 1920s. In other parts of the city, however, many black musicians still encountered discrimination. The Los Angeles local of the American Federation of Musicians, Local 47, denied membership to blacks. In response, black musicians founded Musicians Local 767, which operated independently until the early 1950s.

The narrow range of jobs open to blacks in Los Angeles had a self-perpetuating effect, as one Depression-era scholar discovered when interviewing a sample of white Angelenos. "The Negro," he wrote in 1931, "is mostly thought of as a 'servant' and 'entertainer' by 90 percent of the white participants."[61] This perception, and the limits it imposed on employment opportunities, would be devastating during the Great Depression.

The Great Depression, Labor, and Black Politics

The Great Depression unnerved African Americans in Los Angeles as it did elsewhere. Faced with the double burden of racism and Depression-induced poverty, black people struggled to survive. Ersey O'Brien, a black worker who grew up in Depression-era Los Angeles, remembered the scarcity of the era:

Twice a week, sometimes three times a week, my mother and I would get up early in the morning. I'd take my little wagon, we'd go to the market and pick up spoiled fruit that they had discarded, cut the bad part off. And just as I would do it, I'd see 25, 50 more kids and I'd come home, walk home. You got a wagon full of fruit or potatoes, maybe a little spoiled, and you couldn't sell it in the market but it was still good.[62]

Skyrocketing unemployment threw blacks into deepening poverty. In the first years of the Depression, an estimated 30 percent of black men and 40 percent of black women were unemployed; by 1934, half of all black Angelenos were out of work.[63] Because blacks were disproportionately employed in the service sector, they were particularly vulnerable to the economic crisis that forced even well-to-do residents to scale back on luxuries like keeping servants, dining out, and traveling by rail.

For those of all races, the Great Depression presented American workers with unprecedented hardships and misery, but also with an extraordinary new opportunity. The creation of the Congress of Industrial Organizations (CIO) in 1936 brought into the American labor movement legions of unskilled and semiskilled workers who had long been excluded by the narrow craft unionism of the AFL. In Los Angeles, where the labor movement had languished under well-organized employer offensives, workers responded quickly. Union membership rose from 20,000 at the beginning of the Depression to more than 150,000 by 1938.[64] In cities like Detroit, Chicago, and Birmingham, where blacks were a substantial part of the automobile, steel, and meatpacking labor forces, the CIO became a potent ally in the battle for racial equality, often joining with local civil rights groups and churches to campaign against racial discrimination at work and at home.[65]

But in Los Angeles, where blacks were either excluded from most industries or limited to unorganized custodial work in factories, they were prevented from garnering the benefits of the CIO's official commitment to egalitarianism. Mexican workers, however, did benefit from organized labor's growing strength in Los Angeles, where the CIO became a vehicle for their politicization. Organizing warehousemen as well as textile, agriculture, steel, and transportation workers, the CIO fought against the "Mexican wage" and actively recruited new workers in the Mexican community. The Los Angeles CIO Council created the Committee to Aid Mexican Workers, which protested police harassment and encouraged Mexican Americans to become active participants in the American electoral process. By the end of the Depression, the CIO had organized more than fifteen thousand Mexican workers in the Los Angeles area.[66]

With the exception of several integrated locals of the AFL's Waiters, Letter Carriers, and Bricklayers unions, most union activity involving African Americans in prewar Los Angeles was limited to black-only unions. The Southern Pacific's redcap station porters organized in Los Angeles in 1932 and gained an AFL charter in 1933. Though small, with approximately eighty members in 1938, this union was powerful because white preference for black servants in Los Angeles effectively gave black redcaps a monopoly on their positions. In 1937, the Red Cap Station Porters Federal Local 18329, which represented West Coast redcaps, negotiated the first contract in the nation between an all-black redcap union and a railroad company, the Southern Pacific. The contract governed hours of service, rate of pay, and working conditions for West Coast redcaps. Most important, it abolished the classification of redcaps as "voluntary workers," a classification that had allowed the railroad not to pay these workers, forcing them to survive on tips alone.[67]

In 1925, porter Charles Upton organized a Los Angeles local of the independent Brotherhood of Sleeping Car Porters (BSCP). But the BSCP ran into more difficulties in Los Angeles than the redcaps had encountered. Until the passage of the Amended Railway Labor Act of 1934, which protected railroad workers' right to organize, Pullman Company representatives threatened Upton for his union activities, forcing him to hold meetings in his car and other secret locations. He reported that this intimidation was highly effective at discouraging porters who "were married, had responsibilities and were either buying or owned their homes; for those reasons they could not come out into the open with their union activities." Yet, even after 1934, Upton complained that "a number of the older men retain a reticent attitude and do not ally themselves with the unions," an explanation for why fewer than half of Los Angeles porters were union members in 1938. Nor were those porters who joined the union particularly enthusiastic "union men." Upton complained about dwindling attendance at union meetings and grew exasperated when Los Angeles porters failed to donate a portion of their wages to the defense fund for labor radical Harry Bridges in 1939, writing privately that his porters were "a bunch of reactionaries."[68] More likely, however, porters in Los Angeles were neither "reactionaries" nor naïve. Rather, their dream of life in Los Angeles was one of comfort rather than conflict.

If Los Angeles blacks benefited only minimally from organized labor's sweeping Depression-era campaign, the anti-poverty programs of FDR's New Deal proved far more ameliorative. According to Douglas Flamming, Mayor Frank Shaw, a Republican, elicited tens of millions of dollars from the federal government and oversaw 444 New Deal projects in Los Angeles, employing approximately forty thousand workers. For blacks, New Deal programs paradoxically both provided vital job opportunities and perpetuated racial segregation. The National Youth Administration (NYA), the Civil Works Administration (CWA), and the Civilian Conservation Corps (CCC) unabashedly discriminated against African Americans; in the case of the CCC, black and white youths were often divided into separate work camps. Nonetheless, the heavily segregated NYA ultimately employed more than two thousand black youths in California at the height of the Depression. Similarly, the CCC hired numerous black workers to help maintain California's parks and roads. Twenty-year-old Ersey O'Brien worked at a CCC camp just north of San Diego, earning thirty dollars a month fighting fires, digging ditches, building roads, and driving trucks. Despite segregation, O'Brien remembers, his CCC days were important, not only because they provided a much-needed paycheck but also because "most of us had never been anywhere away from home and this taught us how to live with other people" and instilled a sense of discipline.[69]

However, for many politically active African Americans in Los Angeles, the perpetuation of racial segregation in federal programs was intolerable, whatever the real economic, and perhaps social, benefits such programs conferred. Floyd Covington, Urban League director and local caseworker for the State Emergency Relief Administration, inveighed against segregation in the NYA; and the local NAACP vigorously protested discrimination in the CWA. Although these particular protests met with only limited success, black organizations played a central role in anti-poverty efforts in the Los Angeles black community. The Urban League's job placement program, for example, proved to be a highly effective complement to the New Deal programs. Statistics from the early years of the Depression suggest that more blacks sought employment through the Urban League than through California's expansive State Employment Agency.[70] More broadly, the Los Angeles NAACP aggressively challenged racial discrimination in education, housing, and job training. For example, attorney and Los Angeles

NAACP president Thomas L. Griffith sued the suburban Monrovia school district for forcing the area's black and Mexican students into a segregated school building deemed structurally unsound by the State Architect Department.[71]

While these organizations fought to expand educational and employment opportunities, the black press of Los Angeles played a crucial role in politicizing its readers. More than simply conveying newsworthy information, the *California Eagle* and the *Los Angeles Sentinel,* the city's two most influential black newspapers, prodded their readerships to challenge racial discrimination. Owned by South Carolina native and indomitable firebrand Charlotta Bass, the *Eagle* had been a Los Angeles institution since 1912, when she took over the paper from ailing newspaperman John Neimore. Charlotta and her husband, Joseph Bass, ran the paper jointly until his death in 1934, after which she ran it single-handedly.

In 1932, Charlotta Bass hired a recent migrant and young reporter with impeccable recommendations, Leon Washington. The ambitious Washington quickly tired of reporting and, with a loan from an influential cousin, started his own newspaper, the *Los Angeles Sentinel.* Like the *California Eagle,* the *Los Angeles Sentinel* railed against racism in Southern California. Washington personally investigated, photographed, and then published serialized reports on the effects of discrimination along Central Avenue (see figure 2). Among blacks, Washington was most well known for his direct-action tactics against segregation during the Depression, including his "Don't Spend Where You Can't Work" campaign, which he advertised in his newspaper.[72] In this campaign, which occurred simultaneously with similar campaigns in other cities, Washington led blacks in boycotting businesses that had discriminatory hiring policies. Rarely mincing words, he announced publicly that "refusal to employ Negroes will bring quick and decisive action."[73]

Leon Washington's influential cousin, Loren Miller, was a University of Southern California law school graduate and rising black luminary. While finishing law school, Miller began writing for the *Eagle* and earned a reputation in the black community as an articulate and outspoken defender of African Americans. In his fiery columns, Miller attacked not only white racism but also the "accommodationism" of Los Angeles's black middle class. In a 20 May 1932 editorial in the *California Eagle,* Miller railed against the black middle-class leadership in the city, "that great army of stuffed shirts." "No city," Miller concluded, "is more in need of intelligent leadership than this one where mountebanks flourish at every street corner."

FIGURE 2. Leon Washington, editor of the *Los Angeles Sentinel* and organizer of the "Don't Spend Where You Can't Work" boycott campaign during the Great Depression, ca. late 1930s. Courtesy of the Southern California Library for Social Studies and Research.

Miller was particularly irritated at the Los Angeles NAACP for its failure to take a public stand of support for the "Scottsboro Boys." In 1931, nine young black men who had been riding a rail car in Alabama were convicted of gang-raping two young white women. Despite overwhelming evidence that the defendants were not guilty and that their accusers were famously manipulative, mendacious, and promiscuous, all nine young men were quickly handed a death sentence. The first and most ardent defender of the Scottsboro Boys was the International Labor Defense, an affiliate of the American Communist Party. The Communist Party's efforts on behalf of the Scottsboro Boys drew African

Americans around the country toward more radical politics. The Los Angeles branch of the party, established in 1919, was based in the multiracial community of Boyle Heights and initially directed its appeals to Jewish garment workers. But in the late 1920s, party members had a growing presence on Central Avenue, where they picketed Jim Crow businesses, and the Scottsboro trial accelerated this trend. Although blacks made up only a small proportion of the Los Angeles Communist Party's approximately seven hundred members during the Great Depression, the organization did attract the support of a small and loyal group of African Americans, including Lou Rosser, Frank and Hursel Alexander, and Pettis Perry, who would become one of the Communist Party's leading black spokespersons in the 1940s and 1950s.[74]

Perry had migrated from Alabama in the 1920s, finding work in the Imperial Valley as an agricultural laborer, an unusual occupation for blacks in Southern California. There he had immediate contact with communist organizers for the Cannery and Agricultural Workers Industrial Union, who sought to organize the area's multiracial but predominantly Mexican labor force. He again came upon communists along Central Avenue, where they distributed handbills about the Scottsboro Boys. These encounters made a lasting impression on Perry, who "began to give every free hour to spreading the news of the Scottsboro case to as many people in my community as I possibly could. I went from door to door with petitions, with leaflets, magazines, or whatever was available."[75]

But whatever community-based support Perry might have generated for the Communist Party among black residents was limited, in prewar Los Angeles, both by fears of political repression and by the patent disconnect between the rhetoric of communism and the daily lives of most African Americans. Police Chief Davis, who believed that one of the primary goals of communist ideology was to encourage sexual liaisons between white women and black men, encouraged his red squad to brutally disrupt any gatherings of suspected radicals.[76] More important, the limited influence of the Communist Party in prewar black Los Angeles also reflected organized labor's minimal influence in that community. Communist rhetoric about the "shared class exploitation" of all workers must have sounded somewhat fantastic to African Americans, who were generally not industrial workers in large plants. For most blacks, the only meaningful division in daily life was racial. White students attended one school; blacks, Mexicans, and Asians attended another. White workers lived in white neighborhoods; black workers lived with

Mexicans and Asians. Whites and Mexicans worked in manufacturing industries, but blacks usually did not. And when blacks went to work, they almost always worked with other blacks, and they were often serving whites. It is not difficult to see how most black people would be uninterested in a political movement that emphasized a shared class experience that did not match their reality.

But if Perry, Miller, and others were frustrated by the black community's unresponsiveness to either the Scottsboro Boys trial or the overtures of the Communist Party, they underestimated the assertiveness of that community. As it had throughout the history of black Los Angeles, the African American church played a vital role in mobilizing the city's black residents during the Great Depression. From the Depression through the 1940s, one of the most influential crusaders for black equality and opportunity in Los Angeles was Reverend Clayton Russell, the "fighting pastor" of the People's Independent Church. A Los Angeles native who graduated from Jefferson High and the University of Southern California and later studied theology in Denmark, Russell became the second pastor of the People's Independent Church in 1935.[77] True to its name, the People's Independent Church became a vehicle for community mobilization, establishing cooperative markets, a boys' home, and job relief programs, all of which Russell publicized on his weekly radio show. Summarizing his philosophy of the church's secular responsibility, Russell declared: "I consider it a sin to stand up in the pulpit and preach to hungry people and not help them to get a job or get some food."[78]

Los Angeles's prewar black community also took electoral politics very seriously. During the Depression, African Americans across the country made an historic shift away from the party of Lincoln to the Democratic Party. In 1934, African American Augustus F. Hawkins ousted black Republican Frederick Roberts in the Sixty-Second State Assembly District. A light-skinned Louisiana migrant who grew up in an upper-middle-class South Central home, Hawkins presented himself as a pro-labor, pro-welfare candidate and made overtures to a broad group of Democratic voters, including white craft union members.[79] Once in the assembly, however, Hawkins found that his support for the party was rarely reciprocated. He proposed some of the most progressive legislation in California during the Depression, including a proposal for low-cost housing, a bill prohibiting discrimination in public employment statewide, and a bill protecting what the Wagner Act failed to protect—economic rights for domestic workers.[80] But his party peers refused to back Hawkins, who remained the only African American in the state legislature until Berkeley's William Byron Rumford Sr. was elected in 1948.

At the local level, blacks lacked political representation on either the city council or the Los Angeles County Board of Supervisors. While Chicago and New York had produced local black representatives in the 1920s and 1930s, Los Angeles remained stubbornly resistant to African American representation. This was largely a function of the city's unusually large council districts, whose vast size eliminated the chance of black near-majorities. The large size also made the districts easily susceptible to racial gerrymandering, a practice that, while never documented, was nonetheless widely recognized in the black community.[81] Until the size of the black population increased, African Americans had to rely on nonblack candidates to adequately represent their interests, a dubious arrangement anywhere in the United States before World War II.

Black Los Angeles on the Eve of War

On the eve of World War II, African Americans in Los Angeles were justifiably ambivalent about their progress, their current status, and their future prospects in a city still widely heralded as a paradise for their race. A much higher proportion of black residents owned homes than in any other major city. They did not live in racially isolated "black neighborhoods," but rather in interracial neighborhoods. Their children attended decent public schools that were also patchworks of racial intermixture. Perhaps most important, they lived, for the most part, free from fear of physical violence.

Yet, despite all the tangible assets Los Angeles offered, it was as rigidly defined by race as any southern hamlet. While the geographic boundaries of the Central Avenue area had expanded in the prewar years, stretching south to Slauson Avenue and west to Main Street by the time of the 1940 census, restrictive covenants and overt white resistance severely circumscribed black residential mobility. In 1942, this was made painfully apparent when the members of a local black family, the Laws, were arrested for moving into their own home because they had violated a racially restrictive covenant.[82]

Largely excluded from the Depression-battered industrial economy, blacks benefited little from the new policies of racial equality pursued by organized labor. Forced to find work in low-paying and often demeaning service jobs, African Americans struggled, mostly on their own, to keep their heads above the tide of poverty the Depression brought. And unlike blacks in Chicago, New York, and several other cities, blacks in Los Angeles had minimal political representation. Most distressing, little on the immediate horizon portended any great transformation in the lives of black Los Angeles residents. Little, that is, until the attack on Pearl Harbor on 7 December 1941.

CHAPTER 2

The Great Migration and the Changing Face of Los Angeles

Today there can be no question that Los Angeles is destined
to be one of the great centers of Negro life in America.
Carey McWilliams, *Southern California:
An Island on the Land,* 1946

World War II initiated a fundamentally new era in African American life
and history. The deepening labor shortage, coupled with the rising demand for defense production, forced employers to reconsider, often re-
luctantly, their exclusive preference for white male labor. Accelerating
this trend was the Fair Employment Practice Committee, which threatened to revoke federal defense contracts from discriminatory employers.
Throughout the country, African Americans responded to these circumstances by journeying to the nation's burgeoning defense centers in
search of better jobs and racial equality.

Generally in their twenties and early thirties, and often parents,
members of the "Great Migration generation" resolved to improve
their own lives and the lives of their children.[1] Informed by their sur-
prisingly diverse experiences with race in the South, these migrants
would ultimately define the priorities and politics of black urban
America for approximately two decades. They also wrought great
change in their new homes. Most affected was Los Angeles's prewar
black population, which viewed the Great Migration with some un-
certainty. Some celebrated the influx, because it brought families together, signaled further advances for the race, or, more pragmatically,
brought potential new customers and business opportunities to the De-

pression-battered economy of Central Avenue. Others perceived the waves of new migrants as a serious threat to the black community, whose proportionally small size had allowed for its relatively peaceful, if always tenuous, existence.

More broadly, the Great Migration thoroughly transformed Los Angeles and other American cities because it forced white citizens and public officials to meet head-on the high social costs of segregation. Having long ignored the causes of residential segregation, Los Angeles city government was suddenly confronted by its debilitating effects, including the severely overcrowded neighborhoods of Central Avenue and the slums of Little Tokyo, recently vacated by its Japanese residents, who had been sent to wartime internment camps. More universally, the Great Migration permanently transformed the nature of race relations in urban America by undermining the most fundamental rules separating black workers from white workers, black neighbors from white neighbors, and even black men from white women.[2]

Such transformation was evident in many American cities during World War II, but it was particularly pronounced in Los Angeles, which, seemingly overnight, became the nation's second largest industrial manufacturing center. Outranked only by the Detroit area, Los Angeles received more than $11 billion in war contracts, built twice as many warplanes as any other production area, and rivaled all other areas in shipbuilding. By 1943, more than half a million people were employed in ship, plane, and steel production in Los Angeles. The War Manpower Commission nonetheless reported a labor shortage of at least sixty thousand workers, ensuring a continuing stream of migrants.[3] But while Southern California's sprawling factories forged new armaments, the region itself became a highly volatile crucible in which old patterns of race relations mixed with renewed black aspirations for equality.

The Great Migration: A View from the South

The migration of blacks that began during World War II and continued into the late 1960s marked a decisive turning point in African American history because it brought almost five million black people out of the South and exposed them to unprecedented political, occupational, and educational opportunities. Traditionally, scholars have referred to this as the "Second Great Migration," an extension of the more thoroughly studied "Great Migration" from the rural South to the urban North in the first half of the twentieth century, and particularly during World

War I. But the later migration was not merely an extension of the earlier journey; rather, it was a fundamentally new social phenomenon, the true Great Migration.

It differed, first and most obviously, in size: 1.8 million blacks left the South between 1910 and 1940, but more than twice that number departed between 1940 and 1970. Second, the vast size of the migration, combined with the multinodal nature of World War II defense production, caused a much wider geographic dispersal of migrants. In 1940, 78 percent of African Americans still lived in the South; by 1970, that number had been reduced to 53 percent. This broader geographic dispersal was most evident in the West, whose share of the nation's black population rose from less than 1 percent to about 8 percent during the same period. Third, African Americans became much more urban: whereas only 50 percent of blacks were urbanites in 1940, 80 percent lived in cities in 1970.[4] Fourth, the migration begun during World War II was heavily influenced by—and would ultimately influence—federal support for black civil rights. In addition to opening up actual jobs, the FEPC created among migrants the expectation that the federal government could and would intervene on their behalf, an expectation that would have great implications for the emerging civil rights movement.

Finally, just as their destinations were more diverse than during the first half of the century, so too were the origins of these later migrants. It was striking that the vast majority of black migrants to Los Angeles, and probably to many other war production centers, came from metropolitan areas rather than rural and farm areas. In 1950, more than 85 percent of the city's recent black migrants had come from metropolitan areas and only about 8 percent from farms; in the 1950s and 1960s, between 60 and 70 percent of migrants were from metropolitan areas.[5] Most migrants came from Texas (24.2 percent), Louisiana (18.8), Mississippi (7 percent), Arkansas and Oklahoma (6.2 percent), Georgia (5.2 percent), Alabama (4.2 percent), Missouri (3.4 percent), Tennessee (3.2 percent), and Kansas (2.4 percent).[6]

Often traveling on the Southern Pacific's Sunset Route, which had brought the first porters to the city fifty years earlier, migrants came from cities such as Baton Rouge, Shreveport, and New Orleans in Louisiana and Fort Worth, San Antonio, and Houston in Texas. Though often described by contemporaries and historians as dislocated and unsophisticated ruralites, these migrants, in fact, arrived with remarkably complex personal histories and life experiences. As a number of impressive studies have already demonstrated, black migrants to California brought with them rich southern traditions, from Baptist religion to family recipes to blues music, and made important cultural contributions to the state.[7]

Less well understood is the way in which the social and political experiences of migrants from different parts of the South influenced their expectations of Los Angeles and their reactions when those expectations were not met. Virtually all blacks in the South shared common experiences with odious racism, but the effects of that racism differed from community to community, producing distinctive experiences with ethnic competition, labor relations, and political activity. The cities of Shreveport, New Orleans, and Houston, for example, demonstrate the diversity of those experiences.

Located in the fertile northwestern corner of Louisiana adjacent to the Red River, the city of Shreveport was founded in the 1830s as a trading post for cotton and lumber and was heavily dependent on slave labor. Because of Shreveport's disproportionate racial distribution (fifteen blacks to one white), whites were vigilant about maintaining control. During Reconstruction, the single black man who dared to vote Republican in a Caddo Parish election was swiftly executed with impunity. In the early years of the twentieth century, Shreveport became a major Ku Klux Klan recruiting center; between 1900 and 1931, at least nineteen blacks were lynched in Caddo Parish, more than in any other Louisiana parish. As one local NAACP member put it in 1923: "This place is one of the most intolerant in the whole Southland."[8]

More frustrating to the NAACP was that the campaign of terror waged against blacks in Shreveport was a highly effective deterrent to black protest against racial segregation. The NAACP attempted several recruitment drives in Shreveport in the 1930s, each one broken up by the local sheriff, who personally administered brutal beatings to participants. An NAACP field organizer from Washington, D.C., was astounded by the atmosphere of fear and accommodation he encountered among blacks. In a telling 1937 letter to NAACP president Walter White, the field agent wrote that "the colored people there are still a bit skittish," always fearful of white mob violence. Another agent explained that low attendance at Shreveport NAACP meetings was a function of the fact that "the colored people are scared and stay away."[9] Blacks in Shreveport likely resisted their degradation and achieved a measure of dignity through creative, sometimes surreptitious ways. But under the circumstances, black resistance remained "infrapolitical," to borrow Robin Kelley's notion, rather than explicitly political.[10]

In an atmosphere of such intense repression, blacks in Shreveport could do little to combat the racial discrimination that kept them employed only as laborers and domestics and kept their children stuck in segregated and dilapidated schools. During World War II, the city grew rapidly as white Louisianans sought work at Barksdale Army Air Field, one of the world's largest airfields at the time, but blacks continued to be excluded from all but the most menial positions. Bitterly resentful of their status but fearful of racial violence, a growing number of black residents "voted with their feet" by fleeing Shreveport. Some whites were so frightened by the prospect of losing their black menial and domestic workers that they encouraged local bus and rail ticket agents to refuse to sell tickets to blacks.[11] But those African Americans who were determined enough simply could not be stopped.

Many first went south to New Orleans, long a popular destination for blacks within Louisiana. New Orleans did not have Shreveport's history of racial violence, but occupational discrimination there was as intense as anywhere in the South. Since the late nineteenth century, the bustling docks of New Orleans had provided ample employment for blacks. But black workers also faced competition and harassment from white longshoremen, whose unions often sought to restore white power on the docks.[12] This situation changed in the 1930s, when the racially egalitarian International Longshoremen's and Warehousemen's Union (ILWU), led by Harry Bridges, came to New Orleans to organize black dockworkers. Initially skeptical about the white-led union, black workers joined in increasing numbers and found the ILWU to be a true champion of black equality.[13] More educated African Americans in white-collar positions in New Orleans benefited from the egalitarianism of the CIO's United Office and Professional Workers of America, a communist-dominated union that treated both black and white workers with equality and dignity.[14]

But these hopeful developments were overshadowed by the outright exclusion of blacks from the new employment opportunities opened by World War II. Most frustrating was their exclusion from the vast Delta Shipyard, one of the leading southern producers of warships. Delta's management remained intractable on the issue of racial integration, refusing to hire blacks even when the company was understaffed by 40 percent. In 1943, an FEPC field agent reported that the Delta yard "was making the slowest progress [toward integration] of any shipyard in the country."[15] Like blacks in Shreveport, black residents of New Orleans could no longer brook such intransigence. Between 1941 and

1944, more than thirty-six thousand blacks—20 percent of the city's African American population—left New Orleans.[16]

Houston's history imparted distinctive racial lessons to its black population. Relatively unburdened by racial violence, Houston developed a reputation among southern blacks as a safe and promising city. One young black scholar surveying the racial landscape in 1930 remarked that "race relations" were "very good here for a Southern city."[17] This observation was corroborated by a series of interviews conducted by black sociologist Charles Johnson under the auspices of the famous Carnegie-Myrdal study. The interviewees were remarkably consistent in asserting that, despite the obvious limitations imposed by racial segregation, blacks in Houston lived free of fear and were not expected to wear the mask of degraded inferiority that was compulsory elsewhere in the South.[18] In addition, African Americans in Houston celebrated the city's attractive housing opportunities and the high proportion of black homeowners, only slightly less than in Los Angeles.[19]

Yet, as in Shreveport and New Orleans, employment opportunities for black workers remained severely circumscribed. Most black women worked as domestics, and Houston's black men were relegated to the hardest, heaviest, and dirtiest jobs.[20] Exacerbating black economic deprivation, and complicating the southern standard of race relations, was Houston's large Mexican population. One of the only areas in which black men held a monopoly was on Houston's busy docks—only because, according to one black observer, the work was "heavy and in the sun" and "whites and Mexicans dislike it."[21] Charles Johnson concluded that despite Houston's benefits, the social status of blacks was indeed inferior to that of Mexicans: "In the ordinary social relationships, the Mexican is accorded recognition on the same level as the white man, but the freedom which is accorded him isn't of the same degree of intensity as that possessed by the white man. On the other hand, the fact that it exists at all makes the status of the Mexican superior to that of the Negro."[22] Like blacks in Los Angeles, blacks in Houston often found themselves at the bottom of a tripartite racial hierarchy.

Undeterred by the threat of racial violence, African Americans in Houston were outspoken opponents of racial discrimination and organized an aggressive civil rights movement in the late 1930s and early 1940s. The Houston branch of the NAACP quickly became one of the most influential in the country, and the national organization lauded the "aggressiveness and pugnacity of Texas negroes." "This bunch," the assistant field secretary for the NAACP wrote of the Houston branch, "means business."[23] The Houston NAACP campaign focused on integrating buses, challenging police brutality, building health facilities, and integrating black labor into all jobs, particularly those created by public funds.[24] In one of the more successful protests, the NAACP organized a group of black teachers, who threatened to strike in protest of unequal wages. The Houston School Board initially balked, but after the women walked off the job, school administrators were forced to equalize salaries. Similarly, when the NAACP organized a massive demonstration in front of the Kress drugstore in downtown Houston, protesting the store's refusal to serve blacks at the lunch counter, Kress management reversed its policy.[25] Finally, when black Houstonian Dr. Lonnie Smith—local dentist and NAACP member—was denied the right to vote in the Democratic primary, Thurgood Marshall took his case to the U.S. Supreme Court and won a landmark 1944 decision, in *Smith v. Allwright,* outlawing the so-called white primary.

Nevertheless, the coming of World War II revealed that Houston's politically active black community was no match for the intransigence of racism in the workplace. Following the bombing of Pearl Harbor, black Houston businessman B. F. Haile founded the Houston Colored Aircraft School, a trade school that trained African Americans to work in Houston's booming wartime aircraft industry. Shortly after opening its doors, however, the school's enrollment began to plummet because blacks were leaving Houston. Haile and the Houston Negro Advisory Board were stumped. Why, they asked, "were so many Negro skilled workers having to leave Houston to go to . . . the West Coast to help build airplanes and ships when there are plants right here in our back yards?"[26] The answer, of course, was that no amount of industrial training could force Houston's aircraft employers to hire black workers. Moreover, Houston's two big shipyards, Todd Shipbuilding and Brown Shipbuilding, refused to hire blacks.[27] The only major industrial plant where blacks made inroads was the city's sprawling Hughes Tool plant, where workers were represented by the CIO's United Steelworkers of America (USWA). There, African Americans not only got jobs but were given equal representation on the union's negotiating committee, earning the union, and the CIO in general, great accolades in the local black press.[28] Clearly, however, Hughes was the exception to a rule that had become intolerable to Houston's assertive black population.

Black migrants from Houston, Shreveport, New Orleans, and dozens of other small cities and towns wrote back to relatives about the opportunities in California. Houston's black newspaper, the *Houston Informer,* often printed the letters from former Houstonians. One black migrant wrote to his family about his experiences in Oakland: "Well, I am here and what's more, I am a full fledged welder on the pay roll at $66.32. I am going to school . . . to try and make first class in about two or three weeks . . . Now, the jobs are here. They are hiring all they can get." Though housing was overcrowded, this Houstonian didn't care: "Money is what I want." [29] These letters encouraged others to migrate, much to the dismay of one black community leader who lamented the departure of so many Houstonians. "Our people," he complained "are leaving here at the rate of more than 1000 a week." Furthermore, "the majority of those" migrating to California were "fairly substantial citizens." [30]

Regardless of what communities black migrants came from, they all shared a common revulsion at the stubbornness of Southern racism. As the nation fought to protect democracy and human dignity, creating thousands of new jobs in the process, southern blacks transformed their revulsion into resolve and left the South in record numbers. At the peak of the migration in 1943, more than six thousand African Americans came to Los Angeles each month, and more than two hundred thousand arrived in the 1940s. Beyond their shared antipathy toward discrimination, however, Los Angeles's black migrants brought to the city varying experiences with racism and, more important, varying experiences combating it. Migrants from Houston, for example, had experienced an atmosphere of political awareness and civil rights activism that would affect their reactions when they encountered discrimination in Los Angeles. Some migrants from New Orleans brought with them a legacy of affiliation with organized labor and even communism, which also shaped their activities in Los Angeles. In contrast, many of Shreveport's migrants probably found sufficient satisfaction in simply being able to walk the streets of Los Angeles free from fear. Whatever their origins, however, the African Americans of the Great Migration would exercise a profound influence on both black and white Los Angeles, and particularly on the black community's ongoing struggle for racial equality.

The Great Migration: A View from Los Angeles

The vast influx of African Americans from the South permanently transformed Los Angeles. Small and isolated enough to be virtually invisible to white Los Angeles before World War II, the city's black population grew so fast that even the most determined could not ignore it. Whites were now forced to interact with blacks to a degree unimaginable in pre-war Los Angeles, a situation that generated unprecedented racial conflict and more frequent articulations of racist sentiment throughout the city. Both blacks and whites feared that the new population explosion would undermine the previous relative tranquility of race relations in Los Angeles, and many white residents openly protested the arrival of more migrants. Longtime members of the black community were also concerned that the resources of the geographically confined African American community were being seriously taxed; many new migrants were forced to live in overcrowded slum conditions until they could earn enough to resettle. The city and county governments of Los Angeles responded to the migration by openly acknowledging the fact of racial discrimination in Los Angeles and, more important, by earmarking county and city resources for the improvement of black neighborhoods and black housing.

Migrants who had read the NAACP's special issue of *The Crisis* in 1942 must have been stunned when they arrived in Los Angeles. In honor of the organization's national convention in Los Angeles that year, editors filled the pages of the journal with photos of the famously wide, tree-lined streets, accompanied by effusive descriptions of Southern California as the land of "fun and frolic": "There are attractive residential districts with California bungalows and more pretentious mansions flanked by spacious lawns, nestled in shrubbery, and shaded by palm trees. Flowers are everywhere."[31] But the seventy thousand black migrants who resided in Little Tokyo during World War II experienced a very different Los Angeles. Dorothy Baruch, of *The Nation*, captured the circumstances in which they lived:

In place after place children lived in windowless rooms, amid peeling plaster, rats and the flies that gathered thick around food that stood on open shelves or kitchen-bedroom tables. Ordinarily there was no bathtub; never more than a single washbowl or lavatory. Sometimes as many as forty people shared one toilet. Families were separated only by sheets strung up between beds. Many of the beds were "hot," with people taking turns sleeping in them.[32]

Formerly home to Los Angeles's sizable Japanese population, who had been swiftly relocated to internment camps during the war, Little Tokyo became the port of entry for new black migrants. Located just south of Union Station, where the Southern Pacific ended its route from New

Orleans and Houston, "Bronzeville"—as it came to be called—became the center of the black migrant community and a visible symbol of the worst effects of residential segregation.

Shortly after the Japanese internment, property owners in Little Tokyo capitalized on Los Angeles's wartime housing shortage by subdividing small, single-family apartments into multiple-occupancy "kitchenettes." Also a popular arrangement in other cities during World War II, kitchenettes were grossly substandard, commonly characterized by flimsy partitioning, dangerous overcrowding, and inadequate plumbing and sewer systems. A study by the Los Angeles County Health Department demonstrated that Little Tokyo's eighty thousand residents were crowded into a community designed to house fewer than thirty thousand. Wartime kitchenettes were breeding grounds for rodent-borne typhus, tuberculosis, and head lice. It was not uncommon, the Health Department reported, to find "families consisting of two adults and five or more children eating, living, and sleeping in a single hotel room." Furthermore, "gas plates connected with rubber hose were used for cooking and heating; foods were kept without refrigeration or adequate storage facilities; dishes washed in the community bath; cockroaches, rats, bedbugs and vermin infestations were almost impossible to control."[33]

As deplorable as conditions were in Little Tokyo, many migrants had few options. Those with family ties in Los Angeles often doubled up with family members on Central Avenue rather than settle in Little Tokyo. As one observer noted: "The better adjusted Negro in-migrant usually goes to the south or western areas of L.A. and only the friendless and helpless come to Little Tokyo."[34] Surveys of Little Tokyo showed that 35 percent of residents were from Louisiana and 25 percent from Texas, a suggestive ratio, given that each state sent approximately the same number of migrants during the war. Because fewer native Louisianans resided in prewar Los Angeles, wartime migrants from Louisiana arrived with fewer family connections and probably faced even greater challenges than their Texas counterparts. But even those migrants who went to Central Avenue often found themselves in severely overcrowded circumstances. In fact, so many moved directly to Central Avenue that the Southern Pacific made an ad hoc station stop at Fortieth and Central, three miles short of its official stop at Union Station.[35]

As they did in Little Tokyo, many new arrivals on Central Avenue crowded into recklessly subdivided apartments, but many more found shelter with relatives. Louisiana migrant O'Neil Cannon remembered that his family and friends all passed through Mama Bullen's house at one time or another.[36] A distant relative of Cannon and a native Mississippian, Bullen rented affordable rooms to new arrivals in her large Long Beach Avenue house. She also referred them to job placement programs through the Urban League and the United States Employment Service (USES). While family networks eased migrants' transition into their new community, the community itself was barely capable of sustaining the influx. During World War II, intense racial restriction throughout the city kept the geographic boundaries of the Central Avenue area from expanding significantly, though the population increased by more than forty thousand people. The citywide housing shortage, which affected both black and white wartime migrants, was incalculably worse for blacks, who faced housing shortages in black areas and racial restriction elsewhere.

The overcrowding of Little Tokyo and Central Avenue, however, coincided with swiftly expanding employment and sharply rising incomes for many African Americans in Los Angeles. The concurrence of these developments produced an urban anomaly: the prosperous ghetto, where residents often lived in slums but not always in poverty. Although only a temporary wartime phenomenon, the prosperous ghetto deeply influenced postwar expectations among blacks, many of whom enjoyed discretionary income for the first time in their lives. While they were forced to live in squalor, many African Americans could afford, nonetheless, to spend their hard-earned paychecks after hours in Little Tokyo and along Central Avenue. In Little Tokyo, they patronized Shepp's Playhouse and Club Finale, which featured nightly performances by jazz greats Gerald Wilson, Coleman Hawkins, and others. Even more popular among recent southern migrants were the gospel, blues, and R&B acts that came to the Downbeat Club, the Flame, and the Casablanca along Central Avenue.[37]

On a Saturday night in 1943, Deputy Mayor Orville Caldwell toured Little Tokyo at the behest of the mayor. What he saw appalled him: "On Saturday nights they have more money in their pockets than they had before in a year. Many will use it to buy liquor and marihuana."[38] Certainly, revelry was a real part of life in Little Tokyo: between 1942 and 1944, forty-seven liquor stores, as well as numerous storefront brothels, were opened in a four-block area of the community.[39] Though surely exaggerated, Caldwell's remarks accurately captured migrants' newfound prosperity and their freedom to spend their money not only on what they needed but also on what they wanted. This freedom generated considerable pride among migrants, who quickly renamed the area Bronzeville and even helped to create a Bronzeville Chamber of Commerce in 1943.[40] Not only did economic opportunity represent a break from the past for most newcomers, but it also set a standard for the future. Having enjoyed the freedom of a discretionary income during the war, blacks would fight to retain that freedom long after the war.

If life in Bronzeville brought new economic and recreational opportunities to migrants, it also brought them into closer, and often more intimate, contact with whites. While the residences of Bronzeville were almost exclusively black, its nightlife was not. Before the war, well-to-do whites, including Hollywood celebrities, would occasionally patronize black clubs on Central Avenue. During the war, Bronzeville attracted a much larger and wider group of white thrill-seekers, including war workers, servicemen, and local youths, who flocked to the community to dance, drink hard, and pick up prostitutes. Despite Mayor Fletcher Bowron's imposition of a 2 A.M. curfew on alcohol sales in 1940, enforcement in black neighborhoods was particularly lax, a fact well known among young revelers. Many of these pleasure seekers had also learned that Bronzeville's many storefront "shoeshine parlors"—often several per block—were fronts for brothels.[41] It is difficult to know how blacks and whites perceived their encounters with one another in Bronzeville, but the frequency of street fights and bar brawls between the two groups suggested that such encounters were acrimonious at least as often as they were amicable.[42]

Outside Bronzeville, white reaction to the wave of wartime black migration was considerably more hostile. The concentration of brothels and after-hours bars in Bronzeville created the impression among some whites that blacks were disproportionately prone to illicit activity. "I hear that Colored People," one white man wrote to California Governor Earl Warren, "controll all the vise [sic]."[43] Others believed that the sudden growth in the black population was sure to produce an upsurge of violent crime. One Angeleno blamed blacks for the "crime wave that has broken out in Los Angeles." He continued: "I have it from good authority, that the negroes are gettin' all the guns they can and are having their old ones fixed up."[44] (In fact, FBI crime statistics do reveal a sharp rise in crime during the war—particularly larceny and auto theft—but the statistics are not broken down by race.)[45]

His primary complaint, one shared by many whites, was that the growing numbers of black people were ruining the state of California.

He had "refrained from joining the 'Native Sons of the Golden West,' because I am beginning to think that this state is rapidly deteriorating in good citizenship." "In southern states," he continued, "they have laws that keep the niggers in their places, but unfortunately for the white race in this state, there is nothing to control them. I wish that this state was back to where it was before this scum of the nation came here, before the war."[46]

Rather than articulating specific grievances, many whites simply employed long-standing anti-immigrant and anti-Okie rhetoric in their attacks on blacks. A white woman in California's Central Valley drew on stereotypes of the white migrants who had left Oklahoma during the 1930s when she complained about the "thousands upon thousands of negroes from the deep south [that] had been shipped into Los Angeles. . . . These negroes in Los Angeles, according to people there, are very stupid and unable to learn very much. They represent a future great drain on the unemployment insurance and old age pensions of the state as well as a menace to labor in general." Ultimately, she concluded, their motives were identical to those of the Okies: "I live in a rural section where we have seen what a racket has been made of relief by the lazy element of okies and how they never miss a trick when it comes to unemployment insurance and old age pensions."[47]

Others compared the black migration to Mexican immigration. One southern California woman, stationed with her husband in Parris Island, South Carolina, during the war, took time to write to the governor to express her anger:

We get disquieting letters from our friends in So. Calif.—to the effect that Negroes are invading Calif. at the rate of 10,000 or so per month. After living in this awful country [South Carolina] for 14–15 months where negroes outnumber the whites—we feel *sick* to hear such news!!! The Mexican situation there is bad enough—but to add negroes—! The negroes here are practically savages! Please don't let our Calif. be ruined—war or no war! We do not want to return to a ruined native home place![48]

Apparently, the "native home place" could bear the presence of Mexicans, but certainly not that of blacks. For some local whites, many of whom profited directly from Mexican labor, Mexicans were a necessary evil, while blacks were both unnecessary and evil.

Oddly enough, the "Zoot Suit" riots of June 1943—in which white U.S. Navy officers stormed through Mexican neighborhoods in Los Angeles, beating young Mexican men and tearing off the popular, brassy outfits the youths wore—exacerbated whites' fear of black violence. Although these riots were instigated by whites and primarily affected Mexicans, they nonetheless raised the specter of widespread racial violence to a new level. Moving quickly to divert criticism of its rampaging white servicemen, the Navy announced a formal investigation into the causes of racial friction, which it almost immediately assigned to the "Negro problem." Commander Clarence Fogg, senior naval patrol officer in Los Angeles, argued that something must be done to prevent a "racial out-break in Los Angeles [which] could occur at any moment and without fore-warning." Fogg warned civic officials: "The existing local racial situation grows more tense. It appears to spring directly from an aggressive campaign sponsored by local, state, and national representatives of the negro race. Apparently this campaign is founded upon a planned policy of agitation designed to promote unrest and dissatisfaction among the local Negro population." In the event that attacks by "negro hoodlums" culminated in a riot, Fogg devised an elaborate "3 wave" retaliation plan involving the Marine Corps and the Coast Guard under the direction of the Navy.[49] Race riots in Beaumont, Texas; Mobile, Alabama; Detroit; and Harlem that summer further aggravated anti-black sentiment among white servicemen and civilians.

The black community's response to the Zoot Suit riots was largely one of self-preservation. As Kevin Allen Leonard has shown, interracial political coalitions proliferated during World War II, and black leaders in Los Angeles openly lobbied on behalf of the less politically active Mexican community. During the riots, for example, local NAACP president Thomas L. Griffith wrote to President Roosevelt and Governor Earl Warren, demanding that they intervene to stop the violence against the Mexican community.[50] Having grown up in neighborhoods with Mexicans, many members of the prewar black community in Los Angeles likely shared this sympathy.

At the same time, however, African Americans also closed racial ranks, publicly distancing themselves from the event. Responding to allegedly sensationalist accounts in the *Los Angeles Times* and the *Daily News,* which referred to the incident as a racial "civil war," the *California Eagle* reminded readers that there had been "no mass rioting by Negroes" nor had there been "a serious outbreak by the Negro people."[51] But there is also evidence that blacks were prepared for a "race war" and were quite willing to defend their community whatever the cost. Loren Miller remembered that when the marauding sailors declared that they were going down to Central Avenue, blacks "sent back the word that said to come over here and take somebody's trousers off over here, cut somebody's hair. We'll be ready for them. So they never showed up." Miller even contacted Mayor Bowron, telling him that if the sailors made their way to South Central, "somebody was going to get killed and I didn't think it was going to be Negroes." According to Miller, "the Negroes always felt that Mexicans were far too tame during the riots."[52]

The relationship of new black migrants to the existing black community was no less knotty than their relationship to Mexicans and whites. Because so many African Americans in Los Angeles had been migrants themselves, they understood the dynamics and difficulties of migration better than anyone. In many cases, these residents were particularly sympathetic to the aspirations of newcomers and were eager to help where they could. African Americans who opened their homes and garages to new arrivals often took pride in accommodating the city's latest black residents. One migrant even remembered hearing a black woman boast, "I got a sharecropper," only to be outdone by another who replied, "Honey, I got me three sharecroppers!"[53]

Others, however, viewed the newcomers as a source of potential embarrassment and feared that rough-hewn migrants would confirm popular stereotypes of black people. Chester Murray, a black migrant from Morgan City, Louisiana, remembered that longstanding black residents viewed him and his family as "country people" and expected them to "have beer cans in the yard" and to be "screaming [and] playing music all night." New Orleans native O'Neil Cannon remembered that older African Americans considered the newcomers "less acculturated and perhaps a bit more aggressive, and they became a source of embarrassment to people who were getting along fine with their neighbors all along."[54]

Given that most black migrants did not come from farms, descriptions of them as unsophisticated "sharecroppers" were clearly not literal. Rather, these were figurative ways of conveying trepidation and opprobrium. Many black residents were not embarrassed by newcomers as much as they were fearful that the newcomers would upset the tenuous balance that had been struck between activism and accommodation before World War II. New arrivals from utterly repressive communities like Shreveport often availed themselves of their new freedoms and made their presence known to both whites and blacks in Los Angeles. One editorialist for the *California Eagle* opined that the "incoming Negroes from the South" needed to be taught "the basic rules of culture. . . . Unseemly loudness in public places by Negroes fresh from the lower strata of Southern life is understandable. At home they were not permitted to enter so-called 'white' theaters and restaurants; it is no wonder that they sometimes revel loudly in the non-segregated freedom of Los Angeles."[55] But beyond being boisterous, black migrants also often exhibited an uncommonly aggressive attitude toward whites. One black woman worried that "some of them are very belligerent," and an Urban League researcher in Little Tokyo observed that the "newcomers have a freedom they haven't experienced before, and sometimes they become wild."[56]

Others in the black community admired the aggressiveness of the new migrants and recognized their potential for invigorating the campaign for civil rights in Los Angeles. In 1944, Revels Cayton, African American civil rights leader and vice president of the California CIO Council, explained, "One thing is certain: the thousands of Negroes who have come west intend to remain. They are determined to stay, become integrated in their communities and attain full citizenship." Cayton viewed the vast increase in black voter registration as a particularly good sign. "The Negro people," he optimistically stated, "are in the forefront of the West Coast progressive movement."[57] Cayton must surely have been delighted by Charlotta Bass's candidacy for the Los Angeles City Council. Emphasizing postwar job security, affordable housing, expanded public health services, and a reduction of water and power bills, Bass lived up to her slogan as the "people's candidate, the people's champion for jobs and security."[58] Although she lost to white council member Carl Rasmussen in a runoff election, her campaign demonstrated the growing influence of the black electorate as a result of in-migration.

A journalist for the Los Angeles magazine *Fortnight* interviewed a number of recent black migrants in the early 1950s and reported that "the newcomer is generally young, aggressive, and sure of himself. He has no patience with the older generation and its more cautious ways. These newcomers feel they discovered California and it belongs to them."[59] Though overstating the cautiousness of the "older generation," this journalist accurately captured the defiant spirit of the migrants as well as their determination to improve their lives, whatever the costs.

But many new arrivals also needed help getting on their feet, and some within the black community saw it as their responsibility to assist them. As he had before the war, Reverend Clayton Russell continued to use the People's Independent Church as a vehicle for community relief.

During the war, however, he also turned his, and the church's, attention toward protest by creating the Negro Victory Committee. Russell's committee—composed of both old and new members of his congregation—protested discrimination in employment and housing. One particularly successful campaign was the Negro Victory Committee's 1942 protest against the USES, which dropped its discriminatory placement policy for black women as a result.[60] The Urban League, which was not a protest organization like the Negro Victory Committee, continued to play an important part in expanding opportunities for blacks and acclimating migrants to Los Angeles. In addition to its ongoing role as an employment referral service, representatives from the Los Angeles Urban League participated in numerous closed-door meetings with defense company representatives, encouraging them to hire black workers.[61]

Though the wartime influx of black migrants to Los Angeles provoked ambivalent responses from blacks and hostile responses from whites, the responses of the Los Angeles city and county governments were considerably more measured. Despite Deputy Mayor Orville Caldwell's remarks criticizing Bronzeville's residents and his proposal of a state ban on black in-migration, Los Angeles's city hall quickly developed a relatively enlightened set of policies to accommodate the changes wrought by the new arrivals. African Americans benefited from the tenure of Mayor Fletcher Bowron, a reformer and a progressive Republican. Silent on racial matters before World War II, Bowron quickly recognized that the overcrowding in Bronzeville and the rising racial friction throughout Los Angeles had the potential to bring the city to its knees. Desperate to avoid the outbreak of racial riots that plagued other defense production centers, Bowron implemented several policies aimed at improving the quality of life for new migrants.

Throughout his fifteen-year tenure (1938 to 1953), Bowron consistently pushed for more abundant and more affordable housing. After a wartime mayors' conference, Bowron told the Los Angeles County Board of Supervisors, "I am convinced that the present over-all housing shortage in Los Angeles is unequalled in any other major city in the United States."[62] Recognizing the unique obstacles faced by blacks in the restricted housing market, Bowron created a wartime housing committee, appointing respected black businessman Norman O. Houston as chairman and Los Angeles Urban League director Floyd Covington as a board member.[63] Bowron also aggressively sought federal funding for the development and expansion of public housing, a position that

FIGURE 3. A city inspector sent to Bronzeville/Little Tokyo to document slum conditions talks to one of its residents, a young black boy, 1944. Courtesy of the Los Angeles Public Library.

did not sit well with real estate developers and lobbyists but was favored by most African Americans. Toward that end, Bowron sent city inspectors into Bronzeville during the war to document slum conditions so that the city had proof of its dire need for an expanded public housing program (see figure 3).

Bowron's immediate wartime agenda focused on improving conditions in Bronzeville. The crowning achievement of this agenda was the creation of Pilgrim House, a community center in the heart of Bronzeville that focused on integrating migrants into Los Angeles, improving health, and bettering race relations. Sponsored jointly by the City Health Department, the Los Angeles Chamber of Commerce, and several religious bodies, Pilgrim House became an all-purpose community center providing much-needed day care, health and spiritual services, and job referrals. Pilgrim House even launched a remarkable, if limited, exchange program through which black children spent a weekend with a white family and white children visited with a black family.[64]

This exchange program fit well with Bowron's desire to improve race relations in the city. In 1944, he sponsored another body, the Committee on Home Front Unity, half of whose members were African American. In that same year, white county supervisor John Anson Ford created the Commission on Interracial Progress (later the Los Angeles County Committee on Human Relations), which sought to promote deeper understanding of the causes of racial tension and to prevent racial conflict. Ford proved particularly determined to improve Bronzeville, badgering the State Board of Equalization to deny further applications for liquor licenses in the community. Ford believed that the "unwholesome" environment of Bronzeville, which drew thousands of thrill-seekers, "aggravated racial problems."[65]

It is doubtful that the efforts of Bowron and Ford radically improved the quality of life for residents of Bronzeville during World War II, nor was their commitment to equal opportunity shared by all city and county government officials. In fact, the city council stubbornly refused to extend the life of the mayor's committee, arguing that it would tend to "mollycoddle" African Americans and "make a bad situation worse."[66] Nonetheless, for the first time in the region's history, representatives of the city and county governments openly acknowledged the deleterious effects of racial segregation and took concrete steps to mitigate the harshness of those effects. The first wave of the Great Migration had, by its sheer size, forced the city to confront its racial history and prepare for its racial future.

The Future of Race in Urban America

In 1941, the up-and-coming black writer Chester Himes and his wife took a Greyhound bus from Cleveland to Los Angeles. Thirty-two years old and completely exasperated by the racial discrimination he had encountered in Ohio and his boyhood home of Mississippi, Himes hoped Los Angeles would be better. However, like so many migrants, Himes was immediately confronted by the fact that his migration had not freed him from hurt. In his first autobiography, *The Quality of Hurt*, Himes excoriated the hypocrisy of overt racial discrimination in a city fabled for its relatively moderate racial climate:

Los Angeles hurt me racially as much as any city I have ever known—much more than any city I remember from the South. It was the lying hypocrisy that hurt me. Black people were treated much the same as they were in any industrial city of the South. . . . The difference was that the white people of Los Angeles seemed to be saying, "Nigger, ain't we good to you?" [67]

For Himes, perhaps nothing was more frustrating than his inability to find a job commensurate with his skills. During his youth, he had learned considerable job skills from his father, the head of mechanical departments in various southern agricultural and trade schools for blacks. By the time he arrived in California, Himes had amassed substantial training:

I could read blueprints; I understood, at least partially, most of the necessary skills of building construction—carpentry, plumbing, electric wiring, bricklaying, roofing; I understood the fundamentals of combustion engines; I could operate a number of machine tools—turret lathes, drills, milling machines, etc.; and I was a fairly competent typist. [68]

Possessing greater talents than the deskilled shops of the city's booming defense industries required, Himes nonetheless found himself systematically excluded from skilled work because of his race. In his three years in California, some of which he also spent in the San Francisco Bay Area, Himes worked at twenty-three different jobs in wartime industries. Only two of them required any previous training. Himes's frustration with racial discrimination in Los Angeles informed his first two published novels, *If He Hollers, Let Him Go* (1945) and *Lonely Crusade* (1947), both searing indictments of racism, underemployment, and the emasculation of African American men in the 1940s. [69]

Just as Himes was initially optimistic about the wartime industrial opportunities Los Angeles offered, so too were thousands of other black migrants. As tragic as the bombing of Pearl Harbor was for all Americans, many blacks also recognized that World War II could radically improve their economic opportunities. Several days after the bombing, George Beavers of the Los Angeles NAACP proclaimed that the "doors of the defense industries are now practically wide open . . ." and predicted that "qualified workers will be drawn from our group as well as others." [70]

For black sociologists St. Clair Drake and Horace Cayton, writing at the beginning of the war, the Great Migration of blacks to defense centers portended great things for the race. "Negroes in America," they wrote in 1945, "are becoming a city people, and it is in the cities that the problem of the Negro in American life appears in its sharpest and most dramatic forms. It may be, too, that the cities will be the arena in which the 'Negro problem' will finally be settled." However, Drake and Cayton recognized that the resolution of the "Negro problem" was contingent on the economic progress of blacks after World War II. The most important question they posed was whether African Americans "will remain the marginal workers to be called in only at times of great economic activity, or will become an integral part of the American economy and thus lay the basis for complete social and political integration."[71]

Although the answer to this question varied from city to city and from industry to industry, generally speaking, white employers and unions had one answer to that question, and black workers had quite another. Although not enough of the participants recognized it, the outcome of racial struggles in the metal shops, automobile plants, tire factories, and busy docks of postwar Los Angeles would have long-term and wide-ranging implications.

CHAPTER 3

The Window of Opportunity

Black Work in Industrial Los Angeles, 1941–1964

Who can deny that the next six months will see the greatest
expansion of opportunities for Negro workers in the history of
this nation?

Charlotta Bass, *California Eagle*, 16 July 1942

World War II initiated an era of economic prosperity in the United
States that would continue for more than two decades. Sustained by the
country's heavy manufacturing industries, this boom created thousands
of new jobs and laid the foundations of a new standard of comfort for
American workers that included union membership, home and automobile ownership, and expanded discretionary income. Having been
swiftly integrated into the nation's industrial workforce during the war,
California's African Americans stood poised to share in this postwar
prosperity. One 1947 survey concluded that Los Angeles and San Francisco were among the ten cities providing the best employment opportunities for black workers.[1] And in the twenty years following World
War II, blacks in Los Angeles made the greatest economic advances they
had ever experienced, becoming a steadily increasing proportion of the
industrial workforce, joining unions in rising numbers, purchasing
homes, and occasionally approximating the middle-class standards of
life often thought to be the sole province of whites.

But there were also many barriers—old and new—to black economic progress. Both within and outside the workplace, African Americans encountered disheartening and capricious restrictions that made
economic parity with whites virtually impossible. To suggest that World

War II presented the country with an opportunity to completely resolve its deeply entrenched "race problem" would surely be an overstatement. But by drawing heavily on black labor, forcing the racial integration of previously all-white plants and departments, and stimulating the support of the federal government for workplace desegregation, the wartime defense production effort certainly initiated a new era of racial and industrial relations that could have, at the very least, put black and white Americans on equal economic footing. Instead, the new era healed some of the historic wounds caused by workplace discrimination, while simultaneously creating many new ones.

The Postwar Industrial Metropolis and the New Standard of Blue-Collar Life

The establishment of defense industries in Southern California during World War II laid the foundation for extensive industrial growth in the postwar era. Though many Americans still associated Los Angeles with the glitz and glamour of Hollywood, the city rivaled Chicago and New York as the nation's leading industrial producer. During the war, the shipbuilding and aircraft industries dominated the economy. After reconversion, the aircraft, motion picture, automobile, rubber, petroleum, furniture, and food processing industries continued to flourish as they had before the war, and the electronics industry rose quickly in the 1950s. Between 1946 and 1955, more than $2 billion were invested in the construction and equipping of manufacturing plants in Los Angeles. By 1963, the Los Angeles Chamber of Commerce proudly announced: "Los Angeles Area Gives Chicago a Run as Number Two U.S. Industrial Giant." Indeed, only Chicago produced more than the city of Los Angeles, and Los Angeles County was unrivaled as the largest manufacturing county in the United States.[2]

Nationally and in Los Angeles, workers benefited from the postwar boom.[3] Determined to share in the prosperity, organized labor undertook the most extensive recruitment drive in the nation's history. In 1954, when postwar union membership was at its peak, 25.4 percent of all American workers were in unions.[4] This progress was most remarkable in Los Angeles, once the "cradle of industrial freedom." A 1962 survey revealed that 26 percent of homes in Los Angeles County had at least one union member.[5] Furthermore, the postwar years witnessed a rise in both per capita income and employment.[6] Most promising for industrial workers of all skill levels was the continuing rapid expansion of the manufacturing sector. While Detroit experienced a gradual postwar decline in unionized blue-collar jobs as early as the 1950s, Los Angeles experienced remarkable growth in those jobs through the 1970s.[7]

Workers also benefited from the region's phenomenal housing boom. Stimulated by the Federal Housing Administration (FHA)—which aided both homebuyers and developers by offering mortgage insurance and an extended repayment period—real estate developers created vast new subdivisions of affordable, single-family homes. Often developed in conjunction with aircraft manufacturers, these new subdivisions offered blue-collar workers tremendous opportunities for lives of security and comfort unimaginable in Depression-era Los Angeles. Connecting these new subdivisions was a rapidly growing freeway system, designed to reduce commute times and provide greater mobility. During the 1950s and early 1960s, the new Golden State (I-5), Harbor (I-110), Long Beach (I-710), San Diego (I-405), and Santa Monica (I-10) freeways were built; and the older Pasadena (SR110), San Bernardino (I-10), and Hollywood (U.S. 101) freeways were extended. Automobile ownership skyrocketed in Los Angeles, and many working families owned more than one vehicle.

All of these developments heralded the emergence of a new blue-collar standard of living in Southern California. In 1953, *Life* magazine recognized this new standard in a photo-essay titled " . . . And 400 New Angels Every Day."[8] Focusing on the fast-growing suburb of Lakewood, largely inhabited by aircraft workers, *Life* showed rows of new homes loaded with appliances and new cars in the driveways. When *Life* announced that "patios, pools, and a pleasant way of life" typified life in Southern California, the magazine was, of course, simply rearticulating the historic trope of the mythical city. But for white workers, this trope was anchored by real accomplishments: rising incomes, home and car ownership, and increased material comfort.

Despite initial optimism among African Americans that they too would share in this prosperity, it quickly became clear that access to this new standard of blue-collar life was determined by numerous factors, many of which were beyond their control. First, and most universally, industrial employers and managers played a critical role in the pace and tone of industrial desegregation. Most engaged in racially discriminatory hiring and promotion practices, even as they actively recruited black workers to replace white workers who were eager to find lighter, cleaner, and better-paying work.

Second, organized labor played an ambiguous role in the integration process. With a few important exceptions, unions did not lead the charge for the racial integration of America's workforce. Rather, they responded to employer-initiated integration. Yet, even within that reactive role, organized labor wielded important power over the meaning of integration. In some cases unions operated almost entirely as defenders of white privilege, whereas in others they legitimately sought equal rights for their black members.

Third, America's workers themselves shaped the integration experience. On a daily basis, black workers decided how to approach employers, interact with unions, and combat the inequities perpetuated by both. White workers' responses to black workers, as well as their perception of what distinguished "good jobs" from "bad jobs," deeply influenced how employers viewed racial integration and colored the experiences of black workers. Mexican workers, too, played a crucial role, one that has been relatively unexamined. In some industries, their very presence was considered as foreign as the presence of black workers. In most industries, however, as chapter 1 noted, they were already considered a "normal" part of the workforce—albeit not quite white. In the postwar years, many Mexican workers parlayed their "near-white" status into concrete job gains as they jockeyed for better-paying positions in older industries. Black workers increasingly, and quite correctly, perceived Mexicans as competitors in the job market, and Mexican labor as yet another barrier to occupational advancement.

Finally, the federal government influenced workplace desegregation, if only haltingly. After the wartime FEPC was dismantled in 1946, black workers were left without an important tool for fighting discrimination. But, starting with the Truman administration, the federal government's gradual steps toward fighting workplace segregation improved conditions for African Americans in selected industries and culminated in the historic Civil Rights Act of 1964.

These, then, were the players who acted in the drama of postwar racial integration. Though too few appreciated it at the time, what was at stake in the outcome of this drama was nothing less than America's most cherished principles of individual freedom and equality. The first act of this drama, of course, began shortly after America's entry into World War II.

The Politics of Wartime Racial Integration

Throughout the nation, African American leaders shrewdly recognized that World War II presented a window of opportunity to completely integrate American society. In addition to supporting A. Philip Randolph's monumental March on Washington movement, African Americans lobbied for the desegregation of the armed forces and the home front workforce. The NAACP, in particular, exerted constant pressure on the federal government to abolish segregation. "Now is the time," the editorial page of *The Crisis* blared in 1942, "*not* to be silent about the breaches of democracy here in our own land."[9]

Black workers needed little encouragement from leaders, however. Emboldened by their own migrations, as well as the FEPC, black industrial workers proved doubly aggressive about securing their place in the new economic order. To be sure, some preferred to accept discrimination rather than jeopardize their hard-won gains. As one African American worker in Los Angeles put it: "My family was more important than a political fight . . . I went in every day and just did my job. . . . I would not have been given a good recommendation when I tried to get another job."[10] But many more black workers actively challenged their white employers and union leaders and demanded total equality with white workers.

Black workers manifested this sense of entitlement in many ways, some small and personal, others large and well organized. In 1942, for example, personnel at the Los Angeles office of the United States Employment Service (USES) were caught off guard by a highly organized group of black women. State employment agencies across the country had been placed under the direction of the USES, which served as a referral service for local industrial training schools and defense plants. Because the USES was an extension of the War Manpower Commission, a federal agency, it was beholden to the FEPC. Not only was the USES supposed to avoid discrimination itself, but it was required to report discriminatory job listings to the FEPC. However, many USES employees, including those in Los Angeles, brazenly ignored this stipulation and succumbed to local prejudices by filling—and even encouraging—discriminatory employment requests.[11]

As the labor shortage deepened in July of 1942, management at several of Los Angeles's larger defense plants contacted the USES seeking female labor. The companies made it clear, however, that they did not want to hire black women. The local USES allegedly consoled management by reporting that black women were regarded as "no problem since they showed a lack of interest in war work training." When word of this remark spread into the black community, many African American women who had been seeking defense work were outraged. The Negro Victory Committee organized a group of several hundred black women who expressed their ire by flooding the offices of the USES, demanding equal treatment and shouting: "This is our war! We must win it! We cannot win it in the kitchen; we must win it on the assembly line!"[12] By the sheer force of their determination, these black women reversed the discriminatory policies of the Los Angeles USES.

During the war, African Americans also demanded that the FEPC fulfill its obligation to abolish discrimination in wartime industries. African Americans sought the FEPC's support in breaking the discriminatory hiring practices of the Los Angeles Railway (LARY). Though disproportionately patronized by low-income African Americans, LARY refused to hire blacks (or Mexicans) as rail car conductors or bus drivers. In 1943, LARY acknowledged that 47 cars a day were kept idle daily because of a "manpower shortage."[13] By 1944, only 493 of a normal 800 streetcars were in use, and almost one-third of the buses were idle.[14] Black protest, pickets, and letter writing drew the FEPC's attention to the LARY situation. FEPC investigators reported in 1944 that "hostile feelings in the Negro community have become so violent that there are almost daily attacks upon operators working lines which run through colored neighborhoods."[15] Finally the War Manpower Commission suspended LARY's manpower rating, preventing LARY from recruiting workers through the USES. This action forced LARY to capitulate, and African Americans became conductors and drivers.

In addition to acting as individuals and marshaling the resources of the FEPC, black workers quickly came to view the CIO as a potential ally in their struggle for equality. After near-total quiescence on the issue of black equality before World War II, the CIO in Los Angeles began actively courting black workers. "There has been a growing movement within various minority groups," the California CIO Council reported in 1945, "towards self-expression and a militant advancement of their rights and interests. We welcome these manifestations of group solidarity within the various communities and seek to play a helpful and cooperative role."[16] The CIO's advocacy on behalf of minority workers had focused exclusively on Mexicans in prewar Los Angeles. But the swift integration of black workers into the labor force during World War II, and their determination to receive equal treatment, changed the way organized labor thought about African Americans and the way African Americans thought about the labor movement in Los Angeles. Organized labor realized that it had much to gain by advocating black equality, and black community leaders saw in organized labor the prospect of a mass movement for civil rights. Black labor leader Revels Cayton believed that the Los Angeles CIO could become nothing less than "the core of a progressive people's movement in America."[17]

The heart of this new relationship was the Los Angeles CIO Industrial Union Council, under the leadership of Philip "Slim" Connelly. His nickname belying his three-hundred-pound frame, Slim Connelly had been active in Los Angeles radical politics since the 1930s. Head of the Los Angeles chapter of the American Newspaper Guild (a CIO union) in the late 1930s, Connelly was elected as the first president of the newly formed California CIO Council in 1938. He became secretary-treasurer of the Los Angeles CIO Council the next year, a post he held for a decade. In 1947, he married Southern California Communist Party organizer Dorothy Ray Healey; and he took over as editor-in-chief of California's communist newspaper, the *Daily People's World,* in 1948. Under his leadership, the Los Angeles CIO Council became the hub of virtually all employment-related civil rights activities for African Americans in the 1940s and early 1950s. Under Connelly's tenure as secretary-treasurer, blacks were appointed to several leadership positions on the council. African Americans John Dial of the Shipbuilders Union and Arthur Morrison of the Packinghouse Workers, for example, both rose through the ranks of the council under Connelly's leadership.[18] But perhaps Connelly's most important appointment was Walter Williams.

Born in Georgia in 1918, Williams had been raised in Depression-era Los Angeles. After graduating from high school in 1936, he worked in a Civilian Conservation Corp camp to help support his mother, who was a domestic worker in Hollywood, and his brother. He then became a truck driver for a Japanese produce firm. His first experience with racism in the labor movement came from the Teamsters union, which fired Williams in order to replace him with an unemployed white driver. Infuriated, Williams vowed to fight this blatant racism but was dissuaded when a carload of Teamsters with guns pulled over his brother and threatened to kill both of them. "What the hell, we can't win here," Williams recalled saying, but "somewhere down the line maybe we'll learn how to cope with this crowd . . . maybe we'll figure out a way."[19]

In 1940, Williams secured employment at a metal foundry. He was immediately disgusted to find that blacks were denied employment in anything other than menial jobs. He approached the CIO about starting a union at the foundry and began organizing. Though he was quickly fired for his union activity, he was hired as an organizer for the Los Angeles CIO Council. Like many other African Americans in the 1940s, Williams saw in the CIO great promise for African Americans: "I had put my faith in the CIO . . . they tended to organize people and be democratic and they taught you not to discriminate, not to make first or second class citizenships out of our memberships." [20] From within the labor movement, Williams became one of the most important advocates of equal employment opportunities for blacks in wartime and postwar industrial Los Angeles.

Under the leadership of Slim Connelly and with constant pressure from Walter Williams, advocating equality for black workers moved from being a fringe position in the Los Angeles CIO Council to a central one. Under an astute and increasingly multiracial leadership, the Los Angeles CIO proclaimed the right of African Americans to work and receive fair union representation. Furthermore, African Americans rose to key leadership positions in the city's CIO organization at a time when blacks were still denied leadership positions in most American institutions. And local black CIO leaders actively recruited African Americans in their neighborhoods in South Central. For all these reasons, it is fair to say that the CIO, at the national level and at the level of the Los Angeles CIO Council, was genuinely committed to organizing African Americans and treating them with dignity and respect. Unfortunately, however, the most important decisions made by the labor movement regarding integration happened on the shop floors and in the local union halls. There, the relationship between black workers and the labor movement was much more troubled. In postwar America, the much-celebrated solidarity and communion of unionized workers was as often a barrier to integration as it was a facilitator. [21]

Trouble on Terminal Island

Terminal Island, the bustling port at the southern tip of Los Angeles, was a critical center of Southern California's economy during and after World War II. Home to the wartime shipbuilding industry and the longstanding shipping and freight industries, Terminal Island was also the front line for the integration of African Americans into Southern California industry. For black migrants from Houston, New Orleans,

and other Gulf Coast cities, Terminal Island was a natural place to begin the search for work. Many black men had already worked as longshoremen before moving to Los Angeles, and many more had longed
for lucrative shipbuilding jobs in Houston and New Orleans.

But their experiences on Terminal Island during and after the war
challenged the faith of even the most optimistic migrant. In both the
shipbuilding and longshore industries, African American workers found
that organized labor, far from being an ally, was the greatest barrier to
equality. Black workers fought against such barriers in several well-
organized civil rights campaigns. But, in a pattern that would become
common in other industries in the postwar years, victorious battles for
integration often bore little fruit. In the shipbuilding industry, whose
leading companies ceased operations in Los Angeles after the war, this
fact was quickly and painfully apparent. In longshore, where intransigence on the part of white workers was deep, the battle was more pro-
tracted but also more effective. Yet in both cases, blacks accurately perceived that organized labor's first priority was the defense of white
workers.

The integration of African Americans into ship production along the
entire West Coast was shaped by the outcome of a heated battle between the AFL and the CIO, both seeking to capitalize on potential
membership gains during the war. In the Bethlehem Steel Shipbuilding
yard and the Los Angeles Shipbuilding and Drydock yard, the CIO's International Union of Marine and Shipbuilding Workers of America
(IUMSWA) won easy victories over the AFL's International Brotherhood of Boilermakers (IBB). For black workers in those yards, this was
a boon. From its inception in 1933, the IUMSWA had rejected racial discrimination and had great success organizing on the East Coast. After
affiliating with the CIO in 1936, it began to be successful in other regions. Even before World War II, minority workers were welcomed into
Los Angeles Local 9 of the IUMSWA, and this pattern continued into
the war.[22] By 1943, Mexicans made up approximately 10 percent of the
union, and blacks also accounted for 10 percent. Yet these yards were
quite small and never employed more than about two thousand African
Americans.[23] More than 80 percent of black workers employed in shipbuilding worked for the "Big-3" shipyards—Western Pipe and Steel,
Consolidated Steel Corporation's Shipbuilding Division, and the
sprawling California Shipbuilding Corporation (Calship), one of the
largest shipbuilding operations in the nation. In these three yards, there
was a very different racial arrangement.

Large CIO strikes in Southern California's aircraft industry in 1940 and 1941 struck fear into the hearts of major shipbuilding companies. Most important, the continuous agitation by the United Automobile Workers (UAW) at North American Aviation in Inglewood, which culminated in the famous strike of 1941, in which the National Guard was ordered to intervene, convinced shipbuilders that they should quickly make whatever compromises were necessary to ensure uninterrupted production. In 1941, the Big-3 shipbuilders quietly struck an agreement with the AFL's Metal Trades Division.[24]

Known as the Master Agreement, this legally dubious back-door deal stipulated that the Big-3 would be closed-shop yards for the duration of the war and that the IBB would be the sole bargaining unit for all the workers. Unique to California, the Master Agreement had a tremendous impact on race relations in the state. Whereas in other war production centers such as Mobile, Alabama, the AFL was forced to make concessions to the largely black labor force in order to remain competitive with the CIO's racially integrated shipbuilding union, the Boilermakers easily secured a labor monopoly on the three biggest shipyards in Los Angeles, which employed almost ten thousand African Americans.[25]

The Boilermakers, however, had a "whites-only" membership policy, which dated back to the inception of the union in 1880. In fact, the only significant change in this early policy had been to transfer the "whites-only" clause from the written constitution to the admission rituals of local institutions, thus allowing the Boilermakers to retain the policy without publicly acknowledging it.[26] Eventually conceding that the time had come to deal with the question of black labor, the Executive Council of the IBB voted in 1937 to establish "Negro Auxiliaries."[27] A black auxiliary bore little, if any, resemblance to a legitimate union. The auxiliary was totally subservient to the white local with which it was affiliated, had no right to participate in IBB conventions, had no grievance committee, provided very little hope of job advancement, offered only limited insurance programs, and conferred no universal rights of transfer. Its membership was susceptible to punishment for small infractions such as drinking on the job, while white union members were not.[28] In fact, the only similarity between the auxiliary and the white local was that members both paid the same dues. The auxiliary became the vehicle for the Boilermakers' "compromise" between wartime exigencies and their vision of the union.

Particularly galling to Los Angeles's black shipyard workers was the way the "whites-only" policy was enforced. In a policy that was "demoralizing and confusing for Negro and also white workers," Walter Williams complained, "Mexican, Chinese, Italian, German, Filipino, etc. are awarded full membership while American Negroes are denied such privileges."[29] Indeed, Mexicans, who were rarely accepted into the ranks of the Boilermakers before the war, were quietly accepted with full membership once the war began. Thomas Doram, a light-skinned African American, recalled that the union believed that he was white, "or at least not a Negro," and that he kept his identity a secret. Accordingly, he was initiated into the union along with other white members, given his insurance policy and union book, and advanced from being a janitor to a burner in two weeks. In January of 1943, he became an instructor of burners and served in this capacity for half the year. When the union foreman discovered that Doram was indeed African American, he threatened to fire him. After Doram pleaded for several days, pointing out his excellent work record and good rapport with co-workers, the foreman agreed to a compromise: "I will let you work," the foreman told him, "but I will put you on at nights where other Negroes won't see you and therefore won't get the idea that they all can do the same thing. . . . The workers will think that you are Mexican and won't pay it much attention at night."[30]

Walter Williams completed a wartime training course in September 1942 and was given a referral to work at the Calship yard. Williams recalled that in January 1943, after he had worked at Calship for four months, he noticed that his insurance policy covered far less than the policies of his nonblack co-workers.[31] Williams immediately organized and sought recruits for a new organization, the Shipyard Workers Committee for Equal Participation (SWCEP), a group of black workers who dedicated themselves to fighting, as they said, "taxation without representation." "We pay the same dues, get half the insurance of white workers, don't know where our money goes, and get no union protection," one black worker complained.[32] By March, Williams had established an SWCEP office at Forty-Sixth and Central and had recruited upward of eleven hundred members for SWCEP; he would have more than four thousand by October of that year.[33]

But the IBB leadership remained staunchly opposed to accepting African Americans as equals, and union representatives flatly refused to appear at the FEPC hearings in Los Angeles. Earlier, Charles J. MacGowan, vice president of the Boilermakers, had sent a telegram to the FEPC stating, "There is no foundation for the charge that there has been any discrimination on the part of our local union."[34]

Several weeks after the hearings, MacGowan wrote a letter to Western Pipe and Steel in which he reminded them of the provisions of the Master Agreement and insisted that "the provisions of the agreement be adhered to in the future as they have in the past regardless of any opinion to the contrary by the President's Committee on Fair Employment." MacGowan stated that the SWCEP's grievance was "purely an inter-organizational problem which can be settled only at a proper convention." The FEPC directive, MacGowan insisted, was an "arrogant attempt to destroy the collective bargaining agreement [and] . . . alienate the good will of Organized Labor and its support of the War Effort." Finally, MacGowan summed up his feelings on the FEPC: "It is further our position that the president's Committee on Fair Employment Practice is wholly without constitutional and legal jurisdiction and power to issue an order having the force of law. . . . It is also our position that the President's Executive Order no. 9346 was intended as a directive and not to be construed as having the force of legislation." [35]

Much to the chagrin of Williams and other advocates of workplace desegregation, MacGowan was right. The IBB could act with impunity because Roosevelt was loath to antagonize organized labor and risk a wartime strike among the most powerful forces in West Coast shipbuilding. Initially, the companies felt more at risk than the union—after all, they were receiving lucrative war contracts. Yet even they appeared unwilling to comply with the FEPC's directive. Consolidated Steel's shipyard kicked off the New Year by allowing Lodge 92 to fire twenty-four black workers who refused to pay union dues.[36] Thus, the actual impact of the FEPC hearings was quite limited. On the surface, their only function was to "expose racism," whose existence was a foregone conclusion for the members of the SWCEP.

Williams organized a group of litigants to seek a temporary injunction against the shipyards, to keep them from firing the black workers who were "not in good standing" with the union. In June 1944, they were granted a temporary injunction against the companies, but it lasted for only three months. In August, Superior Court Judge Emmet H. Wilson ended the injunction and reaffirmed the companies' conviction that they had no control over union laws. As the SWCEP struggled along, however, a similar body of black shipyard workers in the San Francisco Bay Area had taken their case to the California Supreme Court. Under the leadership of Joseph James, a professional singer-turned-welder for the Marinship Corporation in Sausalito, the Committee Against Segregation and Discrimination had fought since November 1943 to end the Boilermakers' policy. On 2 January 1945, Chief Justice Phil Gibson ruled that an "arbitrarily closed union is incompatible with a closed shop." In *James v. Marinship,* a victory for racial equality had finally been scored.[37] In Los Angeles, the decision was hailed as a moral victory and "an historic swing from the narrow-minded social thinking of the past era,"[38] but the SWCEP knew that its fight was far from over. While the *James* decision set an important precedent, it applied only to the Bay Area's Boilermakers. Los Angeles's black shipyard workers were still on their own.

Because of the *James* decision and Williams's threat to sue any company that pulled the cards of black shipyard workers for failing to pay dues, the Big-3 shipbuilding companies in Los Angeles finally announced a change in policy in February 1945. In a victory for the SWCEP, the Big-3 stopped firing black employees for nonpayment of dues. Black workers still had no union rights, but for the first time they would not be forced to pay for segregated unions.[39]

In June 1945, Los Angeles Superior Court Judge Raymond Thompson issued a permanent injunction against Lodge 92. Handed down in the name of shipyard worker Andrew Blakeney, the injunction affected more than five thousand black shipyard workers still employed in Los Angeles. Thompson ruled that unless the Boilermakers were willing to forego their closed-shop agreement with Los Angeles's Big-3 companies, they would have to give African Americans their full rights. In *Shipyard Workers v. Boilermakers International and Local 92,* Thompson ordered that black shipyard workers must be fairly, not just equally, treated. For example, in response to a wealth of data on the circumstances of black employment presented by the SWCEP, Thompson wrote: "It is well known . . . that mortality among Negroes is higher than among Whites, and insurance rates are higher. It would therefore seem to be entirely proper that insurance benefits [provided by the union] afforded plaintiffs and other Negroes should take these factors into account." Thompson knew, however, that he could not force the white Boilermakers to befriend blacks. He thus gave Lodge 92 the option of forming a separate but equal lodge for African Americans with "identical rights and privileges, by-law provisions, voting powers and other rights, the same as possessed by Local 92."[40]

But two months after Judge Thompson's important ruling, V-J Day ended the Second World War. As quickly as they had risen, the vast shipbuilding companies of Los Angeles closed down operations. The Bechtel Corporation shut down the Calship yard and expanded into other large-scale civil engineering projects. Western Pipe and Steel and Consolidated Steel's Shipbuilding Division quickly reconverted to steel production for civilian uses. On the East Coast, and on the West Coast in Seattle and the San Francisco Bay Area, shipbuilding companies stayed in business, and blacks made headway in those regions, even advancing into white-collar positions by the early 1960s.[41] But in Los Angeles, only a few small ship repair shops remained in San Pedro, employing fewer than four hundred people total; the shipbuilding industry had all but vanished from Terminal Island. In its wake, it left more than ten thousand African Americans who had experienced the best and worst of the new era, earning unprecedented incomes while encountering rampant discrimination. Their experiences in shipbuilding likely whetted their appetite for greater inclusion in the postwar economy.

While most African American defense workers were employed in the shipbuilding industry, a smaller group of black men sought work on the busy docks of Terminal Island, Los Angeles's booming harbor, surrounded by the working-class residential communities of Wilmington and San Pedro. For blacks in Los Angeles, many of whom had recently migrated from Gulf Port areas where the longshore labor force was as much as 60 percent black, it seemed like a logical choice. But black workers quickly discovered a thick wall of resistance to their presence.

This resistance was largely based on anti-black racism, but the culture and community of longshore work in San Pedro also reinforced it. San Pedro's growth, economy, and culture had long been tied to the harbor. After the completion of the modern port in 1912, San Pedro attracted a rich mixture of Swedish, German, Norwegian, Italian, and some Mexican immigrants, willing and eager to work on the busy docks of Terminal Island. Absent from this mixture were African Americans, who were systematically excluded from longshore work in prewar Los Angeles. Mexicans were allowed to work, although they experienced discriminatory treatment by both the shipping companies and the ILWU's precursor, the International Longshoremen's Association. But potential black workers were driven off the docks by physical intimidation and violence. This exclusion was reinforced by the widespread use of racially restrictive covenants in both San Pedro and Wilmington.[42]

The famous waterfront strike of 1934 was the fulcrum on which local history and memory pivoted in San Pedro. The strike fundamentally changed the nature of longshore work along the West Coast, abolishing the dreaded "shape-up" system through which workers competed daily for a chance to work. The continuous efforts of longshoremen to improve their conditions enlisted the support of the entire town. Dock-worker Corky Wilson remembered that, during strikes, barmaids and waitresses in local restaurants would call him if scabs came into the restaurant. "I got three finks in here, come and get 'em," Wilson remembered them saying. "Those women knew we made our bread and butter here. This was a workingman's town."[43]

Thus, when San Pedro's Local 13 of the International Longshoremen's and Warehousemen's Union emerged in 1937, it was made up of workers who shared a sense of both workplace and community solidarity. Like many ILWU locals, Local 13 institutionalized this fraternal pride in its membership rituals. Preference was always given to male family members in a system known informally as the "Sons and Brothers" program and later as the Sponsorship program. As Local 13 official George Love recalled, "It's natural for relatives to get into the same industry as their fathers and neighbors and uncles are in. . . . I mean the waterfront had always been a livin' even during the hard times . . . it was a natural thing."[44] Yet even "sons and brothers" were queried about their labor militancy. Local 13's membership committee gave preference to those "sons and brothers" who had participated in some way during the strikes of 1934 and 1936.[45] Clearly African Americans, who had been excluded from longshore work before World War II, would have a difficult time satisfying these requirements.

Yet the rise of the ILWU in San Pedro, coupled with the extensive labor shortage engendered by the war, opened a door for racial inclusion. Under the leadership of renowned labor radical Harry Bridges, the ILWU became perhaps the most egalitarian union in the CIO. Not only was an anti-discrimination clause included in the union's by-laws from its inception, but equality was put into practice on the local level, especially in the San Francisco Bay Area, where Bridges presided over the International union as well as the San Francisco local. During the war, Bridges frequently used the pages of the *Dispatcher*, the organ of the ILWU, to remind members of the importance of racial tolerance.[46] Under Bridges's leadership, the Bay Area ILWU local was one-third black by the end of the decade. Furthermore, blacks would progress from representing 1 percent of California's longshoremen in 1940 to 24 percent in 1950.[47] But this dramatic increase was most apparent in the Bay Area, where Bridges directly oversaw local affairs. Because he did not preside directly over San Pedro's Local 13, racial equality was not given the same attention in Los Angeles.

In fact, black workers there encountered bitter hostility from the union. As the white labor shortage in Los Angeles deepened, ILWU Local 13 had to hire numerous African Americans to fulfill the obligations of their closed-shop contract. In November 1942, the first two black members of ILWU 13, both recent migrants from Galveston, Texas, signed membership cards.[48] Yet black workers were also required to sign an oath that they would leave the longshore labor force after the war. White workers consistently reminded them that blacks would not be working after the war. "You're only temporary workers," white workers told Walter Williams, who had moved to longshore work in 1943, in hopes of securing more permanent employment. "This union was lily-white before you guys came down here," white workers reminded Williams, "and after the war it's going to be lily-white again." Nor was there a shortage of explicitly racist language. White workers left little doubt about their beliefs when they referred to a round, black winch mechanism on the dock as a "nigger head."[49]

Walter Williams, despite his experience with the labor movement in Los Angeles, was nonetheless surprised by the conditions on the waterfront. "I found it strange at first because, hell, I thought stevedoring was almost typical for black guys, you know . . . in the Gulf ports."[50] But under the leadership of L. B. Thomas, many of the white members of Local 13 made life on the docks as unpleasant as possible for black workers. African Americans were subjected to constant harassment. During a union meeting at the Wilmington Bowl, president Thomas allegedly vowed to make the union "lily-white" after the war. Whites often manipulated the hiring hall by refusing to work with blacks in certain areas, and black workers were often given only the hardest jobs, like unloading bananas.[51] Furthermore, the ILWU's Local 13 unanimously rejected an invitation to support the minorities committee of the CIO, a commitment that was almost taken for granted in other CIO unions.[52]

Bridges was well aware of the events in San Pedro. In fact, Local 13 was a thorn in his side and had a reputation as a "renegade local." When Bridges came to Los Angeles in 1943 to convince Local 13's members that a wartime speed-up would aid the defense effort, he was met with hostility, laced with anti-communism, that he had not experienced elsewhere. When Bridges proposed an increase in the number of sacks per sling load, a rank-and-file longshoreman confronted him with the statement, "I never thought that I'd hear Harry Bridges tell us to give up our conditions just because of a little old war." He called Bridges's proposal "horse shit" and said, before a jeering crowd, "Just because your pal Joseph Stalin is in trouble, don't expect us to give up our conditions to help him out." When the speaker finished, three thousand longshore workers showed their support for the sentiment with a standing ovation.[53] The great strength of the ILWU was its hiring hall, but the hiring hall system gave the local great autonomy—and nobody, not even Harry Bridges, was going to tell longshoremen in San Pedro how to run their local.[54]

As war production slowed down in 1945, L. B. Thomas apparently acted on his "lily-white" promise and quickly deregistered the four hundred longshoremen who had joined the union during the war, the majority of whom were black. According to hiring hall rules, these workers still retained seniority and would be the first hired when more work was available. Instead, however, someone in Local 13's leadership made and sold approximately three hundred phony identification cards establishing certain "sons and brothers" of older longshoremen as more senior than the deregistered workers.[55] In fact, many of those who received the cards had little experience, as a legal consultant for Local 13 later noted: "Many of these ID card holders have not worked recently as longshoremen; some of them use their ID cards only during school vacations, holidays or weekends."[56] The effect of deregistration was dramatic: approximately 90 percent of the ILWU's black membership was quickly and deliberately eliminated from the labor force on Terminal Island immediately after the war. Shortly after the war, fewer than thirty black men worked on the docks of Terminal Island.

Mexican Americans, who had been accepted into the labor force before World War II in the worst positions, made much greater progress than blacks did after the war. In a pattern that was increasingly evident across Los Angeles's industrial landscape, the specter of black integration mitigated, to a degree, anti-Mexican sentiment. Once the darkest and most isolated group on Terminal Island, Mexicans now found themselves increasingly accepted as fellow "white" members of Local 13. As veterans of the labor battles of the 1930s, Mexicans often shared with white workers their hostility toward new black workers. Henry Gaitan, a Mexican American Local 13 member from the 1930s through the 1960s, remembered:

When World War II started and Black workers came on the waterfront, White guys would say, "I don't want to work with that nigger." When the Blacks started comin' in, even the Mexicans had a tendency to feel the same way. I said, "Wait a minute, what's the matter with you, damn fools, they're takin' the pressure off of our neck." By the end of World War II, the White longshoremen who hadn't liked Mexicans had changed their mind.[57]

Unlike black longshoremen, Mexicans advanced to leadership positions within the union after the war. There, too, ambivalence and hostility marked relations between blacks and Mexicans. When John Martinez, the first Mexican American walking boss of Local 13, got in an argument with several black workers, he said: "I'll tell you, back in '33 and '34, and in 1936 and '37, . . . I pounded bricks for this union, when you all were still back in Africa."[58]

The increased demand for labor during the Korean War did not initially expand opportunities for blacks. Local 13 tried to prevent deregistered workers from returning, or any new black workers from applying, by passing a resolution in 1951 that required all applicants to have been residents of Los Angeles County for ten years. Because many black migrants had come to Los Angeles after 1941, few black men satisfied the residency requirements until the mid-1950s. It was not until the late 1950s that blacks finally became a significant and permanent part of the longshore labor force on Terminal Island. By 1960, almost 10 percent of Southern California's longshore labor force was African American.[59]

Yet, at the very moment blacks were integrated into Southern California's longshore labor force, black and white workers together faced new threats brought about by technological advances in the longshore industry. In 1960, the ILWU and the Pacific Maritime Association hammered out the Mechanization and Modernization Agreement (M&M Agreement) aimed at streamlining the shipping and loading processes on the West Coast. Workers initially welcomed the agreement because it introduced labor-saving conveyance systems that greatly reduced physical stress on workers. The ILWU also negotiated generous benefit packages for its membership. But the M&M Agreement could not stop what would soon become the greatest threat to longshoremen: the disappearance of jobs. Beginning in the late 1950s, containerization slowly but steadily eliminated jobs in San Pedro and other ports across the nation. Black longshoremen entered the decade of the 1960s with considerable trepidation about their future in an industry they had worked so hard to enter.

African American Progress Along the Alameda Industrial Corridor

In the two decades following World War II, black men experienced their greatest gains along Los Angeles's industrial corridor. Straddling

Alameda Street on the east and west, though most heavily concentrated on the east, the industrial corridor stretched from the old central manufacturing district some twenty miles south to the Port of Los Angeles, housing the city's large smokestack industries. East of Alameda were the white working-class suburbs of South Gate, Lynwood, Maywood, Bell Gardens, and Huntington Park. On the west were the largely black neighborhoods of South Central Los Angeles and Watts. In the middle ground of the industrial corridor, black, white, and Mexican workers interacted daily in the corridor's vast steel, meatpacking, automobile, rubber tire, chemical, and petroleum refining plants.

Work in the industrial corridor was not glamorous: in fact, it was hot, dirty, and often dangerous. But it was steady, plentiful, and, most important to recent migrants, increasingly open to black workers. Between 1940 and 1960, the proportion of the black male workforce employed as factory operatives in Los Angeles rose from 15 percent to 24 percent, with most of the growth occurring in metal, automobile, and food industries in assembly, maintenance, welding, and truck driving positions. Over the same period, the proportion of black men employed as crafts workers rose from 7 percent to 14 percent.[60]

Yet this progress was consistently marred by inequities. Despite the real gains blacks made, their work lives were too often negatively affected by circumstances beyond their control. Overt racism still restricted black employment as it had before World War II, but the greatest barriers to full equality were now subtler, though no less insidious. Even as the engine of opportunity for blacks accelerated in postwar Los Angeles, it strained against overt managerial racism, restrictive seniority rules, white workers' preferences, and deepening competition with Mexican workers.

The steel industry was an important component of Southern California's postwar industrial growth. Concentrated in the city of Vernon, as well as the distant suburban community of Fontana, Los Angeles's steel industry grew by 200 percent during the war and continued to expand during the 1950s. For African Americans, this expansion brought some new opportunities. Shut out before World War II, blacks quickly gained entry into the industry. As one field representative for the International Mine, Mill and Smelters Workers Union described it, the integration of blacks into the steel plants was almost entirely based on the fact that "the whites were all going into the airplane plants."[61] The steel industry was complex, composed of many different operations, job classifications, and work environments. Steel work fell into three broad categories: primary steel, which involved the hot and heavy processes of smelting and milling and was disproportionately dependent on unskilled labor; fabricated steel, which relied much more heavily on skilled operatives and crafts workers to manipulate steel into finished products; and scrap steel, made up of scrap steel yards employing small workforces of unskilled laborers and semiskilled crane operators. In these diverse settings, the meaning and tone of integration varied widely from plant to plant, even within the city.

In the primary steel industry, the largest employer of both black and white steelworkers was the Bethlehem Steel plant in the industrial city of Vernon. Purchased by Bethlehem Steel Corporation in 1929, the Vernon plant expanded vastly in the late 1940s, modernizing its furnaces and increasing output by five times. At its peak in the late 1950s, Bethlehem Vernon employed more than two thousand steelworkers.[62] During World War II, Bethlehem Steel's shipbuilding division on Terminal Island willingly hired African Americans for temporary war work; by 1943, the Bethlehem shipyard was more than 10 percent black.[63] During reconversion, Bethlehem Steel allowed newly integrated black workers from the shipbuilding division to work at the main Vernon plant. Bethlehem also accepted new black workers after 1947, when expanded operations created a labor shortage. Quickly and rather quietly, blacks became an important part of the workforce at the Bethlehem plant.

But mere inclusion in the labor force did not guarantee equality for black workers. In the primary steel and automobile industries, both of which were more vertically integrated than other manufacturing industries, workers in one department performed tasks that were very different from those performed by workers in other departments. Under these circumstances, departmental seniority—rather than plantwide seniority—was the determinant of upgrades and promotions. While blacks and Mexicans were easily hired into the industry, they were systematically channeled into those departments whites found least desirable. Thus, the greatest number of blacks and Mexicans at Bethlehem could be found in the furnace department, the hottest and most dangerous department in the plant. Ray Salazar, a Mexican American Bethlehem worker interviewed by Myrna Donahoe, remembered:

There was no discrimination as far as hiring was concerned. But as far as jobs that was different. The white persons had the better jobs like crane operator. That was clean and a little technical because you had to be careful of those below. I never saw a Latin electrician and no blacks either at that time. They never held skilled jobs. I didn't see a black electrician ever.[64]

As long as the rule of departmental seniority prevailed, black and Mexican workers had only one of two choices. They could transfer to different departments as "new" employees and relinquish the seniority they had acquired during their term at Bethlehem, or they could stay in their departments and make the best of whatever limited promotions existed there. Forced to choose between bad and worse, black and Mexican workers usually chose to stay in their departments.

Steelworkers at Bethlehem organized Local 1845 of the United Steelworkers of America, a union whose official position in defense of black civil rights was unassailable. In the South in particular, where African Americans had long been an indispensable part of the workforce in the steel industry, the USWA aggressively challenged the racist policies of steel companies.[65] USWA District 38, which covered the Southwest, including California, had a civil rights department, frequently criticized racial discrimination, and actively supported the local NAACP.[66] But Local 1845 did little to address the specific grievances of black and Mexican workers. The local struck in 1959, demanding increased worker control over shift scheduling, crew size, relief, seniority, and even the course of automation—virtually all of the issues important to steelworkers as a group. Yet plantwide seniority, which would have greatly aided minority workers, was not included in the list of demands. Mexican American steelworker Hermes Paiz remembered that white union members strongly resisted plantwide seniority because they believed that "every Black and Mexican would be after [better] jobs."[67] Local 1845's refusal to push for plantwide seniority gained its members little at the negotiating table: when the strike ended, workers at Bethlehem won few new rights and, in fact, lost several existing ones.

If the USWA's official commitment to racial equality was rendered meaningless by Local 1845's insensitivity to the issue of plantwide seniority at Bethlehem, it was further hobbled by the structure of Los Angeles's fabricated metals industry. This industry employed almost four times as many workers as the primary steel industry, but they generally worked in much smaller shops, with fewer than fifty workers on average.[68] Unlike the vertically integrated structure of the primary steel and auto industries, most fabricated steel companies specialized in one narrow procedure, producing, for example, screws, tubing, rivets, steel tanks, or washers. And unlike primary steel, in which workers spent lifetimes in physically separated departments, workers in fabricated steel worked in close proximity to one another. Furthermore, most workers preferred the fabricated steel industry because the work was generally lighter, cooler, and cleaner than in primary steel. Under these circumstances, white workers exhibited far greater resistance to black workers than they did in the primary steel plants, which became a major cause of slower integration. Whereas blacks represented 13 percent of operatives in primary steel plants in 1960, they represented fewer than 7 percent of operatives in the fabricated steel labor force.[69] If white management and workers considered the fabricated steel industry "white man's work," each increasingly included Mexicans in that category. In 1966, the first year in which comprehensive statistics on Spanish-speaking employees in the industry are available, 20 percent of the labor force in fabricated steel was Mexican, with only 6 percent black.[70]

Perhaps the brightest moment in the story of blacks' integration into the postwar steel industry was, ironically, the rise of ILWU Local 26. Because it organized warehousemen inland, Local 26 developed policies that were very different from those of its parent union, Local 13, the famously racist San Pedro longshore local. Under the leadership of Mexican American labor organizer Bert Corona, Local 26's sizable black and Mexican membership received equal treatment with one another and with white members. Already six thousand strong in 1941, Local 26 expanded to a postwar peak of more than seven thousand members.[71] The local elected its first black president, George Lee, one of very few African Americans at that level in any union in the 1950s. Local 26 continued to expand its influence in many different industries, from stockers in chain drugstores to workers in waste-rag plants and scrap steel yards.

By the mid-1950s, Los Angeles's scrap steel yards were heavily black. Sylvester Gibbs, who had migrated to Los Angeles from Lauderdale, Mississippi, in 1948, was typical of African Americans in the scrap steel workforce. Gibbs first found work torch-burning scrap steel at Calumet Iron and Metal in Wilmington, later joining Local 26 in 1953. After several months of training, Gibbs became a crane operator, a position he held for almost forty years. He credited the union for equalizing pay between white and black workers and felt the influence of the local in his daily work: "This company was fair to its men as far as I am concerned, because of whatever the union agreed—we struck—and whatever we settled on, that's what we got paid."[72] Gibbs' experience demonstrated the great potential of organized labor to provide financial stability and job security for its black membership: in 1952, he bought a new home in the quickly integrating city of Compton, while his peers in primary steel—where the vast majority of blacks in steel were employed—could afford to live only in Watts or in South Central.

In contrast to Los Angeles's primary steel, scrap steel, and meat-packing industries, which accepted African American men relatively easily—albeit always on unequal terms—integration in the automobile industry met with much greater resistance. The industry was Los Angeles's third largest, ranking second nationally just behind Detroit. Fueling its success in Los Angeles was the incredible regional demand for cars. Los Angeles had the highest per capita vehicle ownership of any city in the United States; by 1955, there were more than 2.7 million registered vehicles in the metropolitan area.[73] To keep abreast of demand, the city's automobile, rubber tire, and glass manufacturers hired workers in unprecedented numbers. General Motors and Firestone Rubber had plants in South Gate; Goodyear was located in South Central Los Angeles; and Chrysler, B. F. Goodrich, and U.S. Rubber (Uniroyal since 1967) had plants in Commerce, just east of the industrial corridor.

General Motors and Ford plants in Michigan had hired black workers from the inception of the industry, but their West Coast plants unabashedly refused to do so until after World War II. Shortly after the war, the *California Eagle,* usually quite guarded in its appraisal of employment opportunities for blacks, celebrated the Los Angeles auto industry's "reinvigorated" commitment to black equality, announcing that ten black veterans had been hired at the sprawling General Motors plant in South Gate in July of 1946, "breaking the Jim Crow policy of hiring in Los Angeles."[74] Yet, despite the celebratory tone of this article, eight of these men were assigned to janitorial positions, and the other two were assigned to warehouse positions, both poorly paid, nonunion jobs.

The management of General Motors in South Gate consistently argued, as many employers did, that the wartime influx of white workers from Oklahoma, Texas, and Arkansas made racial integration impossible and undesirable. This GM policy was consistent with attitudes in the surrounding community of South Gate, whose residents perceived themselves as perpetually besieged by their black neighbors to the west in South Central and Watts.[75] A 1949 survey revealed that blacks made up no more than 6.7 percent of the workforce at any plant—and, in most cases, the percentage was much less. By 1960, blacks still represented less than 8 percent of the workforce, but Southern California's racial geography complicated that total, creating wide disparities between plants. Thus, while blacks represented only 1 percent of the labor force at the South Gate General Motors plant in 1949, at the Ford plant in Long Beach—which was surrounded by a sizable community of recent migrants—about 7 percent of the workers were black.[76]

In Depression-era Detroit, the UAW, a CIO union, became a model of racial egalitarianism in the labor movement and the hub of black political activity in the city.[77] But in Los Angeles, where the black labor force remained quite small, the UAW did not serve that function. At the General Motors plant in South Gate, UAW Local 216 did make some overtures to blacks. In the mid-1950s, for example, a shop committeeman recruited black journeymen electricians, carpenters, and plumbers in nearby South Central Los Angeles to disprove the claim by General Motors' management that there were no qualified minorities willing to work.[78] But overall, as in steel, the union was not able to deal with the most significant barrier to black prosperity, strict departmental seniority. Most blacks then were hired into the noxious painting department, where their greatest hope was incremental advancement within that department.

The rubber tire industry, dominated by the sprawling B. F. Goodrich, Goodyear, Firestone, and U.S. Rubber (Uniroyal) plants, proved more willing to hire blacks than the automobile manufacturers were. Though none of these companies hired blacks before World War II, postwar expansion brought in a sizable group of African American men, attracted by the relatively high wages of the rubber tire industry and its proximity to black neighborhoods. By the 1960s, almost 13 percent of California's rubber tire labor force was black. In the U.S. Rubber plant in Commerce, which employed more than two thousand workers at its peak, black workers came to represent up to 20 percent of the labor force.[79]

But, from the perspective of black workers, the most important development in Los Angeles's rubber tire industry was the United Rubber Workers Union (URW). Between 1935 and 1937, all four of the big tire plants were unionized by the URW. Not a large union compared to the UAW or the USWA, the URW nevertheless had great bargaining power over employers because the tight competition and the interchangeability of products in the industry made industry leaders fearful of strikes.[80] Though URW locals 43, 44, 100, and 131—covering Goodrich, U.S. Rubber, Firestone, and Goodyear, respectively—made no special overtures to black workers, they accomplished what the UAW and the USWA had not: they negotiated for plantwide seniority. After a bitter dispute between the URW and two major tire plants in Akron, Ohio, the URW won plantwide seniority, which after 1952 became standard in rubber plants organized by the union.

Also fueling African American gains in the rubber tire industry were changing white preferences. As in primary steel and meatpacking, advances for black workers were always most significant in industries that had ceased—in the minds of white workers—to be desirable or respectable. Thus, a 1969 study of black employment in the rubber industry noted: "In the Los Angeles area, rubber tire work . . . is a less attractive and glamorous source of employment than is aerospace. The tendency of white workers to prefer the latter gives Negroes a greater opportunity in rubber tire plants."[81] Nonetheless, black men and women could earn relatively high wages and make interdepartmental transfers without losing seniority. In few places in the city were blacks closer to being treated equally than in the corridor's rubber tire plants.

African Americans viewed postwar gains along the industrial corridor from many different, and often conflicting, perspectives. From the perspective of Los Angeles's prewar African American community, postwar industrial integration represented clear and unambiguous progress. As longtime black resident Ersey O'Brien put it: "After Pearl Harbor, everything opened up . . . you finally had jobs here."[82] For the Great Migration generation, many of whom could have only dreamed of steady, union jobs in Louisiana or Texas, the progress was also real and important. But black workers' assessment of progress was not so narrowly defined. They did not simply compare present opportunities to past opportunities. Rather, they quite naturally compared their opportunities to those of white workers. Viewed from that perspective, their progress seemed much more uneven. In particular, even the most contented workers along the industrial corridor could not help but notice that the best jobs in the region lay elsewhere.

Race and the Suburbanization of Industry

Although job opportunities in the industrial corridor expanded annually during the two decades after World War II, the most rapid and significant growth in Southern California—in terms of capital investment, labor hours, and long-term economic importance—occurred outside the corridor, in the aircraft/aerospace industry. Fueled by the technological imperatives of World War II, the Korean War, and later Vietnam, the industry enjoyed phenomenal government subsidies. At its peak in 1957, the aircraft industry in Southern California employed more than 220,000 workers, almost one-third of the region's manufacturing workforce.[83] The aircraft industry quickly became the largest manufacturing industry in the United States. As the industry expanded beyond airplane production into space and defense technologies, it stimulated the growth of a booming electronics and electrical equipment sector that employed thousands of additional workers.

These industries were important beyond the mere numbers they employed. In fact, they shaped the landscape of the region, drawing workers farther and farther away from the central city with the promise of jobs and, in the case of the aircraft industry, affordable housing. They also presented an appealing alternative to the hot, back-breaking, and often noxious labor typical of the industrial corridor. By contrast, work in the aircraft and electronics industries was typically light and clean, often performed in spacious, airy warehouses. In both industries, corporate welfare, more than organized labor, provided workers with what they perceived to be a fair deal. And the tight integration of housing development with increased suburban-industrial growth allowed city-weary workers to not only live but also work in suburbs. These postwar industries represented the best of what Los Angeles had to offer working Americans and, in many respects, the best of what the country had to offer as well.

From the 1930s through the 1960s, the fact that workers found employment in the aircraft industry highly desirable acted as a significant barrier to the advancement of blacks in the industry. Employers and workers almost unanimously agreed that aircraft work was white men's work. In August 1940, the manager of industrial relations at Vultee in Burbank flatly told the National Negro Congress: "I regret to say that it is not the policy of this company to employ people other than of the Caucasian race."[84] And while Mexicans had found opportunities open to them in the industrial corridor before World War II, they too were tightly restricted from aircraft work.

The wartime labor shortage forced management to reconsider its priorities, however. As the white male labor shortage deepened, aircraft executives began to accept Mexican men and white women into the workforce. The Los Angeles Aircraft Training Program conceded to train only "Mexican youth with very light complexion."[85] The most telling personnel stipulation came from aircraft executives who agreed to start hiring African Americans in custodial positions, but only if they were "coal black," presumably to maintain the clarity of racial segregation.[86] In an exaggerated version of hiring policies in other industries, aircraft management claimed the prerogative of not only managing the workforce but also, quite literally, managing the color line.

In 1941, the Los Angeles Urban League met with industry leaders, imploring them to integrate.[87] Employers became increasingly receptive as the labor shortage deepened and product demand increased. By February 1943, African Americans had become a vital part of the war industries in Los Angeles: Douglas hired twenty-two hundred black workers; North American hired twenty-five hundred; Lockheed-Vega, seventeen hundred; Vultee, three hundred; and Consolidated, five hundred.[88] The Lockheed-Vega plant in Burbank proved to be, as the black press called it, "the bright spot of local aircraft employment." "We expect Negroes," a Lockheed personnel representative stated in 1941, "to work in any division for which they are able to qualify." Lockheed management was willing to employ blacks primarily because of the labor shortage, but the company also appears to have taken the FEPC seriously and worked closely with the Los Angeles Urban League.[89]

When management forced white workers to work beside black workers, the results were striking. As one black employee stated: "I was struck by the courtesy of my fellow white employees and still marvel at the fact that of the thousands here, I have met with no insult, either open or veiled, and that I am given to feel that the Lockheed man is fair and is an ideal citizen."[90] In a clear example of management's influence over the racial policies of organized labor, Local 727 of the International Association of Machinists defied the national "whites-only" policy of the union in an effort to retain its strength at the integrated Lockheed plant.[91]

But wartime gains were quickly wiped out for most black workers. Because they had entered the industry later than other workers and thus had less seniority, black workers were disproportionately affected by reconversion. Between 1945 and 1949, the proportion of blacks at North American dropped from approximately 7 percent to 3 percent, and from 8 percent to 1 percent at Douglas.[92]

Organized labor played an even less significant role in racial integration in the aircraft industry than it did along the industrial corridor. Since the beginnings of Southern California's aircraft industry in the 1920s, organized labor had made very little progress; at the beginning of the war, few of the young aircraft plants were unionized. With rumblings of war, the UAW sent veteran labor organizer Wyndham Mortimer from Michigan to Los Angeles to unionize the sprawling North American Aviation plant in Inglewood.[93] But when UAW Local 887 launched an unauthorized strike in 1941, the national leadership of the UAW and the CIO fired Mortimer, allegedly for supporting the strike (but probably because of his well-known communist affiliation). The loss of Mortimer was a loss for blacks; during his days with Local 887, he consistently pushed to advance African Americans to skilled jobs and leadership positions within the union. When the National Guard stepped in to end the strike, Mortimer's replacement dropped the "Negro issue."[94] As the war came to a close, it became clear that the union could not—and would not, in any case—apply much pressure to counter anti-black employment policies.

Despite the tremendous demand for new labor in the postwar years, African Americans did not become nearly as significant a part of the labor force in the aircraft industry as they did in industries along the industrial corridor. The black share of aircraft employment never again rose to what it had been during the war; by the 1960s, blacks represented only 4.5 percent of the California aerospace workforce.[95] Black leaders found this trend troubling because, as early as 1950, it was clear that the aircraft/aerospace industry held the jobs of the future. Nor was the slow course of integration as easily explained as in other industries. By the end of World War II, management seldom articulated the racist views that had been commonplace at the beginning of the war. Furthermore, the structure of the industry, which allowed open bidding for jobs rather than basing advancement on restrictive departmental seniority, as in the industrial corridor industries, should have expanded opportunities for black workers.

In addition, unlike the industrial corridor industries, the aircraft/aerospace industry was heavily subsidized by the federal government. Lacking the legal authority to challenge discrimination in private industry, civil rights advocates within the federal government focused their attention on discrimination in government or government-contracted industries. The most significant embodiment of this trend was the President's Committee on Government Contracts, which operated from 1953 to 1960. Unwilling to jeopardize lucrative government contracts, employers in the aircraft/aerospace industry usually complied with directives to diversify the labor force. Yet, despite all this, the employment of African Americans remained quite minimal.

One significant barrier to integration was the increased demand for skilled workers in the suburban aircraft/aerospace and electronics industries. "The labor problem in Los Angeles in the foreseeable future," the Southern California Research Council astutely predicted in 1957, "is not one of numbers but of skills."[96] During World War II, skill requirements in aircraft were greatly reduced to accommodate new workers, but as the industry became increasingly dependent on more sophisticated technologies during the 1950s, the demand for skilled labor again increased. In the postwar years, the occupational distribution of the industry diverged from the typical manufacturing pattern, increasingly employing a much higher proportion of salaried and professional employees than blue-collar workers. For example, whereas 55 percent of the automobile labor force consisted of operatives, these workers made up less than 20 percent of the aircraft/aerospace labor force.[97]

The NAACP, which historically expended most of its resources litigating for civil rights and racial equality, became increasingly sensitive to the skill deficit among black workers in the 1950s. Conducting a series of local industrial surveys that demonstrated the miniscule proportion of blacks in skilled and engineering positions, the NAACP concluded that at the current rate blacks would not have equal representation in skilled positions until the year 2094! In its 1960 report on the matter, "The Negro Wage Earner and Apprenticeship Training Programs," the NAACP placed most of the blame on apprenticeship programs. In addition to facing outright discrimination by union-controlled training programs, the NAACP concluded, blacks were also affected by the geographically specific nature of industrial training, particularly in the aircraft industry.[98] How, the NAACP asked, could aspiring black workers easily receive industrial training in suburban communities where they were not welcome? This question begged other and larger questions about the nature of industrial location itself that were germane to postwar Southern California.

In postwar Los Angeles, the underemployment of black workers in the aircraft/aerospace industry was exacerbated by the suburbanization of the industry. Los Angeles's early airframe manufacturers, including Douglas, Northrop, and Lockheed, started their businesses in the central manufacturing district. Seeking greater space for testing aircraft in the late 1920s, these companies relocated to the suburban areas of Santa Monica and Burbank. In the 1930s, before the dramatic expansion of the aircraft industry, developers, in conjunction with aircraft production plants, proposed carefully planned communities to house both production workers and management in the vicinity of the plants. West Side Village (Mar Vista) was built near the Douglas plant in Santa Monica, Toluca Woods in North Hollywood was built near Lockheed, and tracts in Westchester were built to house workers at North American Aviation in Inglewood.[99]

Throughout the vast wartime expansion, the suburbanization of the industry, its many feeder industries, and their workforces proceeded rapidly. During the war, aircraft production companies maintained that residential proximity to production facilities was not only a convenience but also a military necessity. In 1943, management at Lockheed's North Hollywood plant stated that the company lost about 10 percent of its productivity because of a lack of personnel in the San Fernando Valley, a result of "the lack of housing within a reasonable distance to the plants."[100] After the war, aircraft firms envisioned planned communities in which all of the workers' needs could be fulfilled. Kaiser Homes developed huge tracts in Panorama City near Rocketdyne, Lockheed, and General Motors, in which housing was integrated with schools, hospitals, churches, and commercial centers. Advertised as "Homes at Wholesale," these houses represented the fulfillment of the "American dream" for many white workers in postwar Southern California.

This tight integration of work and community, as well as the distance of these communities from the central city, effectively eliminated blacks from the industry, even when the industry was not explicitly discriminatory. With the important exception of North American Aviation, which was located in Inglewood, adjacent to areas of increased black settlement, and which hired more blacks than any other aircraft company, most aircraft, aerospace, and electronic firms were well outside the central city by the early 1950s, mostly in the San Fernando Valley. The greatest obstacle African Americans faced was the vigilance with which white aircraft/aerospace workers defended their planned communities and housing tracts against the "encroachment" of blacks. Well after the Supreme Court declared racially restrictive housing covenants unenforceable in 1948, residents of the San Fernando Valley developed dozens of strategies to keep African Americans out, as chapter 4 describes.

Although aircraft and aerospace employers had long since abandoned the notion that work in their industry was strictly "white work," the suburbanization of the industry and its workforce actually reinforced that very sentiment. The electronics industry further perpetuated this cycle. In the 1950s, the three largest electronic component manufacturers were all outside the city, as far away as Pomona and Azusa. The regional director of the President's Committee on Government Contracts noted:

The Committee has found that is quite possible for a company to be free of intentional discriminatorial practices and yet, to have no Negro in the work force year after year. . . . We find where Government contractors are located in geographical areas in which Negroes are unable to obtain housing, Negroes are to be found . . . [only] in very small numbers.

Thus, a North Hollywood aerospace company explained that its black employees were so few because "no Negroes are available in the area." Another Burbank electronics firm responded that there was "no Negro residential area nearby" and that the "transportation costs from Negro neighborhoods [are] prohibitive."[101]

The experiences of black Lockheed worker Preston Morris were typical, although his credentials were not. With a master's degree in physics from Howard University, Morris applied for a job as a research engineer at Lockheed's Burbank plant in 1959 and was quickly hired. But for Morris, a resident of South Central, transportation posed a problem: "My wife was working at that time, so she had the car. I thought maybe there was public transportation in the Valley but I found that it was very poor." To ease the commute, Morris and his wife decided to purchase a home at the Rolling Greens Vista Estates, one of the San Fernando Valley's many planned communities. After being quoted a price over the phone by the real estate agent, a white sales representative for the company was sent to show Morris the property. The sales representative, also a worker at the nearby Packard Bell electronics plant and a resident of Rolling Greens, quoted a significantly higher price than had been quoted over the phone and suggested that Morris look elsewhere. Morris then looked at homes in the Northridge area in the northeast Valley. There the real estate agent told him that the owners "would only sell to Caucasians." Morris's next search, in Sherman Oaks, proved equally unfruitful. "Most of my encounters in the Valley," Morris told the U.S. Civil Rights Commission in 1960, "have not been [met] with success. We are still looking and have yet to find accommodations."[102]

Ultimately, the postwar economy developed in ways that reinforced the separation of whites and blacks as often as it reduced it. While the Alameda corridor continued to provide employment opportunities, the popularity and desirability of those jobs declined in the eyes of white workers. Black men happily filled positions that had once been denied to them, gaining steady incomes and, in some cases, useful union representation. Furthermore, these jobs were close to where black workers lived, reducing the stress and wasted time of commuting. Meanwhile, white workers also forged their own new link between the workplace and the community, but this development occurred away from the central city. Even where suburban industries were open to blacks, the vehement resistance of white workers to neighborhood integration made workplace integration undesirable and often untenable for black workers. Thus, postwar economic development and worker responses reinforced, in the minds of both blacks and whites, the notion of clearly defined black spaces and white spaces that would ultimately exacerbate racial distance and tension in Southern California.

Black Women in the Postwar Economy

The deepening racial divide in the postwar economy of Southern California was also shaped by gender differences. Many black women experienced postwar economic opportunity in distinctly different ways than black men did. Though historically black women often suffered "double discrimination" by being both black and female, many now found that their gender, in fact, opened new doors that still remained shut for black men. Like black men, women entered the manufacturing labor force in unprecedented numbers in the postwar years. In 1940, 3.9 percent of employed black women in Los Angeles were manufacturing operatives, but by 1960 this figure had risen to more than 18 percent.[103] Even more promising was the integration of black workers into clerical and public administration jobs, a development that benefited black women more than black men.

More than their male counterparts in Los Angeles and more than black women in most other cities, black women in Los Angeles made dramatic occupational and economic gains in the two decades after World War II. These female workers secured employment and job skills that would benefit them long after the decline of the industrial corridor began in the late 1970s. Interestingly, the importance of these gains was lost on most contemporaries (and many subsequent scholars), who viewed the economic progress of black women primarily as a symptom of "the breakdown of the Negro family," rather than as an important development in its own right. Articulated most famously in 1965 in the U.S. Department of Labor's "Moynihan report," *The Negro Family: The Case for National Action,* this view obscured the critical influence of these gains on the psychology of migrant women and on the economy of America's black families and communities.[104]

During World War II, defense industry employers and labor unions, in contrast to their attitudes toward black male workers, were much more tolerant of and much less threatened by black women workers. This tolerance probably stemmed from the prevalent belief that black women, like all women, would leave the workplace after the war. Because labor leaders and male workers of all races assumed that women would work only "for the duration," the union status of female workers was not the subject of debate or even much discussion among most labor leaders. AFL unions simply and quietly assigned women to "auxiliaries" that were subservient to the union with which they were affiliated. The CIO was at least rhetorically committed to retaining the female workforce after the war and preventing the emergence of "another minority wage earning group," but the CIO locals rarely acted on this stated policy.[105]

In fact, many women in Los Angeles did indeed want to work after the war. In 1944, the Los Angeles County Chamber of Commerce conducted a survey of more than seventy-five thousand war workers and discovered that, although only 3 percent of the city's female war workers had labored in factories before the war, 42 percent wanted to continue their factory jobs after the war. Furthermore, among women workers who had been housewives before the war, more than 30 percent wanted to continue doing factory work after the war.[106] Nevertheless, without a mass feminist movement or popular consciousness of women's right to work, most were quickly laid off during reconversion.[107]

But black women, who had always worked in higher proportions than white women, had little intention of leaving the workforce. Black women's aspirations to continue working in manufacturing were realized most fully in Los Angeles's thriving garment district. The apparel industry boomed in postwar Southern California, and black women's share of garment work rose from a meager 1 percent in 1940 to just over 22 percent in 1960.[108] In prewar years, Mexican and Jewish women had dominated the industry, but after the war employers responded to the expanding market by employing black women. Because the garment industry depended almost exclusively on unskilled labor, with a constant demand for new workers, interethnic relations were not as competitive in this industry as they were among male workers in the industrial corridor. In the garment shops, it appears, blacks and Mexicans did not necessarily view each other as competitors; sometimes, in fact, they viewed each other as allies.

African American Arvella Grigsby, who grew up in Dallas, remembers working in the garment industry in Texas: "We had Mexicans, we had whites and blacks, everybody working together. And it was just like a big family. Everybody would bring lunches and share with each other, and if somebody got sick, everybody would put in money and buy flowers or cards to send them. It was just like a big family." After losing her job in Texas, Grigsby turned her attention to Los Angeles, where some family members already lived. All she knew about Los Angeles was that "they said you could find a job, you know. It might not be exactly what you wanted, but you could find a job and make a living." Shortly after arriving in Los Angeles, Grigsby found work at Rota's Apparel in the city's garment district. Her experiences in Los Angeles were similar to her experiences in Dallas: "[At Rota's] we just mixed with everybody because all kinds of people worked there. There was Asians, there was blacks, there was Latinos, chinamen and everybody. And everybody got along. We shared lunches, cake and everything."[109]

This camaraderie extended to the union, the International Ladies Garment Workers Union, in which black women played an increasingly important role in the postwar years. Yet despite these positive steps, there was no escaping the notoriously low wages paid in the garment industry. Garment workers' hourly wages were typically only two-thirds of the wages paid in the industrial corridor's manufacturing industries. As one sympathetic editorial in the *Los Angeles Sentinel* described, black women "can hardly exist on [garment wages] if they're single people. If they're married persons and heads of families the situation is even worse."[110]

The electronics and aerospace industries seemed to hold more promise. Although black women suffered as men did because of the suburbanization of these industries, and the proportion of black women employees remained small, strong employer preference for black women lured enough female workers to the industry so that they outnumbered black men. In one plant, a manager actually had to be stopped from publishing discriminatory job advertisements that stated a preference for black women.[111] Black migrant Tina Hill, who worked at North American Aviation during the war, was laid off in 1945 and went to work in a garment factory. But when the Korean War renewed the demand for labor, she was called back to work:

When North American called me back, was I a happy soul. I dropped that job [in the garment factory] and went back. That was a dollar an hour. So, from sixty cents an hour, when I first hired in there, up to one dollar. That wasn't traveling fast, but it was better than anything else because you had hours to work by and you had benefits and you come home at night with your family. So it was a good deal.[112]

Hill worked at North American Aviation for almost forty years.

When TRW Electronics opened up its sprawling plant in Lawndale in 1958, black women were hired rather easily. When African American migrant Mary Cuthbertson left Charlotte, North Carolina, and arrived in Los Angeles, she wasted little time searching for a job: "I went to TRW semiconductors and put in an application. They called me that evening and asked me could I come work the next morning. So I stayed there for 21 years." Cuthbertson viewed her employment at TRW in the context of her recent migration: "I liked it. It was something very different, because I had never worked in any kind of company or even a restaurant or even a fast food place. The only place I ever worked was as a domestic . . . it was really degrading to have to do domestic work."[113] For Cuthbertson, and many black women in Los Angeles, leaving domestic service was a personal and, indeed, a cultural victory. Between 1940 and 1960, the proportion of employed black women who were in domestic service in Los Angeles dropped from 68 percent to 24 percent.[114]

The most exciting improvements in opportunities for black women occurred outside the private sector entirely, in the field of public sector clerical work. Before the war, blacks had been strictly relegated to custodial and laboring jobs in the public sector, but the FEPC proved unusually effective at integrating black workers into additional positions during the war. Furthermore, the rapid growth of the California state government during the 1950s and 1960s created thousands of new clerical jobs (see figure 4). While about 8 percent of employed black women in other American cities worked in the clerical sector, on average, almost 16 percent of employed black women in Los Angeles were clerical workers by 1960. In 1970, nearly 32 percent of employed black women in Los Angeles worked in clerical positions.[115] Although blacks, and particularly black men, encountered increased labor competition from Mexican men in many blue-collar occupations, black women were much more likely than Mexican women to obtain clerical jobs because blacks were generally better educated.[116]

Outside the public sector, however, black women had a much harder time securing clerical work. Here, they were often subjected to a more rigid color line than black male industrial workers faced. Lighter-skinned African American women usually had a better chance of securing office work than darker-skinned women. This was especially true in the sales sector, which employed very few African American women of any shade. During the Depression, even black-owned businesses preferred hiring lighter-skinned black women, believing that both black and white men would find them more attractive. One black man refused to recommend employment for a young, dark-skinned black woman in

FIGURE 4. Typical of the growing proportion of black women employed as clerical workers in the public sector, an African American woman works at the Los Angeles Police Department in 1957. Courtesy of the Los Angeles Public Library.

a local black-owned cafe because they "hired girls only of fair complexion."[117] In the postwar years, white employers often turned first to Mexican women, although the color line was drawn sharply for them also. One representative of the AFL Retail Clerks union in 1952 observed: "The lighter skinned Mexicans have no trouble—they're very flexible, and scattered all over. But the darker ones are at a disadvantage."[118] Despite black women's real gains in office work in the postwar years, black and white male perceptions of female beauty often reined in those gains.

For black mothers, new work opportunities required creative and often communal solutions to child care. Because most black women still worked in low-paying industries, many took on additional night jobs to supplement the family income. But women had to rely on one another to handle these increased workloads. Arvella Grigsby remembered that during conventions at the famous Biltmore hotel, she would leave her children with neighbors in Watts: "I'd go down there at night. They had a big convention coming in, and my girlfriend that lived across the street her daughter would baby-sit for us, and so sometimes I'd work in the day. And then we had a friend who worked there who said we need extra [help]—she was a housekeeper—and you had to clean 16 rooms. It wasn't bad. We'd do it quickly." Because most black women were in similar circumstances, they rarely paid one another for babysitting services. Instead, they often exchanged favors:

A lot of times when you get home, they would have cooked and fed the kids and everything. Most of the neighbors were from the South, like Texas and Louisiana—there were some cooking people from there! Whatever they cooked, they would share with everybody. "What' you cook today?" "I cooked this, that and the other." And then you'd give them some of what you had. Some of them like to bake cakes, some of them like to bake pies and I just like to cook the vegetables and the meat. So we'd divide up.[119]

These communal solutions sustained black mothers as they took on important new responsibilities in postwar Los Angeles.

Bringing It All Home

In the two decades after World War II, black men and women in Los Angeles vastly improved their lives. Thousands of black men advanced from the most menial labor and service positions into stable careers as operatives in the city's burgeoning manufacturing industries, affording them steady, if modest, incomes. Black women, whose opportunities before the war had been even more limited than men's, took giant steps, abandoning en masse the degrading routine of domestic service. Instead, they worked their way into manufacturing industries and, most promisingly, into office jobs. A rising number of African Americans, particularly women, found clerical positions, gaining contacts and skills that would continue to be useful even after Southern California's postwar boom. And if unemployment rates remained inexcusably high for African Americans in Los Angeles, these rates did decline during the 1950s. Between 1950 and 1960, black female unemployment dropped from 10.9 percent to 8.7 percent, and black male unemployment decreased from 12.4 percent to 9.4 percent.[120] Although an intricate web of racially restrictive policies—some explicit, some incidental—consistently set limits to the progress of both black men and women, this progress was nonetheless real and meaningful to those workers who experienced it.

But the limits were glaring nonetheless. By the 1960s, it had become clear that the industrial jobs for which blacks had long fought were now slowly disappearing. Furthermore, figures from the Equal Employment Opportunity Commission suggest that the preference of industrial employers for Mexican over black workers—especially in the metal and food industries—had become thoroughly entrenched, further eroding opportunity for black workers in blue-collar occupations.[121] Of course, the deepest "opportunity gap" was still that between blacks and whites. Throughout the postwar years, white workers increasingly availed themselves of employment opportunities in new, lighter, and cleaner industries far outside the city, in communities where blacks were prohibited from living. Perhaps most frustrating, whatever economic gains blacks made after World War II were often tempered by how circumscribed their residential opportunities remained. But, as they had in the workplace, African Americans stubbornly refused to be "Jim Crowed" in housing.

CHAPTER 4

Race and Housing in Postwar Los Angeles

In the two decades after World War II, few issues evoked more passion from average Americans than the racial integration of neighborhoods. Most passionate about the issue were African Americans, who suddenly found that significant barriers to integration had begun to crumble. The landmark Supreme Court decisions *Shelley v. Kraemer* and *Barrows v. Jackson,* handed down in 1948 and 1953, respectively, effectively abolished racially restrictive housing covenants, the most entrenched barrier to neighborhood integration. And more African Americans than ever were earning incomes that allowed them to consider buying homes, especially in Southern California, where housing prices remained relatively low. Furthermore, the housing stock in Los Angeles expanded by approximately one-third in the 1940s.[1] Perhaps most important, a growing number of African Americans wanted to move out of areas where blacks had traditionally been concentrated. A 1956 survey of 438 black families in Los Angeles, for example, revealed that 84 percent would buy or rent in a "nonminority" neighborhood if they could.[2]

Thus, in postwar America, African Americans entered a booming and relatively affordable housing market in unprecedented numbers, determined to enjoy the fruits of their labor. Like whites, blacks sought nice homes in safe and conveniently located neighborhoods. Most important, black families longed for integration into communities that could provide superior schools for their children. For African Americans, residential integration was always about more than simply owning property—it was about dignity, opportunity, and their children's future.

White opponents of residential integration framed their opposition in similar terms. From their perspective, integration was a threat to the moral, aesthetic, and financial character of their neighborhoods, and thus a threat to their opportunities as working Americans. The more moderate opponents of integration emphasized its deleterious effect on property values rather than the racial inferiority of blacks. The most extreme opponents argued that integration was merely a vehicle for the real goal of miscegenation. Both moderate and extreme opponents almost universally shared the view that the most unsettling, if not dangerous, aspect of neighborhood integration was its effect on local schools. Most white parents did not want to subject their children to what they perceived as "experiments" in integrated schools. This conflict between black ambitions and white ambitions ensured that long after racially restrictive housing covenants were declared unconstitutional, residential integration would proceed very slowly or, in many places, not at all.

In Southern California, as in much of the nation, the pace and tone of integration were determined by many forces. Arguably the most important was the overt resistance of white homeowners, who devised dozens of tactics to keep African Americans out of their neighborhoods. As Los Angeles's black population continued to grow, the front line of white resistance expanded from the city to the white working-class suburbs surrounding the South Central area.[3] In the city of Los Angeles, as well as in these suburbs, whites often found that their efforts at exclusion were buttressed by the policies of the California and Los Angeles real estate boards, lending institutions, and even the federal government.

But white resistance was only one part of the story. Also influencing the trajectory of postwar housing trends was the changing economy of the black community. African Americans' uneven postwar economic gains, explored in the previous chapter, greatly affected the urban landscape of black Los Angeles, sending better-paid black workers in search of housing outside South Central, while limiting the mobility of others. In addition, the changing status of other ethnic groups affected segregation and integration in surprising ways. The multiethnic neighborhoods in which blacks had lived before World War II often became solidly black neighborhoods, while Mexicans, Asians, and Jews experienced varying degrees of acceptance in formerly white neighborhoods.

For black home seekers in Southern California, the combination of these pressures created a relatively wide range of experience that belies most accounts of African Americans in postwar urban America. Numerous excellent studies have emphasized the ways in which segregation deepened in the postwar era, creating a new underclass of "hypersegregated" black Americans.[4] And for blacks in Southern California, the most prevalent experience was, indeed, increased concentration in the various neighborhoods and communities of South Central. Although blacks in Los Angeles remained slightly less segregated from whites than was the case in many northern cities, they did become much more concentrated in certain areas after the war. Furthermore, in South Central, black families increasingly found themselves sending their children to all-black schools.

Yet African Americans who could afford to move to outlying neighborhoods such as West Jefferson and West Adams had very different experiences, often gaining access to better schools, better housing, and a greater share of municipal resources than their counterparts in South Central. In still another trajectory, some better-employed blacks also began integrating the formerly white working-class suburbs adjacent to South Central. Most apparent in Compton, this integration has generally been interpreted by scholars as "ghetto sprawl," but for black families establishing residences in Compton, it represented something quite different. In Compton, blacks gained access to the much-vaunted suburban lifestyle for which Southern California was famous.

Between World War II and the late 1960s, the geographic area in which African Americans could buy and rent property in Southern California expanded far beyond its prewar borders. This expansion, however, rarely kept pace with the continuing influx of migrants. More important, it absolutely did not keep pace with the expectations of black families. Their determination to further broaden the areas in which they could live generated an unprecedented wave of anti-black hostility and violence among white homeowners, forever undermining the relative racial peace that had characterized the prewar years. Within the black community, the expansion of housing opportunities was cause for optimism, but it also exacerbated the material and psychological effects of economic divisions among blacks. Black flight from South Central frequently engendered resentment among the area's remaining black residents, who perceived the out-migration as a drain on the local economy and even, in some cases, as an act of racial renunciation. Ultimately, African Americans' uncompromising resolve to move beyond the confines of their prewar boundaries permanently transformed the racial geography of Los Angeles and deeply influenced the social and political climate of the city in the postwar years.

Challenging the Legal Ghetto

The Great Migration of African Americans to Los Angeles severely overtaxed the city's already crowded black neighborhoods. During World War II, fifty thousand new residents packed into the prewar boundaries of Central Avenue, ten thousand new residents moved to Watts, and seventy thousand crowded into Bronzeville/Little Tokyo, a community that originally housed no more than thirty thousand residents. Immediately after the war, Central Avenue and Watts became even more crowded, as each absorbed the continuing waves of black migrants. Furthermore, many black residents of Bronzeville/Little Tokyo began to move south to Central Avenue and Watts, leaving Little Tokyo to the city's Japanese residents, many of whom had recently returned from wartime internment.[5]

Yet, despite the immense new burden of overpopulation, the geographic boundaries of black Los Angeles remained largely unchanged, still demarcated by Slauson on the south, Broadway on the west, and Alameda on the east.[6] In contrast, however, the general attitude of its residents had definitely changed. Certainly, blacks in Los Angeles had long chafed at the racial restrictions they faced in their search for housing. But after World War II, the city's African Americans proved remarkably insistent about expanding their housing opportunities, launching dozens of suits against white neighborhood associations and real estate brokers.[7]

This political assertiveness found its apex in the famous "Sugar Hill case" of 1946. Originally known as the Heights, because of its slight elevation, Sugar Hill had long been a coveted area for well-to-do white residents.[8] Located in the northeast corner of the West Adams district, Sugar Hill boasted some of city's stateliest homes, many of them Victorian mansions built in the late nineteenth and early twentieth centuries. The surrounding area of West Adams consisted of more modest Craftsman and Spanish revival–style homes, mostly built in the 1920s.[9]

As early as 1935, some elite African Americans managed to buy houses on unrestricted blocks of West Adams, bringing them within one mile of Sugar Hill. Then, in 1938, black business owner Norman Houston purchased a home in the heart of Sugar Hill. Hesitant about subjecting himself to racial hostility and slurs, Houston initially rented to a white tenant. In 1941, however, he decided to move into his home, despite the vehement opposition of the local white homeowners organization, the West Adams Heights Improvement Association. Within the next three years, several more wealthy African Americans moved into Sugar Hill, including Academy Award–winning actress Hattie McDaniel, actress Louise Beavers, former Los Angeles NAACP president J. A. Somerville, and Horace Clark, owner of the Clark Hotel, one of the preeminent cultural centers of black Los Angeles.[10] By the end of World War II, Sugar Hill was still predominantly white, but the richest and most famous African Americans in the city also lived there.

In 1946, members of the West Adams Heights Improvement Association filed a lawsuit in the California Superior Court, arguing that by selling to blacks, white Sugar Hill homeowners had violated racially restrictive covenants that supposedly covered those properties until the year 2035. When Judge Thurman Clarke ruled that such restrictive covenants were unenforceable, the homeowners association appealed the decision to the California Supreme Court.[11]

Representing the defendants was renowned NAACP attorney Loren Miller, whose fiery Depression-era journalism had earned wide respect in Los Angeles's black community. As an attorney, Miller brought the same keen intellect and incisive rhetorical style to the courtroom. Longtime friend and client Don Wheeldin remembered that Miller was so dynamic that other lawyers would actually postpone their own cases just to hear him.[12] Throughout the postwar period, Miller was Los Angeles's leading crusader against racial discrimination in housing. Later in life, he described the impetus for the postwar crusade to desegregate urban America: "Negro newcomers and old residents alike were hemmed in, penned up in racial ghettos—those sprawling black belts lying in the residentially least desirable heartlands of America's great cities."[13]

The luminaries of black Los Angeles turned out at the California Supreme Court for the appeal hearing. The ubiquitous Carey McWilliams, who also attended, described the procession of the "brightest social lights in the Negro community": "Conscious of the occasion, the wives appeared in all their finery and elegance, and the atmosphere was such as to make one wonder if the Judge would pour tea during the afternoon recess."[14] This display of finery was matched by Miller's dynamic defense, in which he not only developed a technical critique of the covenant but also lambasted the utter absurdity of invoking claims to a "pure white race" as a requirement for residence. Miller won the case and resolved to carry his message to the Supreme Court of the United States.

In 1947, the U.S. Supreme Court responded to nationwide appeals, and to an aggressive campaign by the NAACP, by finally agreeing to review challenges to the 1926 *Corrigan v. Buckley* decision, which had up-held the judicial enforcement of racially restrictive housing covenants. The NAACP immediately sent Loren Miller to Michigan to prepare a case defending Orsel and Minnie McGhee, a young black couple who had purchased a home in Detroit in 1944. The local neighborhood as-sociation demanded that the two leave for violating the covenants that prohibited any person except "those of the Caucasian race" from pur-chasing a home in that area. When the association filed suit, Michigan courts ordered the McGhees out of their home. A similar case from Washington, D.C., was presented to the U.S. Supreme Court, and both cases were combined under the title *Shelley v. Kraemer*, named after a third case from Missouri. Thurgood Marshall and a team of lawyers that included Miller presented persuasive arguments about the sociological effects of restrictive covenants and the constitutionality of state actions sanctioning discrimination. After several months of review, the Supreme Court handed down its historic decision in May of 1948, ren-dering racially restrictive covenants unenforceable.

The *Los Angeles Sentinel*, like other black newspapers across the country, welcomed the decision as a great triumph for African Ameri-cans: "California Negroes Can Now Live Anywhere!" the front page read following the decision. Above a large picture of Hattie McDaniel's opulent home, another headline proclaimed: "Homes Like These No Longer 'Out of Bounds.'"[15] Legally, however, one more hurdle re-mained in the battle to end restrictive covenants. In *Shelley*, the Supreme Court had not ruled that covenants were void but only that they were legally unenforceable. White homeowners were still free to voluntarily enter into covenants and demand that their neighbors do the same. In fact, determined white covenantors realized that they could continue excluding blacks by suing fellow covenantors for breach of contract if they sold property to blacks.

Thus, when Leola Jackson, a white woman and a covenantor, de-cided to sell her property to African Americans in Los Angeles, another covenantor, Olive Barrows, sued her. Again Thurgood Marshall, with the assistance of Miller, took the case to the Supreme Court. In its 1953 decision in *Barrows v. Jackson*, the Court ruled that to allow covenan-tors to sue for damages would indirectly compel them to violate the *Shelley* ruling. Together, the *Shelley* and *Barrows* decisions effectively abolished racially restrictive covenants in the United States. The efforts of the Sugar Hill defendants, and the thousands of politically minded African Americans like them throughout the country, had paid off.

Many believed, and even more hoped, that racial segregation in housing, like slavery and lynching, would soon be a thing of the past.

Defending White Neighborhoods

As the legal barriers to the geographic dispersal of the black community
fell, the economic and social barriers to that dispersal became much
more significant to both blacks and whites. While the postwar period
brought unprecedented gains for African Americans, it also brought a
crushing wave of virulent anti-black racism the likes of which the city
had never known. As long as the black population remained relatively
small and well contained, as it had before World War II, whites had little
reason to express racist sentiment overtly. But as the black population
mushroomed during and after the war, and the legal tools of racial
containment were struck down, white homeowners became much more
adamant in their defense of racially segregated neighborhoods and
communities.

Certainly, many white homeowners in South Central Los Angeles reacted to the influx of black residents by quietly selling their homes and
moving elsewhere. Lloyd Fisher, a researcher for the American Council
on Race Relations, studied the racially mixed, solidly middle-class West
Jefferson neighborhood in 1947 and found that many whites, "having
planned to move soon in any case to more modern neighborhoods, are
not averse to receiving the premium prices the Negroes are willing to
pay for their property." [16]

But in the two decades following the war, a rising number of ordinary white homeowners became outspoken—and sometimes violent—
opponents of residential integration in Los Angeles, especially in blue-
collar communities whose white residents could not easily afford to buy
homes elsewhere (see figure 5). Using data from the Los Angeles
County Commission on Human Relations (earlier known as the Committee on Human Relations), the Los Angeles Urban League identified
no fewer than twenty-six distinct techniques used by white homeowners to exclude blacks. [17] These techniques ranged from payoffs by neighbors to discourage home sales to prospective black buyers, to vandalism,
cross burnings, bombings, and death threats. [18] White resistance surfaced in the formerly white neighborhoods of South Central, in the
more distant San Fernando Valley, and, most stridently, within the ring
of white working-class suburbs surrounding South Central, including

FIGURE 5. A white mob gathers at the home of W. H. Whitson at 1863 East Seventieth Street in 1949. Whitson intended to sell his home, in this still-white section of South Central, to African Americans. Courtesy of the Los Angeles Public Library.

the cities of Inglewood, Hawthorne, Gardena, Compton, Lynwood, Huntington Park, and South Gate.

Within the city, those "transitional" neighborhoods in which blacks were slowly buying property became the focus of white resistance. White residents of Leimert Park, for example, vigorously defended segregation. Located on the western edge of South Central, Leimert Park had been created by architect Walter Leimert in 1927 as an upscale white "bedroom community." But in the late 1940s, African Americans slowly began purchasing homes in and around the area, provoking growing white hostility. For example, shortly after African American John Caldwell, his wife, and his sixteen-year-old daughter moved into their home at 543 Sixth Avenue in 1951, they awoke to the crackling sound of a four-foot cross burning on their lawn.[19]

Similarly, William Bailey, a World War II veteran and the head of the science department at nearby Carver Junior High School, moved with his wife to a modest bungalow in a predominantly white area just north-

FIGURE 6. Schoolteacher and World War II veteran William Bailey (*left*) surveys the wreckage from a bomb that exploded at his house at 2130 Dunsmuir in 1952. Although Bailey and his wife were unharmed, dozens of other black residents in this area received bomb threats in the following months. Courtesy of the Los Angeles Public Library.

west of South Central. In the twilight hours of Sunday, 16 March 1952, a dynamite bomb destroyed their home at 2130 Dunsmuir (see figure 6). Although Bailey and his wife were unharmed, dozens of other black residents in the area and in South Central received bomb threats in the following months. Two days after the bombing of the Bailey house, Mrs. Bertha Pitts received a threatening phone call at her home at 1207 West Sixty-Fourth Street, then the western fringe of black South Central. "Get out in ninety days," the caller told Pitts, "or you'll be bombed out." [20] Between 1950 and 1959, the County Commission on Human Relations reported six bombings and four incidents of arson against black homes in Los Angeles County. [21]

White resistance was also strong, if less violent, in the remote San Fernando Valley. Though part of the city of Los Angeles, the Valley was a suburban locale, and its residents enthusiastically embraced the popular distinction between "the Valley" and "the city." As "the city's" population became increasingly black in the 1950s, white homeowners in the Valley closed ranks against integration. Approximately 17 percent of racial "housing incidents" reported by the County Commission on Human Relations between 1950 and 1959 occurred in the Valley, most in the blue-collar suburb of Canoga Park, home to many aircraft and aerospace workers.[22] Mrs. Marguerite Herrick, of the Valley community of North Hollywood, wrote to the Los Angeles County Board of Supervisors, arguing that the supervisors must be tacitly supporting integration in the Valley, because they had not passed an ordinance against it. According to Herrick, the county supervisors needed to put themselves in her shoes: "Do they want to live next to colored people? Do they want to pay high taxes as we are paying in the Valley to keep a higher class of our people in the Valley, or will they reduce the value of our property when they let the colored people come in? No, I dare say not one of them would care to live next to a colored person. . . . We don't have any grievances to the colored people, but let's just keep them out of the Valley."[23]

Tempers also flared among white residents in the peculiar Valley community of Pacoima during the 1950s. Founded in 1887 on the Southern Pacific railroad route, and zoned for residential use only, the community of Pacoima became an affordable and desirable suburb for railroad workers. Consequently, it drew a small proportion of minority railroad laborers and became the Valley's only interracial community, housing a small population of Mexicans, Japanese, and blacks living east of the Southern Pacific railroad tracks.[24] During the war, about two thousand black migrants settled in Pacoima, as did another six thousand in the 1950s.[25] Pacoima's minority population benefited during these years from the construction of new tract homes that were sold on an unrestricted basis and well advertised in the black press. In the early 1950s, Green View Homes, a tract development with three-bedroom homes, was opened, as was Valley View Village, a 200-acre tract with a thousand three-bedroom bungalows.[26] But even as new housing opportunities emerged, they were always within the racial lines that had existed before the *Shelley* and *Barrows* decisions. Some of Pacoima's Mexican American population had begun to move into white areas, but blacks had much less success.

The experiences of Mr. and Mrs. Emory Holmes, a young black couple with three children, were not uncommon. Emory Holmes worked for a government-contracted defense firm in the San Fernando Valley and sought housing near his work. In August 1959, he and his wife purchased a home from a white homeowner in the white section of Pacoima. When the family moved in, they were subjected to an extended and bizarre campaign of aggravation and intimidation. Neighbors, posing as Mr. or Mrs. Holmes, telephoned dozens of local establishments, requesting rush calls to the house. Thus, within the first week, the Holmes family received visits, often after hours, from a life insurance sales representative, a milk delivery service, a drinking water company, three repair services, several taxis, an undertaker, a *Los Angeles Times* newspaper carrier, a veterinarian, a sink repair service, a termite exterminator, and a pool installer. One night, the couple returned home to find tacks in their paint-splattered driveway, several windows broken by rocks, and a spray-painted sign on their garage reading: "Black Cancer here. Don't let it spread!" During a local election several weeks later, someone tacked a sign to the Holmes's garage reading: "Democrats are for Niggars." Nor was the Holmes family the only target. The white man who sold to them charged that he had been quickly fired from his engineering position at a Valley aerospace company because of the sale. When he moved into his new home in Northridge, neighbors who knew about the sale in Pacoima greeted him with protest and pickets. So many protesters gathered, in fact, that police had to be called to quell the disturbance.[27]

But such vigilance was probably strongest in those white working-class suburbs surrounding South Central. Though increasingly accustomed to working beside blacks in the industrial corridor, just east of South Central, many of these white homeowners vigorously defended their neighborhoods from integration. Many of South Gate's white residents, for example, worked peacefully beside blacks in the local General Motors plant, but then retreated across Alameda Street after work and actively supported racial restriction in their neighborhoods.[28]

During and immediately after World War II, concerned residents of these suburbs wrote frantic letters to the County Board of Supervisors and to Governor Earl Warren, imploring them to prevent blacks from moving into white areas. A white homeowner from Inglewood pleaded with the governor to "help us out about this Negro business. We are going to have a terrible problem with the negroes if we do not stop their way of trying to mix with the white people."[29]

In the neighboring city of Hawthorne, a resident wrote to the Board of Supervisors, suggesting that "blacks in this section should be placed in their own all-Negro communities . . . with their own churches, their own schools and recreational facilities." Claiming to represent the thought of "99% of the people," he concluded that this solution "would certainly be one of the finest things that could happen to this region."[30] A white Huntington Park resident recommended that "there should be separate places for the Negroes to live instead of continually coming to white communities."[31]

White homeowners often had the support not only of their neighbors but also of their community leaders. When a black family bought a home in Eagle Rock, for example, a local uniformed police officer organized a neighborhood posse who burned a twelve-foot cross on the adjacent lot and threatened to "burn a nigger house down." Participants in the cross burning included the local realtor, members of the Eagle Rock Chamber of Commerce, and the president of the local Kiwanis club.[32]

In some communities, opposition to black neighbors became central to municipal politics. At the most extreme, anti-black, anti-Mexican, and, occasionally, anti-Jewish sentiment was refashioned into a positive creed of white power and purity. Although many white homeowners in the suburban city of Glendale worried about new black migrants from Shreveport, they welcomed another Shreveport transplant, white minister and demagogue Gerald L. K. Smith. In 1953, Smith bought a home in Glendale and moved the headquarters of his Christian Nationalist Crusade to Southern California. Smith's incendiary blend of millennial, anti-black, anti-immigrant, and anti-Jewish rhetoric appealed to thousands of Southern Californians through the 1960s.[33]

Real estate agents played a crucial role in maintaining the color line long after the *Shelley* and *Barrows* rulings. Until the late 1950s, the Code of Ethics of the National Association of Real Estate Boards contained a provision explicitly prohibiting real estate agents from introducing minorities into white neighborhoods.[34] Members of the highly influential Los Angeles Real Estate Board informed the Los Angeles Urban League that they would not sell homes to black families in a white neighborhood or cooperate with black brokers in such transactions unless three or more Negro families already lived on the block.[35] This board also refused to admit black members and several times proposed constitutional amendments to reverse the 1948 *Shelley* ruling.[36] In extreme cases, realty agents and neighborhood groups bought available properties themselves, even at a financial loss, to prevent blacks from moving in.[37]

Banks were also unwilling to break the racial lines set by white homeowners and real estate agents. Mortgage-lending institutions typically set higher interest rates for African Americans, believing them to be a significant credit risk. As *Los Angeles Sentinel* owner and editor Leon Washington put it: "Banks won't lend money and title companies won't guarantee titles [to blacks] in what they regard as white communities even when no valid restrictions exist."[38]

Private developers further intensified segregation in postwar Los Angeles. Several tract developers sold homes to blacks, but Southern California's largest homebuilders, including Milton Brock Builders, California City Builders, Lakewood Village Builders, and Julian Weinstock Builders, all refused to sell to African Americans in new tracts and subdivisions, believing that integration would destroy property values. "Few builders," the Community Relations Conference of Southern California reported, "will publicly affirm, but most will privately admit that the exclusion of nonwhite persons from the opportunity to purchase new homes in housing developments is virtually universal."[39] The housing industry itself was not necessarily a bastion of white Anglo-Saxon purity. In fact, two of the largest developers, California City Builders and Julian Weinstock, were Jewish-owned. Yet there, too, anti-black discrimination flourished. A representative of California City Builders explained the company's discriminatory policy to an NAACP representative: "We are Jews; they discriminate against us. We have to be very careful. If we let you Negroes go down there, the white people won't buy."[40]

In addition, the federal government played a determinant—though sometimes unintentional—role in perpetuating racial segregation in the postwar years. The Federal Housing Administration continued to require racially restrictive covenants as a precondition of loans until the *Shelley* decision. After 1948, both the FHA and the Veterans Administration (VA) refused to guarantee home construction loans where racial covenants were on record. Yet both agencies also refused to take an affirmative position on desegregation, demanding that individual complainants provide proof of discrimination rather than creating an institutional mechanism to prevent it.

Proof of the lack of resolve on the part of the FHA and the VA came during Southern California's vast postwar housing boom, dominated by large-scale tract builders who received generous FHA and VA funding but regularly flouted rules regarding racial discrimination. In 1959, the California State Legislature passed a law, authored by Augustus Hawkins, prohibiting discrimination in the sale or rental of any private housing developments subsidized by the FHA or the VA. Even then, however, local VA-authorized brokers often feared integrating neighborhoods. One VA-authorized broker who sold a home to a black aerospace worker in Azusa returned to his office to find pickets and protesters. Out of the 125,000 FHA housing units built in Los Angeles County from 1950 to 1954, only 3,000 (2.4 percent) were open to nonwhites. Nationally, the proportion of FHA units available to nonwhites was under 2 percent.[41]

If anyone had cared to listen, the experiences of the small group of black families who did receive FHA funding could have been quite informative. John E. McGovern, the regional zone commissioner of the FHA, conducted a study in 1948 that examined the records of principal lending institutions and builders in the Los Angeles area and looked at 1,136 FHA loans made to African Americans between 1944 and 1948 in Los Angeles County. Contrary to the popular notion that blacks would default on their loans, McGovern discovered no foreclosures. More significant, the delinquency rate was less than 1 percent, equal to the rate recorded for white borrowers. Furthermore, McGovern's interviews with several developers flatly contradicted the popular belief that African Americans were incapable of maintaining their property. Developers observed, in fact, that black homeowners were fastidious: "There are no better kept subdivisions in the city. As a group, Negroes have put in more landscaping, maintained better lawns and have improved their properties more than residents in 9/10's [of FHA homes]."[42]

McGovern may have exaggerated for effect, but photographs and anecdotal evidence from the era suggest that many black homeowners did take great pride in their property. Nonetheless, the fact remained that in the postwar era many individual white homeowners, and virtually all the public and private institutions in the housing market, did everything possible to prevent African Americans from living outside areas that were already predominantly black.

Creating the Postwar Ghetto

For many African Americans in Los Angeles, the postwar years brought increased social and spatial isolation from the rest of the city. Most striking was the rapid disappearance of the multiracial character of neighborhoods where they had lived before the war. In general, these neighborhoods became increasingly black, a development that quickly erased whatever social and psychological benefits African Americans had accrued from living among other minority groups before the war.

This development was not only a result of continuing black migration and rising white resistance to integration but also a function of the changing social, economic, and political status of other minority groups in postwar Los Angeles. Although nonblack minority groups continued to experience various degrees of discrimination and prejudice in Los Angeles after World War II, the obstacles they encountered usually failed to block their opportunities as completely as did those encountered by blacks. For example, despite being reviled as "traitors" and "spies" during the war, and despite continuing resistance to their presence in certain pockets of the city, Japanese Americans were able to integrate more fully into white neighborhoods than they had before the war, and much more so than blacks.[43] Jews, who had always been more integrated into white Los Angeles than Mexicans, Asians, or African Americans, found that most property, educational, occupational, and social restrictions against them were now in the past.[44]

For African Americans, however, the most significant development was the increased out-migration of their former Mexican neighbors. Census tract figures reveal a steep decline in the population of Mexican immigrants and Mexican Americans living in South Central during the three decades after World War II. For example, at the outbreak of the war, blacks, Mexicans, and whites represented approximately equal proportions of the Watts community. However, by 1958, blacks made up 95 percent of the Watts population.[45] Similarly, in 1940, the multiracial neighborhood of Avalon, also known as the Eastside, was about 60 percent black, with the remaining population composed of Mexican immigrants, Mexican Americans, and whites. By 1960, Avalon was 95 percent black.[46] Mexican residents of these formerly mixed neighborhoods often grew weary of the continuing waves of black migrants. In Watts, for example, Lloyd Fisher found that returning Mexican veterans deeply resented the African Americans who were moving in. In some instances, he observed, these Mexicans "threatened to band together to expel the Negro invaders from the community."[47] In Watts, this tension was sometimes manifested in violent and even fatal confrontations between black and Mexican youths.[48] More often, however, Mexicans, like whites in transitional neighborhoods, simply decided to move elsewhere.

Many Mexicans moved to the unincorporated area of East Los Angeles, which included the communities of Boyle Heights, Maravilla, City Terrace, and Belvedere. In the postwar years, East Los Angeles became almost exclusively Mexican, creating a large and crowded

Mexican barrio where there had once been racially and ethnically diverse neighborhoods.[49] In East Los Angeles, Mexicans experienced many of the same debilitating conditions blacks did in their neighborhoods, including overcrowding, bad schools, an insufficient share of city and county resources, and either inadequate or overzealous law enforcement.[50]

However, the story of East Los Angeles was only one of several important stories about Mexicans in postwar Los Angeles. As one, largely poor, segment of the Mexican population became concentrated in the barrio of East Los Angeles, another group moved out to emerging areas of Mexican settlement and, in some cases, to mixed white and Mexican neighborhoods. According to the 1960 census, only about 12 percent of the documented Mexican and Mexican American population of the Los Angeles–Long Beach area lived in East Los Angeles.[51]

More important, Mexicans gained far greater entry into Southern California suburbs than blacks did. For example, the working-class suburbs surrounding South Central—including Hawthorne, Huntington Park, Inglewood, Lynwood, South Gate, and Bell Gardens—were home to more than nine thousand Mexicans in 1960, but fewer than seventy blacks. In more distant suburbs, the gap between Mexican and black housing opportunities was even more apparent. The outlying suburbs of Alhambra, Arcadia, Baldwin Park, Burbank, Carson, Culver City, Downey, Glendale, Manhattan Beach, Norwalk, Paramount, Redondo Beach, Torrance, and West Covina housed more than forty-seven thousand Mexicans, but only about eleven hundred blacks. Even taking into account the larger size of the Mexican population, these figures reveal that a much higher proportion of the Mexican community, in comparison to blacks, became part of postwar Southern California suburbs.[52] The only Los Angeles County suburbs with sizable black populations in 1960 were Pasadena and Monrovia, where blacks outnumbered Mexicans; Altadena and Santa Monica, where the Mexican and black populations were roughly equal in size; and Pomona, where Mexicans greatly outnumbered blacks.

The difference between housing opportunities for Mexicans and blacks in postwar Los Angeles was largely a reflection of white attitudes toward each group. In 1952, black sociologist Alphonso Pinkney conducted a survey of white attitudes toward Mexican Americans and African Americans in an anonymous Southern California suburb. Pinkney queried 319 "native white American adults" about their willingness to interact with either minority group in different scenarios. He found that, on the whole, the respondents "approved of greater integration of Mexican Americans than of Negroes into the life of the community." For example, 48 percent of whites interviewed said they would tolerate Mexican Americans in social clubs, but only 25 percent would tolerate African Americans. Similarly, 61 percent reported that they would stay in a hotel with Mexican Americans, but only 38 percent would do so with African Americans. Most important, 45 percent of the whites surveyed reported that they would tolerate living next door to Mexican Americans, while only 23 percent would live among African Americans.[53] This relative tolerance of Mexican Americans translated into a much more timid campaign of exclusion against them than the campaign waged against blacks. For example, of the ninety-five racial "housing incidents" reported by the Los Angeles County Commission on Human Relations between 1950 and 1959, seventy were against blacks, nine were against Japanese, six were against Mexicans, and one was against Chinese.[54]

If whites had come to think of Mexican Americans as white or near-white, there is evidence that some Mexican Americans themselves adopted that new identity. Although the most striking development in postwar Mexican American history was the rise of the Chicano movement, which embraced Mexican ancestry, other Mexican Americans simply considered themselves white. For example, Charles Gonzalez of Los Angeles wrote to Mexican American city council member Edward Roybal in 1953, complaining about a traffic citation he received on a Los Angeles freeway. Gonzalez did not object to the ticket and admitted to speeding, but he did object that the officer had written "Mex" for Mexican under the race category on the ticket. "Now both of us know," he wrote to Roybal, "that there is no such thing as a Mexican race. The proper division for identification, as I understand it, is either Caucasian, Negro, or Oriental."[55] Similarly, World War II veteran Anthony Perez wrote to Roybal in 1950, encouraging him to further expand housing opportunities for Mexican Americans. Distinguishing himself from recent Mexican immigrants, this man argued that Mexican Americans were "modern citizens who do not delight in speaking Spanish." He continued: "We must learn to live with our non-Latin fellowmen. As members of the white race there are many of us who would make fine neighbors."[56]

In a glimpse of black attitudes toward increased Mexican integration into white society and neighborhoods, Mrs. Freita Shaw Johnson of Watts observed: "Mexicans get an education, the thing they do is move away from the area where they have lived and move over some place else and they are no longer Mexicans. They are Spanish-speaking people."[57] As the rising Chicano movement of the 1960s made abundantly clear, expanded housing opportunities hardly eliminated the disadvantages of being a racial minority in Los Angeles. Rampant discrimination in employment and education, as well as racially motivated abuse by law enforcement officials, constantly reminded Mexican immigrants and Mexican Americans of their second-class citizenship.[58] Nonetheless, the fact that Mexicans enjoyed far greater residential opportunity and mobility qualitatively distinguished their experiences from those of most blacks.

For a rising number of African Americans, residence in overcrowded, poorly serviced, and exclusively black neighborhoods was a typical experience. The community of Willowbrook was representative of the worst effects of racial segregation. An unincorporated portion of Los Angeles County south of Watts, Willowbrook underwent one of the fastest racial transitions of any South Central community. Typically multiracial and only 11 percent black before World War II, Willowbrook was approximately 80 percent black by 1960 and approached 100 percent in most tracts. During the same period, the population of the community rose by 400 percent.[59] Because this was an unincorporated portion of the county, Willowbrook residents found municipal services severely lacking. In 1962, a researcher for the Welfare Planning Council observed:

Some sections of Willowbrook appear rural in character, with unpaved roads and old houses; low rentals and low dwelling unit values predominate in such sections. There are no large shopping centers to focus community activity or traffic. Willowbrook gives the impression of being largely unplanned; some areas show marked over-crowding, in contrast to large patches of land with relatively low population density.[60]

In 1954, the Housing Authority of the City of Los Angeles (HACLA) opened its Imperial Courts public housing project on the Imperial Highway between Willowbrook and Watts, further contributing to the "unplanned" appearance of Willowbrook. Despite the high unemployment rate among residents of Imperial Courts, the rest of the Willowbrook community was typical of postwar black neighborhoods in South Central, in that it was composed mostly of working-class residents through the 1960s. If Willowbrook had become a ghetto by virtue of its racial concentration and overcrowding, it was, nonetheless, a working ghetto. Willowbrook's black men were industrial operatives and laborers; its employed black women were service workers and industrial operatives, and a few were even clerical workers.[61]

But the black working-class residents of Willowbrook and the rest of South Central increasingly found that the neighborhoods in which they had invested much of their time and energy were deteriorating rapidly. Continuing a prewar trend, the Los Angeles city government consistently diverted municipal funds for traffic safety, sewage, and street repairs away from the city's poorer black neighborhoods and ignored or relaxed zoning ordinances to accommodate commercial growth in residential areas.

This trend was particularly apparent in the Avalon area of South Central. Bordered by Alameda Street on the east, Avalon became home to many smaller chemical companies and food processing plants that could not find space in the booming industrial city of Vernon. It was not uncommon in the postwar era for Avalon residents to find pockets of their neighborhood littered with industrial debris and saturated by industrial liquid runoff. Debris fires and even factory explosions became increasingly common in the Eastside community. "One may purchase a beautiful home next to a vacant lot," Leon Washington inveighed in the pages of the *Sentinel,* "and in a few days, find a heavy manufacturing or some other industrial plant as his next-door neighbor."[62] Washington's dire assertion that South Central had become the "dump-yard of the city of Los Angeles" was borne out by a 1949 plan by the City Planning Commission to build a giant trash incinerator at Avalon and Slauson.[63]

In addition to the physical deterioration of South Central neighborhoods, African American residents also lamented the declining effectiveness of public transportation in their communities. Because a disproportionate number of blacks lacked the savings or the credit to purchase automobiles, efficient public transportation was indispensable. Though the popularity of the Red Cars had waned considerably among Angelenos by World War II, the Pacific Electric (PE) railway system remained a critical transportation network for blacks in South Central until its demise in 1961. When the PE stopped running Red Cars through the Watts and Vernon stops to San Pedro and Long Beach in 1948, Watts residents were outraged. They created an ad hoc committee called the Watts Citizens Welfare League, which protested to PE officials. The Watts and Vernon stops were reinstated, but this incident foreshadowed the ultimate defunction of the PE.[64]

Recognizing that declining PE service created a transportation crisis in Watts, and overtaxed by transportation problems throughout the city, the Los Angeles Public Board of Utilities granted contracts to dozens of small upstart bus companies. Unfortunately, these bus services were notoriously unreliable and inconvenient. The Landiers Transit Company was typical: it provided no bus shelters, took arbitrary and inconsistent routes, and adhered to no discernable schedule.[65]

For African Americans with automobiles, the construction of the Harbor freeway during the 1950s brought great relief. As one survey of Willowbrook residents revealed, however: "Even when people are able to afford or manage to obtain a used car, it is usually junk and, in a few days or months, inoperative."[66]

Poor public and private transportation narrowed employment and consumer options for African Americans. For those who depended on public transportation, employment outside the Alameda industrial corridor brought unbearable, or at least undesirable, commutes. For example, the bus commute from Watts to Santa Monica, which included several transfers, took up to two hours.[67] The transportation problem also forced many African Americans to shop at expensive local corner stores, engendering deep resentment among blacks toward local store owners. As Loren Miller explained: "The disadvantaged buyer is in no position to reject shoddy merchandise or haggle over prices. He must take what he can get and pay what he is asked."[68]

In another significant development, as formerly multiethnic neighborhoods became black neighborhoods, formerly multiethnic schools became black schools. The three large South Central city high schools, Jefferson, Fremont, and Jordan, which had been multiethnic, became almost exclusively black in the two decades after World War II. The same was true for the area's elementary and junior high schools, including Carver, Adams, Mount Vernon, Edison, Foshay, Markham, and Gompers. Segregation even extended to teachers. The two organizations responsible for teacher placement in the Los Angeles Unified School District (LAUSD), the California Teachers Association and the Los Angeles County Teachers Placement Advisory Service, both accepted discriminatory job requests from LAUSD schools.[69]

As the children of the Great Migration generation completed high school, the problem of higher education also loomed large. Most African Americans in central Los Angeles who attended junior college went to Los Angeles City College. But for those who lived in Watts, this was a fifteen-mile trip. One Watts resident from the 1950s remembered: "How you gonna get your kids to school after they get out of high school? If you didn't have the resources or somebody to get your kid down to Vermont and Monroe [to Los Angeles City College], they're kids without a school."[70]

The Ghetto Within the Ghetto: Public Housing

In postwar Los Angeles, the course of residential integration was also affected by a conservative shift in local politics, a shift fueled largely by the city's hotly contested public housing program. Since its inception, the Housing Authority of the City of Los Angeles had been plagued by controversy. HACLA was the product of the 1937 Wagner-Steagall Housing Act, which provided funds for slum clearance and construction of public housing projects under the auspices of the U.S. Housing Authority (USHA). An effort to fulfill President Roosevelt's commitment to helping the "one-third of a nation ill-housed," the act was designed to create housing for America's "lowest income group" in cities throughout the nation.

But within weeks of its creation, HACLA encountered massive resistance from opponents of public housing, chiefly the Los Angeles Real Estate Board and its several allies on the Los Angeles City Council. One representative from the USHA visited the city to check on HACLA's progress and was amazed at the degree of hostility to the public housing program. "Opposition has been so strong," he wrote, "that it has been necessary for the USHA to make surveys of actual slum and near-slum areas in order to have convincing proof of the need for such slum clearance to present to the City Council."[71] Thus, the USHA and HACLA commissioned a 1939 property survey, which revealed that pockets of Elysian Park and East Los Angeles—inhabited largely by Mexicans—contained up to 100 percent substandard housing.[72]

Confronted with irrefutable proof of slums in Los Angeles, the city council approved USHA funding, and HACLA commenced slum clearance and housing project development late in 1939. Despite the initial hurdles, HACLA quickly produced one of the nation's largest public housing programs. Before World War II, HACLA built Ramona Gardens in East Los Angeles; and during and after the war, it built Pico Gardens, Pueblo Del Rio, Rancho San Pedro, Aliso Village, William Mead Homes, Estrada Courts, Rose Hill Courts, Avalon Gardens, and Hacienda Village, expanding its tenancy to more than twenty-seven thousand residents.[73]

World War II temporarily silenced the critics of public housing because returning veterans, who were guaranteed preference in public housing projects by the Federal Public Housing Administration (FPHA), increasingly inhabited HACLA units. With regard to racial integration, HACLA initially followed federal guidelines stating that the racial composition of projects should match that of the neighborhoods in which they were built. Public housing agencies throughout the country subscribed to this rule, whose consequence most often was the re-segregation of blacks. This was particularly evident in Chicago, Cleveland, Detroit, Philadelphia, and San Francisco.[74] In Detroit, for example, 41 percent of white veteran applicants for public housing made it to the waiting list, whereas only 24 percent of blacks did.[75] And, once admitted, blacks were segregated from whites almost entirely. In Chicago, some projects were racially integrated, but the city council forced the Chicago Housing Authority to "maximize" the proportion of white residents in integrated complexes and restrict black occupancy to less than 10 percent in any one building.[76]

In a dramatic development in 1943, however, HACLA rescinded its racial quota policy and soon adopted a "first come, first serve" policy. As Don Parson has explained, this policy shift was a response to insistent protests by the Los Angeles NAACP, the Urban League, Charlotta Bass, and Leon Washington.[77] The results of the shift were striking. The National Committee Against Discrimination in Housing, a civil rights watchdog group that researched and exposed racially discriminatory housing policies in ten American cities affected by wartime in-migration, was pleasantly surprised by what it found in Los Angeles. Of all the cities the committee surveyed, Los Angeles had "the most enlightened, liberal and complete interracial policy to be effected anywhere in public housing." By the end of the war, leases for units under HACLA contained the following clause: "It is expressly agreed that this lease shall be subject to immediate termination for any disturbance caused, aided or abetted by occupant, including disturbances based on racial intolerance."[78] Furthermore, HACLA's geographically dispersed projects—which stretched from East Los Angeles down to San Pedro—prevented the type of concentration that cropped up in other cities and often doomed neighborhoods to automatic "ghetto" status.

After World War II, thirteen of the original fifteen units built by HACLA were racially integrated. (The only two nonintegrated units had been filled to capacity with whites before the black migration.) Figures from 1947 show a remarkable dispersal of black tenants throughout HACLA units. On average, HACLA's projects were about 26 percent

FIGURE 7. A racially mixed group of children at the Jordan Downs housing project in Watts, 1950. Although this group was typical of the racial composition of units run by the Housing Authority of the City of Los Angeles during the 1940s, public housing became more solidly black in the 1950s as white and Mexican veterans moved out. Jordan Downs itself was almost 100 percent black by the 1950s. Courtesy of the Los Angeles Public Library.

African American.[79] Furthermore, from the perspective of many black migrants, Los Angeles's new public housing was quite desirable. Local architects such as Richard Neutra and African American Paul Williams designed many of HACLA's two-story apartments with personal garden plots, front lawns, and wide courtyards.[80] In these well-built and racially integrated units, children encountered one another in a safe, often convivial atmosphere (see figure 7).

When Louisiana native John Murray, an African American, was discharged from military service, he moved his family out to Los Angeles, where they lived briefly in William Mead Homes. Murray's son Andrew remembered his childhood at William Mead in the late 1940s: "People were really together. It was just a melting pot. . . . Oh, man, it was nice. We danced on Friday and Saturday nights, the Mexicans and [blacks]— it was a big festival every Friday night."[81] For a brief moment in postwar Los Angeles, public housing was clean, comfortable, safe, racially integrated, and, for many, highly desirable as a stepping-stone toward private homeownership.

Initially, most blacks, whites, and Mexicans probably perceived their tenure in public housing as temporary, a way to get "on their feet." In fact, 73 percent of public housing residents stayed fewer than three years, and 31 percent of those stayed less than one year.[82] By the late 1940s and early 1950s, however, as veterans moved out, more poor black families moved in and stayed for longer terms. Unable to afford private housing, many blacks found public housing to be their only alternative. Whereas blacks represented less than 30 percent of HACLA's tenants in 1947, they accounted for 65 percent by 1959. The proportion of Mexicans rose, too, though not as dramatically, from 15 percent to 19 percent. Whites, once the largest group of HACLA residents (55 percent), represented only 14 percent by 1959.[83]

Public housing, both in reality and in public perception, was becoming synonymous with black housing. The extent of this perception was evident in the several battles over the construction of housing projects by the Los Angeles County Public Housing Authority, an organization faced with the unenviable task of finding suitable sites in the largely white suburbs of the city. Proposed county projects in Compton and Santa Monica met with fierce resistance from white residents, who considered them "negro housing," and the projects were ultimately relocated to Watts.[84]

Besieged by mounting white hostility, intense overcrowding, and ever-longer waiting lists for public housing units, HACLA found much-needed relief in the Housing Act of 1949. In this legislation, Congress and the Truman administration reaffirmed the New Deal goal of relieving poverty by granting millions of dollars to expand existing public housing programs throughout the nation. Mayor Fletcher Bowron eagerly pushed the city council to approve funding, and in the same year, with little fanfare, the city signed an agreement with HACLA to build 10,000 new units. HACLA, which already maintained 4,068 units, stood to dramatically expand its operations, becoming the largest housing authority in the nation.

HACLA officials surveyed potential sites and decided that Chavez Ravine was the most suitable, because of both the existing slum conditions and the abundance of land. With the help of the Community Redevelopment Agency, HACLA commissioned proposals from numerous architects, who envisioned the former slum as a carefully planned and beautifully maintained residential-commercial community. By 1950, residents of Chavez Ravine were served with notice that they would have to sell their homes to HACLA and that, in return, they would be given first priority in the Elysian Park Heights public housing development. Preparation of the site began, and the first houses were demolished.

But two years and $13 million into the Elysian Park Heights project, the Los Angeles City Council decided to reconsider its agreement with HACLA. While Mayor Bowron was away on a trip to Washington, D.C., in December of 1951, the city council called a special meeting to issue an ordinance canceling the 10,000-unit project. George Beavers, an African American who chaired both the famous Golden State Mutual Life Insurance Company and the city's five-member Housing Commission, which oversaw HACLA's activities, sent a frantic telegram to the mayor in Washington. But by the time the mayor returned, the council, led by council member Ed Davenport, had already issued the ordinance.

Although the California Supreme Court ruled that the city's attempt to break the agreement with HACLA was illegal, the council placed a referendum, Proposition B, before the voters in the June 1952 local elections. Voters flatly rejected the continuation of the housing project. Shortly after the referendum, Ed Davenport asserted that communists had infiltrated HACLA, and he introduced a council resolution to have the House Un-American Activities Committee investigate the agency. Passing unanimously, the resolution effectively destroyed HACLA. Frank Wilkinson, the outspoken HACLA publicity director and advocate of interracial housing, and four other HACLA employees were fired for invoking the Fifth Amendment at hearings of the California Un-American Activities Committee.

In June 1953, Norris Poulson, heavily backed by the powerful Los Angeles Real Estate Board, became mayor of Los Angeles, with a promise to block any further public housing development. "The city, county or Federal government should not build homes," Poulson stated the day after his election. "Private builders can do it."[85]

Poulson immediately renegotiated the contract with the weakened HACLA, dropping the Chavez Ravine project entirely but allowing HACLA to build four thousand more units in different locations. The last of those units, built in Watts, was completed in 1958. The city proceeded to sell three hundred acres of the now-cleared Chavez Ravine to Walter O'Malley, who built Dodger Stadium there in 1962, home to the recently transplanted Brooklyn Dodgers.

In 1965, shortly after the Watts riots, former HACLA publicity director Frank Wilkinson reflected on the meaning of the Chavez Ravine debacle for African Americans in Watts:

Had the Chavez Ravine and Rose Hill Court Developments been allowed to bear their fruit, 25,000 to 30,000 persons, the majority of them children, could have been lifted from the stifling pressures of the ghettos into the good air of an integrated, beautifully designed and low rent community of good living. And, year after year, as the initial families utilized the new projects as stepping stones to home ownership or private standard dwellings outside the ghetto, another 75,000 to 100,000 persons could have followed. Beyond that, with the pressure of overcrowding in the ghetto alleviated, sound social management could have started the slower process of re-integrating the old ghetto areas.[86]

It must be noted, however, that at the heart of the proposed Chavez Ravine project was a thirteen-story high-rise unit, only slightly smaller than Chicago's infamous Cabrini-Green, which became probably the most notorious housing project in the United States. Given the deepening racial concentration of blacks in Los Angeles's public housing system and the sharp rise in black unemployment in the 1970s, it seems more likely that Chavez Ravine would have eventually resembled Cabrini-Green rather than Wilkinson's optimistic vision.

Nonetheless, the failure of HACLA to build its second round of housing projects outside South Central did have deleterious effects on black Los Angeles. Watts became a dumping ground for public housing developments that were not welcome in other parts of Los Angeles. In addition to Hacienda Village, built in 1942, HACLA built three new projects in Watts between 1953 and 1955: Jordan Downs, Nickerson Gardens, and Imperial Courts. Nickerson Gardens was HACLA's largest project in both physical size and total population, with 1,110 units covering almost 69 acres. Far from HACLA's original vision of integrated, safe, affordable, healthy, and transitional housing, Jordan Downs, Hacienda Village, Imperial Courts, and Nickerson Gardens became self-contained ghettos in which the worst effects of segregated life—including racial isolation, overcrowding, crime, and frustration—were highly concentrated.[87]

African American Mobility and New Class Status: West Adams and Compton

While most African Americans in postwar Los Angeles lived their lives in the socially isolated and physically dilapidated neighborhoods of South Central and Watts, during the 1950s an increasing number moved to adjacent and even noncontiguous neighborhoods, many of which had historically been predominantly or exclusively white. Despite the enormous obstacles they faced, a rising group of steadily employed African American families found housing outside South Central. Most important was the expansion of the black population in West Adams, where battles for integration had been fought and won even before the *Shelley* decision. There, the black population spread farther south and west from Sugar Hill.

But perhaps the most remarkable expansion occurred in the city of Compton, a formerly white working-class suburb southeast of Watts. The growth of Compton's black population was explosive, rising by almost thirty thousand during the 1950s alone. In Compton, West Adams, and the community of Leimert Park, on the far western edge of South Central, African American families found better housing stock, reduced crime, greater integration, and better schools than they had experienced in South Central and Watts. For these families, daily life more closely approximated the mythical Southern California lifestyle of comfort and peace.

Aiding this process of African American suburbanization were black real estate agents and mortgage-lenders. Shut out from the key institutions in the Los Angeles housing market, African Americans created well-capitalized institutions of their own to help other blacks escape the ghetto. Beginning in the 1920s, financial institutions such as Golden State Mutual Life Insurance offered home loans for prospective black home buyers.[88] By the late 1940s, Golden State Mutual was so successful that it expanded its facilities and opened a new office in the heart of West Adams. Designed by Paul Williams, Golden State Mutual on Western and Adams became not only a leading black financial institution but also a source of great pride for the community. In 1947, local black business owner Claude Hudson founded Broadway Federal Savings to further accommodate the financial needs of the expanding black community. In addition, Liberty Savings and Loan Association helped African Americans finance homes from the 1920s until it closed in the early 1960s.[89] Because the Los Angeles Real Estate Board barred blacks from membership until the late 1960s, African American real estate agents created the Consolidated Realty Board, an all-black real estate board, in 1946.[90]

Within the city, West Adams became the most important growth area for these black housing institutions and for blacks eager to move away from Watts and South Central.[91] Since the mid-1930s, a small group of African Americans had lived in the West Adams area adjacent to Sugar

Hill. Max Bond, a sociology student at the University of Southern California in the 1930s, analyzed different black neighborhoods in Los Angeles and concluded that "the people who live on the 'west-side' are representative of those families that have attempted to escape from the masses and attain a higher level of culture."[92] Sugar Hill's location in the heart of West Adams fueled the neighborhood's reputation as home to the elite and rich of the African American community. The local black press encouraged this impression by writing about lavish events and "high society life" in the neighborhood.[93]

The story of the neighborhood's residents was considerably more involved, however. In fact, the occupational profile of black men in West Adams differed only slightly from that of black men citywide. To be sure, a slightly higher proportion in West Adams were professionals and managers, compared to the general black male population. But many worked in blue-collar manufacturing occupations in the service sector.[94] What separated black men in West Adams from those in other parts of the city was not so much their occupations, but rather the occupations of their wives.

In the postwar years, the ability of African Americans to move out of the ghetto had as much to do with the income women brought in as it did with the income earned by men. Black men in West Adams were doing roughly the same work as men in other black neighborhoods, but black women from that community were employed in much better jobs and were earning much more money than black women in other parts of Los Angeles. Compared to black women citywide, a slightly higher proportion of West Adams black women worked in professional and managerial positions; but the most striking difference was in clerical work. While 9 percent of employed black women in Los Angeles were clerical workers, 28 percent of employed black women in West Adams held clerical jobs. The link between women's work and residential mobility was also apparent in the Leimert Park/Crenshaw area.[95] Leimert Park generally attracted more black professionals than West Adams did. Seventeen percent of Leimert Park's employed black men and 19 percent of its employed black women were professionals in 1960, compared to a citywide average of 8 percent for black men and 9 percent for black women. As in West Adams, 27 percent of Leimert Park's employed black women were clerical workers, a fact which often made the decisive difference in the family economy.[96]

As part of the process of black residential mobility, the act of leaving South Central shaped African American perceptions of class. Residents of West Adams were not rich by any measure, but they increasingly identified themselves—and were identified by other African Americans—as middle class, not simply because of their slightly higher incomes but also because of where they lived. For the black community, class distinction had always been more nuanced than it was for whites. For example, the economic distinction between the black "elite," or middle class, and other blacks had never been as great as the distinction between the white elite and other whites. This was particularly the case in the first half of the twentieth century, when Jim Crow effectively put a ceiling on the earnings potential, educational attainment, and residential opportunities of blacks. Forced to live beside one another regardless of education or income, many African Americans conceived of "class" as a social rather than an economic distinction before World War II. Thus, "refinement," which included genteel behavior, impeccable church attendance, and a predilection for fine clothing, was the primary indicator of superior class status. But as the barriers of employment and residential segregation began their steady descent in the 1950s, economic distinctions between African Americans became more significant. Accordingly, class indicators and categories in the black community began to more closely resemble those of white communities. In postwar black Los Angeles, few class indicators were more significant than the ability to buy a house in a well-maintained neighborhood of steadily employed homeowners.

After the war, an emerging class of black property owners in Los Angeles began, quite naturally, to perceive their interests in broader terms, forging identities that transcended the narrow confines of race. For example, members of the all-black Small Property Owners League of West Adams wrestled with the competing demands of racial loyalty and their roles as landlords. The league was formed in the late 1940s by a small but influential group of African Americans who lived in West Adams and owned large apartment complexes in West Adams and South Central. The league's members were also active in the social life of black Los Angeles and were avid supporters of the NAACP. But in 1950, the league found itself embroiled in a conflict with the NAACP over the issue of rent control. Since a majority of NAACP constituents and African Americans in general had always been renters, the Los Angeles NAACP consistently fought for rent control in the postwar years. This, of course, conflicted with the league's financial interests as apartment owners.

Mrs. Rosa Lee Mitchell, head of the Small Property Owners League, wrote a frustrated letter to the Los Angeles NAACP in 1950:

Now property owners believe in fairness to both sides. I am sure many property owners have given their time and money to the NAACP as much or more so than the tenants. But if the NAACP is in accord with [rent control,] I can assure you that . . . the NAACP will receive very little future support from any Los Angeles property owner.

Mitchell also wrote that "the NAACP feels that it is right and fair for the tenants to have higher wages than what was paid in 1940 and for the tenants to have television sets, fine cars, fine clothes, take vacation trips and live the life of a king." Ultimately, Mitchell and the Small Property Owners League of West Adams renounced their NAACP membership: "We shall not buy from the NAACP or any other organization, any more than we would buy string to hang ourselves with."[97] For the league and dozens of similar organizations throughout black Los Angeles, the protection of personal financial interest often took precedence over traditional racial loyalties.

At the same time, black homeowners in West Adams united with their neighbors to combat what they believed to be racially motivated developments affecting their community. In their most determined battle, West Adams residents vigorously protested the proposed route for the Santa Monica (I-10) freeway. Early in 1954, the California State Highway Commission selected a freeway route that cut a 500-foot-wide swath through what the *California Eagle* proudly described as the "most prosperous, best kept and most beautiful Negro-owned property in the country," including Sugar Hill.[98] Believing that the selection of this route was at best insensitive and at worst racially motivated, a group of West Adams residents immediately formed the Adams-Washington Freeway Committee, choosing several delegates to present the community's grievances to the commission in Sacramento.

On 18 February 1954, former Urban League director and Sugar Hill homeowner Floyd Covington and two other West Adams residents, including one Japanese American man, presented their case before the Highway Commission. Arguing that West Adams's minority residents were in a unique situation because of their inability to buy houses in other parts of the city, Covington and his fellow homeowners pleaded with the commission to reroute the freeway on the northern side of Washington Boulevard, then still predominantly white. African Americans in Santa Monica also protested the proposed freeway route, which bisected the independent coastal city's small black community.[99] As a result of the protests, the Highway Commission delayed its decision for several months, although it ultimately insisted on following its original plan, citing transportation convenience and cost effectiveness.[100]

Outside West Adams, African Americans viewed black "blight flight" with considerable ambivalence. Longtime Central Avenue native Ersey O'Brien remembered: "When the war broke out, it let people go other places—move to other parts of Los Angeles. That brought South Central down a little bit because . . . the people that had a chance to move out of there would move."[101] "Bringing the area down" most often meant that black business owners moved elsewhere. Loren Miller described this process: "As soon as individuals are able to buy elsewhere, they attempt to buy elsewhere, and for that reason we lose constantly what might be considered to be the more substantial citizens, those who have higher incomes, and those who have lived in the city for any length of time."[102] To be sure, the loss of "substantial citizens" represented expanding opportunities for those citizens, a sure sign of progress for African Americans. At the same time, however, their disappearance contributed to the isolation of poor black people along Central Avenue and engendered a deep feeling of betrayal among many of those left behind.

As mentioned earlier, the most remarkable postwar demographic shift occurred in an unlikely place: the all-white city of Compton, one of Los Angeles County's oldest suburbs. Straddling the Alameda corridor south of Watts, Compton emerged as an important industrial and residential city in the Southern California economy. The Hub City, as its boosters called it in the 1920s, was fairly typical of those industrial suburbs east of Alameda that included South Gate, Huntington Park, Lynwood, and Bell. Compton offered its predominantly blue-collar residents affordable suburban homes in the heart of a thriving industrial area. The Compton Chamber of Commerce advertised the city as an "Ideal Home City" and as the "Residential Center for Industrial Workers."[103]

During the 1940s, Compton eagerly annexed almost fifteen hundred acres, hoping that added residential and industrial growth would contribute to the city's already substantial tax base. This tax base allowed the city to develop a strong public educational system, whose capstone was Compton Community College, built in 1927. During the late 1940s and early 1950s, the Compton school district built six new elementary schools, two junior high schools, and one new high school. Typical of Los Angeles County's industrial suburbs, Compton was also heavily race restricted. As late as 1948, fewer than fifty African Americans lived among Compton's forty-five thousand residents. Compton's proximity to Watts and Willowbrook kept white homeowners vigilant about maintaining the color line in their city.

Yet during the 1950s, Compton underwent the most profound racial change of any city in Southern California. Responding to the great demand for African American housing outside the ghetto, a new group of tract home developers and real estate brokers found a niche in the unrestricted housing market. Much of Compton's land annexation during the 1940s had occurred on the western edge of the city, close to areas of black concentration. This undeveloped property became a fertile area for the growth of the city's black population. Davenport Builders, a large developer, quickly built unrestricted tract homes on the western edge of Compton. "I moved to Compton in 1952," African American Sylvester Gibbs remembered, "in a place that was a corn field."[104] This was one of the few places in Los Angeles County where blacks could buy new tract housing. One prominent African American in Compton remembered the significance of the black migration to Compton: "For once, the Negro did not move into slums; for once he came into good housing."[105] Indeed, the 1960 census revealed that 93 percent of blacks in Compton lived in homes built since 1940, with more than half residing in homes built since 1950. Compton's houses were also large: almost 75 percent of black households in Compton had four to five rooms.[106]

White Comptonites reacted violently to the city's first wave of black homeowners in the early 1950s. Trouble began at Enterprise Middle School, an integrated Compton school between Central and Avalon on Compton Boulevard, where black and white students engaged in sporadic clashes in January 1953. The next month, several white property owners were beaten and threatened for listing their properties with the South Los Angeles Realty Investment Company, which sold to both white and black buyers.[107] In the following months, shrewd Comptonites scoured the city codes in search of a way to punish real estate agents who sold to blacks, finally dredging up a law that prohibited solicitation within Compton city limits. As a result, Compton police arrested five real estate dealers, who were later acquitted.[108]

In May, exasperated white homeowners resorted to vandalism and picketing. When African American Korean War veteran Alfred Jackson and his wife, Luquella, moved into their new home in Compton, they were welcomed by a mob of white Compton homeowners who hurled racial epithets. Leading the mob was Joe Williams, an employee at the Long Beach Douglas aircraft plant and a member of UAW Local 148. But the Jacksons were defiant—and well armed. As they moved their furniture into the house, both Alfred and Luquella kept loaded .45 caliber Colt revolvers in their pockets. One of Alfred's friends, also a veteran, stood guard with a rifle. In the following days, Luquella took time off from work to guard her home and children with a shotgun while Alfred was at work in the shipyards. Their armed self-defense appears to have shielded them from anything more than verbal attacks.[109]

After several weeks, the protests died down, and the Jacksons settled into their home. In an example of the disparity between the CIO's official policy on race and the views of its white homeowning members, the UAW quickly and publicly censured Joe Williams for leading the protest against the Jacksons. Williams, who had proudly worn his union badge while picketing, was charged with "actions unbecoming a union member" and temporarily suspended from union voting rights.[110]

Sporadic acts of vandalism continued through the summer of 1953, but white residents increasingly recognized that blacks could not be stopped from settling in Compton. Instead of resisting or cohabitating, many white homeowners decided to leave rather than risk a loss in property value. This reaction, common in transitional neighborhoods throughout Los Angeles County and the United States, was abetted in Compton by white and black real estate brokers who sought to stimulate a "panic selling" frenzy. Unscrupulous real estate agents of both races warned white homeowners that unless they sold quickly, their property value would plummet.

During the 1950s, panic selling and continued black in-migration dramatically reshaped Compton's racial composition. African Americans, who represented less than 5 percent of Compton's population in 1950, made up 40 percent of its population by 1960. In 1961, Loren Miller observed, with some ambivalence, Compton's rapid growth as a black suburb: "I doubt there are any other cities of Compton's size that can boast—if that's the word—a comparable percentage of Negroes."[111] And while the total population of Compton increased by 150 percent, to 71,800, both the proportion and absolute number of white residents decreased dramatically.

Despite the persistence of racism in Compton, African Americans truly benefited from their suburban relocation. Indeed, the much-vaunted suburban dream of peace and comfort came true for the thousands of blue-collar African Americans who moved to Compton during the 1950s. When white novelist and journalist Richard Elman visited Compton in the 1960s, he was amazed by this new black suburbia:

If ever the enforced togetherness of race could be transformed into a positive thing, Compton would be such a place. And that is, apparently, what many Ne-

FIGURE 8. Compton Community College graduation, 1956. During the 1950s, Compton's new black residents increasingly availed themselves of the city's superior school system. Courtesy of the Los Angeles Public Library.

groes were thinking when they came to Compton. . . . Here, it seems, a man has a chance to find decent housing and educate his children. Here it is possible to enjoy the great lower middle class dream of private life without feeling as if one were in a private hell.

Furthermore, Elman observed, Compton's superior racially integrated schools created a much better crop of black students than could be found in the ghettos of Watts or South Central: "Compton has become a city which sends its Negro high-school graduates to state colleges, to Berkeley and UCLA, and some even can afford to go as far away as Fisk."[112] Locally, black families increasingly sent their children to Compton Community College, considered at the time to be one of the state's best community colleges (see figure 8).

As in West Adams, African Americans in Compton perceived themselves (and were perceived by others) as middle class. Elman noticed that in Compton, "people never tire of telling you: 'We're different here than in Watts.'" [113] And they certainly were. Compton's black residents were representative of that group of blacks who secured steady blue-collar employment along the industrial corridor. While unemployment passed 30 percent in much of Watts, it stood at 8.7 percent in Compton. Compared to Watts, a much higher proportion of men and women in Compton worked as full-time factory operatives. Seventeen percent of employed black men in Compton were crafts workers, and 32 percent were operatives. Another 17 percent were professional and clerical workers. Among Compton's employed black women, 24 percent were factory operatives, 20 percent were clerical workers, and 9 percent were professionals. Accordingly, the median income of Compton residents was almost twice that of Watts residents. [114]

Although contemporary observers and subsequent scholars viewed black migration to Compton as "ghetto sprawl," or an extension of the black ghetto, it clearly was not. For Compton's residents, the city was far from the ghetto. Even blacks forced to buy older homes in Compton felt a bit of the suburban dream. Mary Cuthbertson, an African American migrant from North Carolina, remembered how her late husband felt about owning a home in Compton: "It was a very old house, but being the first house he owned in his lifetime, it just meant a lot to him to *own your own house.*" [115]

In contrast to the physical deterioration of Watts, Compton's proud black homeowners had meticulously groomed gardens and, for the most part, well-maintained housing. A white resident of Compton candidly acknowledged that their new black neighbors "are stable; in our neighborhood they are of a good class; many buy their homes and take good care of them; we wouldn't exchange Compton for any other place." [116] A white businessman in Compton grudgingly admitted to a white reporter: "Of course [African Americans are] moving into our city and there's nothing legal we can do to stop it. But you would be surprised—I'll take you through some of the streets they took over—clean as anything you want to see." [117] A reporter for the *New York Times* marveled at the "life styles of Compton" where "nurses and small-business men take meticulous care of their small, frame houses and colorful flower gardens." [118] Although Compton was adjacent to Watts and Willowbrook, it was, for its residents, worlds away. And many intended to keep it that way: four decades after moving to Compton, black homeowner Sylvester Gibbs boasted: "I ain't been to L.A. a hundred times. I know I haven't." [119]

The Urban Crisis Comes to California

During the 1940s and 1950s, Los Angeles became part of America's urban crisis. Once widely regarded by African Americans as an exceptional city, a relative paradise for blacks, or at least a marked improvement over northern cities such as Chicago and Detroit, Los Angeles quickly became representative of the worst effects of segregation. For many African Americans in Southern California, postwar residential segregation seriously undercut longstanding beliefs about the racial tolerance of Californians. According to segregation indexes computed by social scientists in the 1960s, the degree of separation between whites and blacks in Los Angeles was still lower than that in Chicago, Detroit, Philadelphia, Pittsburgh, or Cleveland. Significantly, however, the level of segregation in Los Angeles was substantially higher than in Northern California's large cities, including Oakland, Sacramento, San Francisco, Berkeley, and Richmond.[120] With the highest levels of segregation in the state, Los Angeles County had become the epicenter of California's urban crisis, and the western pole of the nation's.

Yet, by the late 1950s, a growing number of African Americans in Southern California were living in slowly integrating middle-class communities outside the ghetto. "There is another migration of the Negro," the Los Angeles *Mirror News* observed in 1956, "almost as dramatic as the [Great Migration]. It is the shift outward from the overcrowded overgrown central section of the city."[121] Propelled by their substantial gains in blue- and white-collar occupations and the first cracks in the wall of housing discrimination, these African American men and women achieved a higher standard of living than their counterparts in Watts or Willowbrook and found much comfort in that fact. But higher standards of living never guaranteed equality, and middle-class blacks encountered racism and discrimination as often as poor blacks did. Ghetto flight, middle-class African Americans found, solved an important, but limited, set of problems. Thus, even as blacks were increasingly separated from one another—both financially and geographically—they always shared a common experience with racism. That shared experience was the impetus for a burgeoning civil rights movement that forced black demands into the public consciousness of white Los Angeles.

CHAPTER 5

Building the Civil Rights Movement in Los Angeles

America's modern civil rights movement was born during World War II, although most Americans did not recognize its presence until the late 1950s. The Montgomery bus boycott in 1955, the desegregation battle in Little Rock in 1957, and the sit-in campaigns, Freedom Rides, and rallies of the early 1960s grabbed the nation's attention, leaving little doubt that an aggressive movement for black equality was afoot in the United States. But for urban blacks, especially in the western United States, the dramatic events of the 1960s were the culmination of at least two decades of struggle for equality. Leading that struggle were the thousands of African American migrants who had defiantly left the South, determined to finally and fully share in the country's new prosperity. The act of migration itself was the cornerstone of the new movement, bringing black people intent on equality to cities where that equality was conceivable. Further infusing the ranks were returning black veterans, emboldened by military service during the war.[1] Between World War II and 1965, such new forcefulness permanently transformed the relationship between blacks and whites in Los Angeles and in other cities around the nation.

Both locally and nationally, this new assertiveness manifested itself in many profound ways. Perhaps the most conspicuous was a deepened determination among African Americans to harness the power of the state as an agent for desegregation. The wartime FEPC had demonstrated that the federal government, when compelled, could act as a potent force for racial integration. The utter necessity of sustained federal intervention was reaffirmed by the wave of racially motivated layoffs that followed the dismantling of that agency in 1946.

Activism by African Americans in Los Angeles and elsewhere compelled the federal government to make a series of small but significant steps toward protecting black civil rights in the postwar years. The Truman, Eisenhower, Kennedy, and Johnson administrations grappled, with mixed success, with black civil rights in general and with equal employment opportunity in particular. But continued activism was necessary to compel the federal government both to follow through on its new commitments and to extend those commitments to all areas of African American life. In Los Angeles, this necessity was underscored by the Los Angeles Board of Education's painfully sluggish response to the spirit of the Supreme Court's landmark 1954 school desegregation decision, *Brown v. Board of Education.*

African Americans' new assertiveness could also be seen in a widening of traditional demands for equality. Although the black citizens of Los Angeles continued to struggle for the desegregation of schools, workplaces, and neighborhoods, they now also actively sought the desegregation of public space. Throughout the country, blacks had been chipping away at the sharp boundaries that separated "black space" from "white space." But for blacks in Los Angeles, who were generally better employed and better paid than African Americans elsewhere, this battle took on particular importance. African Americans in Los Angeles wanted to enjoy their newfound discretionary incomes, no matter how modest, especially in a city renowned for its vibrant nightlife and its abundant recreational and entertainment opportunities. As veteran black civil rights organizer Don Wheeldin remembered: "There were limits to what [blacks] could do with what they made because they couldn't buy houses anywhere, and they couldn't enjoy themselves, in terms of theaters and other things. . . . They couldn't use that money for purposes of themselves or their families."[2]

After World War II, blacks in Los Angeles made unprecedented challenges to the racial boundaries of the city's public spaces. Many whites erroneously believed that these challenges were primarily motivated by a deep-seated desire among black residents to intermingle with whites. In truth, however, African Americans simply wanted the freedom to enjoy, without harassment, beaches, shopping centers, theaters, restaurants, nightclubs, sporting events, and parks. But this modest goal brought them into direct confrontation with the Los Angeles Police Department, many of whose officers considered it part of their duties to reinforce the racial barriers of urban space. This confrontation would prove to be one of the most explosive in postwar Los Angeles.

In addition, the new assertiveness manifested itself in a deepening and widening scope of political activity. As they had always done, individual African Americans in Los Angeles actively challenged daily indignities on their own. For example, when Louisiana migrant Andrew Murray was denied service at The Witch's Stand drive-in hamburger restaurant on Figueroa and Florence in 1952, he piled his friends into a car and staged a sit-down strike at the restaurant. The management refused to serve black patrons and forbade its employees—waitresses on roller skates—to approach cars driven by African Americans. "We just sat down. We told the guy, 'If you don't let us eat, ain't nobody coming to this one,'" Murray recalled.[3]

Don Wheeldin remembered his own outrage at not being allowed to attend citywide dances in Pasadena: "Blacks couldn't go, and the pretense had always been that there would be a riot if they let blacks in, so finally we decided 'to hell with that.'"[4] Wheeldin and his friends approached the police chief of Pasadena and simply informed him that they would be attending the next dance. They did so without incident. In an extreme and atypical example, eighty-year-old Henry Green of South Central shot and killed a man who called him a "Texas nigger." After his arrest, Green recounted the incident for police: "He came to my house and called me a nigger. I ain't no nigger, so I went into my room, got my gun and loaded it and shot him. . . . Negroes here in this city would kill a man for calling them nigger."[5]

Increasingly, however, African Americans in Los Angeles channeled their daily individual battles for dignity into sustained, well-organized, and ever more public campaigns for total equality. In the twenty years following the war, blacks chose several different vehicles for those campaigns. Because the Los Angeles NAACP, the city's oldest and most respected civil rights organization, spent the late 1940s hobbled by ineffectual leadership and paralyzed by a fear of communist infiltration, blacks often sought support from other groups during that time. In this first phase of the Los Angeles civil rights movement, new organizations emerged to sooth interracial tension in the city and county. The Los Angeles Urban League continued to provide invaluable employment referral services to its black constituents; and the Los Angeles County Commission on Human Relations (LACCHR) became an important advocate for black equality and desegregation. Headed by African American migrant John Buggs, who had gained experience in community relations work in Florida before moving to Los Angeles in the early 1950s, the LACCHR pursued the desegregation of public swimming

pools, neighborhoods, and public housing units and formed community committees to intervene in instances of racial tension.[6]

More ecumenical in its approach was the Los Angeles County Conference on Community Relations, a coalition of dozens of religious,
racial, and social service organizations, founded by African American
George Thomas.[7] Yet, perhaps the most outspoken and militant advocate for black equality in postwar Los Angeles was the Communist
Party. Impressed with the party's confrontational protest tactics, many
African Americans enlisted its support in their personal battles against
racism in general and against police brutality specifically.

But by 1952, the House Committee on Un-American Activities
(HUAC) had effectively reduced the influence of the Communist Party
in Los Angeles and nationwide. Now freed from fears of communist
infiltration, infused with a competent new leadership, and invigorated
by the *Brown* decision, the Los Angeles NAACP reemerged as the preeminent civil rights organization in the city, leading aggressive campaigns for workplace integration and school desegregation and introducing the second phase of the civil rights movement. Rallying the
support of black churches and newer civil rights organizations such as
the Congress for Racial Equality (CORE) and the United Civil Rights
Committee (UCRC), the NAACP wove its crusade for equality into the
daily fabric of Los Angeles life.

Yet, without local black political power, the moral and legal victories
of desegregation remained abstract. Thus, on a parallel track, African
Americans in Los Angeles fought to achieve political representation throughout the 1950s. Their efforts were rewarded in the early
1960s, with the election of black representatives to the Los Angeles
City Council, the California State Legislature, and the U.S. House of
Representatives.

By the early 1960s, Africans Americans had significantly transformed
their status in Los Angeles. Their protests were widespread, their demands were well known, and their political influence—if still uneven—
was undeniable. Most important, African Americans participated in
daily urban life in ways that would have been impossible two decades
earlier. They shopped in stores, ate in restaurants, and went to public
places in record numbers. Long hidden from or ignored by white Los
Angeles, blacks had become an integral part of the city's public life. Yet
this increased public presence also unleashed an angry and aggressive
wave of anti-black racism in the city. This was particularly the case when
blacks attempted to integrate Los Angeles schools, viewed by many

white parents as the last bastion of white privilege. In this respect, the children of the Great Migration generation were on the front line of Los Angeles's desegregation battle.

Black Los Angeles and the LAPD

Few issues troubled African Americans in postwar Los Angeles more than the complete deterioration of their relationship with the Los Angeles Police Department. Under the watchful eye of reform mayor Fletcher Bowron and the expedient leadership of William Parker, who held his position as chief of police from 1950 until his death in 1966, the LAPD evolved from an inefficient, highly corrupt department into one of the most sophisticated agencies in the country. Described in *Life* magazine as the "second most respected law enforcement officer in America behind J. Edgar Hoover," Parker enjoyed a national reputation in the law enforcement community.[8]

But racism within the department only seemed to get worse. Of course, racism in law enforcement was not unique to Los Angeles, but the vast size of the city intensified its effects. Most problematic was the small size of the police force relative to the population. In 1959, the city employed 1.8 LAPD officers per 1,000 residents, a ratio approximately half that found in New York City. Under these circumstances, it was unlikely that officers would be residents of the communities they patrolled. As Chief Parker acknowledged, "We are under a difficult handicap here in that everyone here is a stranger."[9] In a world of strangers, in communities far from their homes, racist LAPD officers often acted with reckless impunity.

Paradoxically, however, under the Parker administration LAPD officers were also expected to be familiar enough with the communities they patrolled to make on-the-spot decisions about who belonged there and who did not. When asked about accusations of racial profiling, Parker responded: "Any time that a person is in a place other than his place of residence or where he is conducting business, . . . it might be a cause for inquiry."[10] White officers most often made that determination based on race. In this respect, even as the legal barriers to residential segregation were falling, many LAPD officers believed that at least part of their duty was to enforce the color line.

Parker's own views did little to challenge these attitudes. In a 1959 presentation before the U.S. Civil Rights Commission in Los Angeles,

Parker flatly told the commission, "There is no segregation or integration problem in this community." When asked about allegations of discrimination against minorities, Parker replied, "I think the greatest dislocated minority in America today are the police."[11]

Regardless of where black men or women lived in Los Angeles, how much money they earned, what jobs they performed, or what education they had, the threat of police harassment plagued them like a chronic illness. Chester Murray, a wartime migrant from Louisiana, recalled being arrested outside the Pantages Theatre in Hollywood, an area that was still largely off-limits for blacks: "I'll never forget, the police pulled us over and said, 'What are you niggers doing down here?' I said, 'We just going home.' They say, 'You busted now,' and took us in."[12] A well-respected African American physician, Dr. Joseph Hayes, who had served three years in the Army Medical Corps during World War II, was pulled over because he "looked suspicious" and was then beaten in the head with gun butts until he passed out.[13]

When African American Don Whitman and his wife were involved in a minor traffic accident in 1959, they were subjected to a vicious attack by the LAPD. When the officers arrived, they handcuffed Mr. Whitman, placed him in a squad car, and beat him repeatedly en route to the precinct station. At the station, officers punched and kicked Whitman, who was still handcuffed, causing severe bruising, a torn ear, a deep gash in his shoulder, and a cut eyelid requiring three stitches.[14] Roberta Washington, also a victim of police assault, wrote a heated letter to Governor Earl Warren, informing him of "the atrocities we suffer by the unchecked brutality of plainclothesmen and policemen in uniform. It has now reached a state where citizens are being subjected to vicious beatings and uncontrolled insults if officers don't happen to like their appearance."[15]

A survey of Watts residents corroborated the frequency and routine occurrence of police abuse: half of the respondents reported that they had been lined up on the sidewalk, frisked for no apparent reason, and "slapped, kicked, etc.," by the police.[16] Conversely, black residents also felt that the police under-patrolled their neighborhoods. This was especially frustrating to those African Americans who had worked hard to escape the poverty and escalating crime of South Central by moving west within the city. In the 1950s, organized groups of black homeowners in West Adams regularly protested the rising problems of prostitution and gambling on the fringes of their neighborhood.[17]

Black distrust of the LAPD was exacerbated by racially discriminatory assignment and promotional policies within the department. Although it was one of the first departments in the country to hire African Americans, the LAPD typically assigned black officers to all-black neighborhoods or to highly undesirable traffic duty downtown. During the 1940s, sergeant was the highest rank open to black police officers. Not until the late 1950s were the first African Americans promoted to lieutenant.

One of those promoted was future Los Angeles City Council member and mayor Tom Bradley, who joined the police department fresh out of UCLA in 1940. Bradley, widely regarded as one of the most highly qualified officers in the department, did not become a sergeant until six years later, a promotion that less-qualified white officers received after only three years of service. Nonetheless, Bradley was determined, he told fellow officers, "to work hard to replace the negative view of the police department within the [black] community, with a feeling of trust and respect."[18] But in this particular task, Bradley was unsuccessful. The LAPD remained largely intransigent, and as late as 1959 only 3 percent of the department's 4,600 officers were African Americans.[19]

For black Los Angeles, the threat of police violence was a daily, and sometimes deadly, reality. Few incidents more dramatically demonstrated this than the murder of Herman Burns. Before World War II, Nelson and Laura Burns, an African American couple, had spent their lives working hard to support their three sons and one daughter in New Orleans. As a carpenter and a seamstress, Nelson and Laura earned enough money to send their children to Catholic schools and sought to raise, as Laura put it, "a decent and respectable family." But the couple continually chafed against the racial restrictions of the Crescent City. America's entry into World War II infused the economy of New Orleans with fabulous new opportunities, but the greatest of those were always reserved for whites. For example, the city's Delta Shipyard became the leading southern producer of ships during the war, providing unprecedented industrial employment. But Nelson Burns, like thousands of African Americans in Louisiana, found the doors of Delta closed. He and his wife were determined to leave Louisiana, and their friends in Los Angeles assured them that opportunities were better there. In fact, Laura believed that in Los Angeles "there would be no discrimination."[20]

Migrating to Los Angeles with his family in 1942, Nelson Burns quickly found work in Los Angeles's bustling shipyards. With their hard-earned savings and Nelson's new job, the Burns family purchased a new home on Jefferson and St. Andrews Place, just south of West Adams. The oldest sons—Herman, a veteran, and John—quickly found work as plasterers and joined the AFL Plasterers Union. The youngest son, Julius, was a carpenter and joined the AFL Carpenters Union. In 1946, Herman moved into a new home with his wife, Virginia, a fellow migrant from New Orleans, and they had two children. The extended Burns family had seemingly fulfilled the most fundamental ambitions of migrants: steady employment, homeownership, and happiness—the "California dream" come true.

But on a hot August night in 1948, that dream was savagely shattered. Herman and his two younger brothers went to the La Veda ballroom in South Central for a dance sponsored by the "Ex-New Orleaners Club," a social group that brought black Louisiana migrants together on a monthly basis. Herman, a teetotaler, danced with his friends while Julius drank at the bar. Not long after arriving at the La Veda, Julius ran upstairs to use the restroom, accidentally bumping into a woman on the way.[21]

The woman's short-tempered boyfriend began shouting at Julius, and within seconds the two men were fighting. During the fight, two LAPD officers moonlighting as private security guards stepped in to break up the fight. The officers clubbed Julius repeatedly until he bled from the head and face. According to one eyewitness, a barmaid at the La Veda, the officers then dragged Julius down the stairs by his collar and along the floor, "beating Julius on the legs as he was being dragged along." Anita Callier, another New Orleans migrant, was in the restroom when she heard the fighting. She peeked out to see Julius, whom she recognized from his work on the house next door to hers, being dragged and punched.[22]

When Herman and John saw Julius at the bottom of the stairs, "groggy and bleeding profusely," they picked him up and rushed him to the car, two blocks away, to take him to the hospital. Before they could reach the car, however, two LAPD squad cars pulled up and immediately handcuffed John and began kicking the already injured Julius. When Herman tried to shield his younger brother, six LAPD officers began beating him and shouting racial epithets. At an inquest, John Burns recalled:

Two special officers seized Herman and Buddy [Julius] while three uniformed officers held Herman by his arms. The two special officers began to beat on him and handcuffed me. We told the officials to leave us alone because we were trying to get Julius to the hospital. They kept beating him. A tall heavy set special officer beat Herman with his blackjack and club on the side of his head, on his neck and wherever they could get a blow. Two white uniformed officers beat him in the side and all over his body with their blackjacks until he fell helplessly to the ground.[23]

When the melee ended, Herman Burns lay dead in a pool of his own blood. The LAPD adamantly maintained that the cause of death was a heart attack, but John and Julius knew that Herman's death had not been from natural causes. At the coroner's inquest, an eight-member, all-white jury declared that there was no evidence of criminal blame on the part of the officers.[24] And with that, the ex-GI, former defense worker, and husband and father of two was laid to rest. The testimony of Herman's mother captured the devastation his family felt:

It was hard to do, but we told little Herman and Rodney, the grandchildren, that their Daddy was killed by the police. Now every time they see a police officer they ask "is that the policeman that killed my Daddy?" If we hadn't been so upset we probably wouldn't have told them, because before we had taught them to respect the police, now none of us have any feeling but fear every time we see one. They are too young to really understand the meaning of death, so we tell them that Daddy is working in heaven, building a house for them.[25]

By ending Herman's life, the LAPD ensured that his children, and perhaps another generation of black youths, would continue to see the LAPD as an enemy, the capricious arbiter of cruel fate.

Communism, Anti-Communism, and Black Civil Rights in 1940s Los Angeles

Within days of the Burns incident, the Civil Rights Congress (CRC), a civil rights organization and subsidiary of the Communist Party, charted a course of action to protest the murder. Inviting several prominent members of the black community, including Charlotta Bass, the CRC formed a "Justice for Burns Citizens Committee." Infuriated by the "shocking increase in police brutality in the city [and] the shameful lack of action on the part of the law enforcement agencies,"[26] the committee sent delegations to all city council members demanding immediate action and began a door-to-door fundraising campaign for the prosecution of the officers and for the defense of John and Julius Burns, who had been charged with disturbing the peace. The committee also successfully solicited donations from several AFL unions that represented Burns family members, including the Plasterers Union, Painters Locals 664 and 1348, the Retail Clerks, and the Carpenters Local 634. Finally, the committee drafted a letter to District Attorney William E. Simpson, requesting a second coroner's inquest and a grand jury investigation of the murder.

Simpson agreed to the coroner's inquest, and the committee quickly secured the services of five physicians and obtained a court order to have Burns's body exhumed. After the coroner conducted a second autopsy and photographed the body, he determined that the real cause of death had been a broken neck, caused by severe blows to the back of the head. Yet, despite the clear evidence of police abuse, Simpson proved unwilling to call for a grand jury investigation. Doggedly, the CRC then sent a delegation of more than one hundred black, white, and Jewish citizens to Mayor Fletcher Bowron's office, where the mayor presented what the *California Eagle* called a "blanket defense of the Police Department." For more than a year after the violent incident, the district attorney gave no reply to the request for a grand jury investigation, and no action was ever taken. Furthermore, the police department never even released the names of the officers involved in the Burns tragedy.[27]

Although it failed to bring the killers to justice, the Justice for Burns campaign heralded the emergence of the Communist Party as an important political force in black Los Angeles. During the 1940s and early 1950s, many African Americans in the city came to view the Communist Party as the most effective and expedient vehicle for civil rights activism. This was especially the case because many black residents were becoming increasingly frustrated with the once illustrious crusader for civil rights, the NAACP.

The vanguard in the fight for equality before World War II, the Los Angeles NAACP blossomed during the war years, expanding its membership from two thousand in 1941 to more than eleven thousand in 1945, making it the fifth largest chapter in the United States.[28] Yet, under the leadership of local attorney Thomas L. Griffith, the NAACP did not translate these membership gains into aggressive political action. Members of the Los Angeles NAACP Board of Directors complained about Griffith's refusal to delegate authority and his insistence on directly controlling virtually every aspect of the organization.[29] When a troubleshooter from NAACP headquarters in Washington, D.C., visited the Los Angeles branch, he concurred that it was hindered by an "inept, confused and personal-interest leadership."[30] Furthermore, the NAACP's failure to support high-profile discrimination protests, such as the one against Bank of America branches on Central Avenue, gave the organization a reputation of indifference. An *Eagle* editorial described the local NAACP as "out of step with events on almost every occasion" and "more noted for its hesitancy than its militancy."[31]

The NAACP response to the Burns incident further alienated black supporters. During the war, Mayor Fletcher Bowron had appointed Griffith to a wartime race relations commission. Throughout the 1940s, the mayor viewed Griffith as a kind of liaison to the city's black community—no small responsibility in a city with no black representation in municipal politics. But when outraged African Americans and the Justice for Burns Committee demanded that Bowron push for deeper investigation of the Burns murder, Griffith found himself in an untenable position. Though likely disturbed by the Burns murder, Griffith was unwilling to jeopardize the important relationship he had forged with city hall. Nor would he align his organization with well-known communist protesters; just one year earlier, the NAACP West Coast Regional Conference had adopted a resolution calling on all affiliates to carefully guard against communist infiltration or associations.[32] Thus, Griffith vigorously defended the mayor. According to one NAACP official, Griffith appeared at the mayor's side, stating that "His Honor is doing the best he can and is working closely with the NAACP." "As long as Griffith is president," the official continued, "it will be impossible to do an effective job."[33]

Local African Americans were outraged by what they perceived as Griffith's choice of personal careerism over the cause of black equality. NAACP headquarters in Washington issued a stern rebuke to Griffith, chastising him for being a "catspaw" for Mayor Bowron.[34] Incidents like these seriously undermined faith in the local NAACP, and the earlier membership gains were quickly erased. From its 1946 high of fourteen thousand, the membership of the Los Angeles chapter plummeted to six thousand in 1948 and continued to drop through the early 1950s.[35]

Partly in response to this frustration, blacks increasingly sought out the Communist Party in their efforts to secure equality in Los Angeles. Since World War II, the Communist Party had reconstituted itself, and dramatic leadership changes had created a newly revitalized organization. The party grew rapidly in California, which became the second largest party district outside New York. A small but vocal minority of African Americans in Los Angeles were immediately drawn to the party's rhetorical commitment to racial equality and its aggressive protest tactics. Party activist and white Willowbrook resident Dorothy Healey recalled that "the fight against racism . . . was the central question as far as we were concerned. There was nothing that had a higher priority. It was something that every party member felt as an absolute obligation, a requirement."[36]

Certainly, other Communist Party members were less interested in racial equality per se than in the immediate practical benefits of organizing the new black migrants, who could help to create a greatly expanded political base. Many contemporaries and subsequent critics seized on this motivation as evidence of the party's duplicity regarding African Americans. The Communist Party, according to these critics, duped naïve blacks into allegiance by disingenuously proclaiming its commitment to racial equality.[37] In fact, however, the interaction of black residents with the party in postwar Los Angeles suggested quite a different relationship. In most cases, African Americans got as much, or more, from the party than they gave up.

African Americans brought to the Communist Party their own expectations and demands. They were not, for the most part, impressed with the "party line" on the perils of global capitalism. Most black members sought out the party because they or someone they knew had been abused by the LAPD, and no one else seemed to care; or because their local supermarket refused to hire African Americans, and no one else was picketing; or because when a cross burned on a black family's lawn in the middle of the night, the communists were the first ones to arrive and demand justice. These priorities brought blacks to the party in increasing numbers. At the peak of the Communist Party's activity in Los Angeles, approximately 10 percent of its members were African American.[38]

Perhaps the most important contribution the Communist Party and its local neighborhood clubs and councils made to black Los Angeles was the political education they dispensed to black residents. Healey recalled that the neighborhood clubs encouraged active political participation: "No matter what political subject was under discussion, people could stand up to speak about their own experiences in a union or in their community. They didn't feel like they had to be experts on national politics or political theory."[39] O'Neil Cannon, a black migrant from New Orleans who owned a small printing shop in Watts, also saw the party's political education as a critical moment in the emergence of the modern civil rights movement: "The kind of leadership among people that was encouraged by the party made it possible for people to understand how to struggle. I think that is the most important contribution made by the Communist Party to the world . . . to teach people to struggle."[40]

Most important, the Communist Party and its neighborhood clubs organized direct action protests when few others were willing to do so. For example, when Ralph's supermarket at Thirty-Fifth Place and Vermont Avenue refused to hire blacks in any positions, local communist clubs led picketing campaigns until the store amended its hiring policies.[41] Similarly, when the Farmers and Merchants Bank refused to hire black or Mexican tellers in its Watts branch in 1949, the Southeast Interracial Council, an organization with communists among its members, organized a picket line, eventually forcing the bank to change its policy.[42]

When black migrant Joseph Brocks faced extradition, after a routine arrest in Los Angeles revealed that he was wanted for stealing a bicycle in Thomasville, Alabama, the Civil Rights Congress wrote letters to Governor Earl Warren asking for his release. Unable to prevent the extradition, the CRC continued a correspondence with Brocks from his prison cell in Alabama and arranged for several of that state's Communist Party members to monitor his treatment. Brocks regularly wrote to Marguerite Robinson, the African American head of the Civil Rights Congress Minority Affairs Commission:

Margie, I realize that you is busy. I want you to know that I appreciate what you have so willingly done for me. Margie, I really don't know what I would have done if it wasn't for you and your staff. . . . you see Margie, the reason I write to you like I do, because I feel that you is a woman with understanding, and you understand my condition.[43]

For Joseph Brocks, and many other African Americans, affiliation with the Communist Party was neither whimsical nor capricious, but expedient.

As Marguerite Robinson's role in the Civil Rights Congress suggests, African Americans not only benefited from the Communist Party's activities but also shaped those activities as leaders of local clubs and organizations. One of the most influential of these leaders was Donald C. Wheeldin. Born in Connecticut, Wheeldin came to Los Angeles shortly after being discharged from the military in 1945. Like Pettis Perry and so many other African Americans nationwide, Wheeldin first became involved with the Communist Party because of its campaign to free the Scottsboro Boys during the early years of the Depression. During that time of economic and social crisis, Wheeldin recalls, "I found that the communists seemed to be the only ones that seemed to have the answers to many of the questions which arose."[44]

During his two years in the Navy, stationed at Oahu, Hawaii, Wheeldin became the editor of an Army newspaper called the *Mananan*.[45] Charlotta Bass, who had heard of Wheeldin's fine writing and editing, promised him a job in Los Angeles after the war. He arrived immediately after being discharged and began his job as a writer, and later editor, for the *California Eagle*. The articulate and passionate Wheeldin quickly rose through the ranks of the California Communist Party and worked as the first African American on the staff of the *Daily People's World*, California's communist newspaper.

When Wheeldin first moved to Watts, he was "very depressed by the extreme stringency imposed on blacks here, so I tried to do what little I could to alleviate some of those things." He lived with Frank Alexander, another black communist and a union organizer for the AFL Carpenters Union, whose membership was predominantly black. In addition to sharing a strong sense of camaraderie, these black leaders were able to make inroads into the new migrant population. Wheeldin and Alexander held street meetings and curbside "political education" sessions, recruited African Americans to neighborhood Communist Party clubs, and canvassed Watts, selling copies of the *Daily People's World*. "If I ran across somebody who was open to discussion on this question," Wheeldin remembered, "I [gave] talks on the Scottsboro Boys, Angelo Herndon—cases [where] the party had achieved some real results for blacks."[46]

Despite the growing number of black leaders in the Communist Party, there was often a gulf between the local leadership—both black and white—and the black rank-and-file and club members. O'Neil Cannon became involved with the party by printing fliers for neighborhood clubs, and he eventually joined the Watts club, but he never aspired to a leadership position. Like many black communists, Cannon came into frequent conflict with the local party leadership. "The party was always trying to keep us in line," Cannon noted, "because in Watts, we had a different breed of people." African Americans, for example, always had a different take on the "Negro question," "not fundamental differences, but how much effort should be put into this":

Many people came to the Communist Party and to the communist movement for many different reasons. Some people were humanitarians, some people like now are mostly involved in the environment, all those good things that the party and the Left and the Socialists fought for. But most of us black folks down in Watts, down our way, came in on the race question. We were talking about trying to get jobs.[47]

This single-minded emphasis on black civil rights led Cannon and others to pursue their own initiatives without official party sanction from the leaders "downtown":

In Watts, we would go out and organize stuff without discussing it with them dudes downtown! Whether them dudes downtown like it or not, this is what's going to happen. They'd look around and see something going, and they'd try to get in there and try to make us respectable, organized kind of people.[48]

Thus, the relationship between the Communist Party and African Americans in Los Angeles was most often reciprocal. Blacks gained an organizational structure they could use to voice their demands, and the party gained new members who could bolster its base.

But almost as quickly as the Communist Party had become a political force in Los Angeles, so too had anti-communism. Los Angeles was a critical target for America's anti-communists because they believed that the film industry was a hotbed of radical activity. First visiting Los Angeles in 1947, the House Committee on Un-American Activities identified a "hardcore revolutionary conspiracy" at work in the city, whose goal was to "carry communist theory into the practical sphere of workaday relations." HUAC claimed that "Communists and their fellow travelers appear in the spotlight as friends of the oppressed and abused" merely to expose the injustices of capitalism. Ultimately, HUAC concluded, the Communist Party was not committed "to the broader issues of civil liberties, but specifically to the defense of individual Communists and the Communist Party."[49]

Ironically, the American Civil Liberties Union, which aggressively challenged HUAC, shared HUAC's view of the Communist Party in Los Angeles. The national director of the ACLU warned A. A. Heist, director of the Southern California chapter, that the Communist Party "does not support defense of civil rights impartially for everyone without distinction but only for those whom they regard as progressive."[50] Similarly, many local NAACP officials shared the national body's belief that communists were more determined, as one editorial in *The Crisis* put it, "to confuse and embarrass Americans and the American government" than to help the cause of civil rights for African Americans.[51]

Despite the important role the Communist Party initially played in Los Angeles's emerging black civil rights movement, party support could also be a liability. In addition to the wrath that associating with communists brought down on noncommunist organizations, the party's ecumenical ideology and uncompromising rhetoric often undercut the largely integrationist ambitions of African Americans. The communist belief that racism was a function of that greater evil, capitalism, did not sit well with established civil rights groups, whose goal was to fully integrate blacks into the American system, not lead them to another. The atmosphere of intense fear generated by anti-communism aggravated this ideological rift, often with explosive results. This was apparent, for example, in a 1948 NAACP campaign to integrate the workforce of the Sears-Roebuck store in Santa Monica.

Like all suburban communities in Los Angeles County, Santa Monica had a long history of racial exclusion. Although the city never officially sanctioned racially restrictive housing covenants, a 1920s editorial directed "to Negroes" in a Santa Monica newspaper left little doubt as to the sentiments of white residents: "We don't want you here; now and forever, this is a white man's town."[52] But the expansion of the Douglas Aircraft plant during World War II permanently changed the city. The overall population grew by some 26 percent during the war, to reach sixty-seven thousand by the war's end. During the peak of wartime production, more than two thousand African Americans worked at Douglas, with many of them settling in residences just north of the plant, along Pico Boulevard. During reconversion, those former Douglas workers, especially many black women, sought work in Santa Monica's bustling retail trade.

Consistent with the California Sears-Roebuck policy, the company's Santa Monica store, on Fifth and Colorado, flatly refused to hire black employees. In March of 1948, two black women who were denied employment at the Santa Monica Sears store immediately contacted the Santa Monica NAACP. Unlike the Los Angeles branch of the NAACP, the smaller Santa Monica branch had been thriving under the steady leadership of Frank Barnes, one of the area's first black postal carriers and a well-respected leader of the black community. Barnes was one of the many African Americans in postwar Los Angeles County who had benefited from the appointment of a new county postmaster in 1945. The new postmaster was remarkably dedicated to equal employment opportunity, and, by 1950, more than twenty-seven hundred black men and women were working for the post office.[53] Well-employed with few political ambitions beyond his leadership post in the NAACP, Barnes was a determined defender of black civil rights. He immediately organized more than two hundred protesters, who picketed outside the store every Friday night for several weeks.[54]

As protests continued, Sears began negotiations with Barnes. Most of the protesters were black NAACP members, but a handful were also white Communist Party members who passed out party leaflets to passersby. Undeterred by the NAACP's official stance on the Communist Party, Barnes welcomed the additional protesters and united with them under the banner of the Community Committee. But this decision cost him dearly. During negotiations, Sears management realized that Barnes's position as a federal employee made him vulnerable. Accusing him of soliciting the aid of subversive groups, a crime under the newly resuscitated Smith Act of 1940, Sears contacted the U.S. Postal Service, and Barnes was immediately notified of his termination.[55] With the protest in disarray, Santa Monica business owners quickly and successfully petitioned the Santa Monica City Council for an ordinance against picketing. Within a month of its initiation, the Sears boycott had been stopped dead in its tracks. Sears did not change its hiring policy until 1955, when it did so voluntarily.

Eventually, Barnes was reinstated at the post office and rose to important leadership positions within the NAACP's West Coast Regional office. But the lesson of the Sears campaign was clear: communist affiliation had become a liability that the black civil rights movement could not afford. The NAACP turned that notion into policy in 1950 with a stern resolution against communism, which empowered the organization to expel any NAACP unit that had come under communist control. By the early 1950s, however, the Communist Party's influence in Los Angeles's civil rights movement was disappearing. Though the events were overshadowed by the arrest of the famous Hollywood Ten, many other party members and civil rights advocates were arrested, blacklisted, and imprisoned, permanently weakening the organization. Communist influence in the city's civil rights movement ended abruptly, only a few years after it had begun in earnest, but its legacy was critical. By encouraging direct action protests like picketing in response to everyday instances of discrimination, the Communist Party not only forced the general public to recognize racial prejudice but also set a standard of militant confrontation that other civil rights organizations would later emulate.

The Rebirth of the Los Angeles NAACP
and the Crusade for Desegregation

In the early 1950s, the Los Angeles NAACP was at its weakest point. Although the city's black population continued to rapidly expand, the membership of the organization was dwindling. The chapter's justified fear of communist infiltration, which could have severed it from the national NAACP, had hampered its efforts on almost every front and prevented it from participating actively in black protests around the city. But the year 1954 marked a dramatic turning point. Most important, the NAACP's victory in the historic *Brown v. Board of Education* decision renewed faith in the organization. Furthermore, local attorney and black luminary Loren Miller, who helped write the legal briefs for the *Brown* case and was vice president of the Los Angeles NAACP throughout the 1950s, bought the *California Eagle* in 1952 and used the pages of the popular black newspaper to reenlist support for the local NAACP.

Perhaps the most highly publicized NAACP campaign, and one that helped to revitalize the organization, was the campaign to desegregate the Los Angeles Fire Department. In 1953, NAACP field investigators discovered a clear pattern of segregation in the department's hiring and promotional structure. Of the fire department's 2,577 uniformed personnel, 74 were African Americans, and only 55 of 1,782 firefighters were black. There were only 6 black captains out of 293. Most discouraging, all of the black firefighters worked at only two fire stations—Stations 14 and 30 on Central Avenue—of the eighty-seven in the city.[56]

Loren Miller and NAACP attorney Thomas Neusom drafted a letter of protest to the newly elected mayor, Norris Poulson, and appeared before the Board of Fire Commissioners, threatening legal action unless Fire Chief John Alderson changed departmental policy. The board denied any wrongdoing. The NAACP pushed on for several months, finally gaining a Superior Court order that Alderson provide a deposition. After meeting with the Board of Fire Commissioners, Mayor Poulson concluded that there were indeed "unsatisfactory policies in personnel assignments, susceptible of criticism." He described racial segregation as "abhorrent" and encouraged the board to agree to a six-month desegregation plan, during which there would be a "correction of the practice of segregation." The board immediately drafted a plan to begin integration. In December 1954, two black firefighters were transferred to the all-white department in Studio City, a San Fernando Valley suburb.[57]

Like Police Chief Parker, however, Chief Alderson resented interference with his department's operations and bitterly opposed any efforts to desegregate the fire department: "As for the transfer of Negroes from the two stations, I will stand on my charter right to run the department in the manner in which I feel is best for all the people of Los Angeles. . . . I have made no agreement to change in six months or in two years." [58] Alderson convinced the board to abandon its agreement with Mayor Poulson. By April, the board officially announced that it did not intend to follow through on plans to desegregate.

Alderson engaged in months of diversionary tactics, including a proposal to empower a fact-finding committee to determine whether claims of segregation were even warranted. Moreover, Alderson threatened to resign rather than permit the integration of the department. "I will not remain," he staunchly declared, "to see the LAFD torn down to a second, third and fourth rate department." Finally, Alderson sent the black firefighters assigned to the Studio City station back to the Central Avenue stations and flatly told the board and Mayor Poulson, "That's all there is to it, my friends. I took this action and I stand behind it." [59]

Although Alderson shared Parker's hubris, he lacked the police chief's influence and power and was fired in December of 1955. Poulson appointed William Miller, who immediately undertook the desegregation plan. After a brief transition period, all of Los Angeles's black firefighters were transferred into seventeen of the city's ninety-one stations, and Stations 14 and 30 were desegregated. For the NAACP, and the principle of desegregation, this was a remarkable success. However, from the perspective of expanding employment opportunities for African Americans, it was far less important. Despite Miller's appointment, the number of blacks in the LAFD did not increase during the 1950s and grew only slightly in the 1960s. [60]

During the battle to desegregate the fire department, NAACP attorney Thomas Neusom ran for the presidency of the Los Angeles NAACP. The young but experienced Neusom ran against respected community elder and dentist Claude Hudson. Hudson, a member of the Los Angeles NAACP for more than thirty years, was widely considered a shoo-in. But the election was telling of a new mood among black civil rights advocates. During the campaign, Hudson ran on a platform of anti-communism, claiming that "evidence of Communist activities in recent membership meetings" compelled him to seek the office: "Community leaders and organizations . . . are concerned over rumors of communist infiltration." Neusom dismissed Hudson's claims and responded that only "lethargy, inactivity, lack of program and direction would allow the NAACP to be infiltrated."[61] Evidently, Hudson had misjudged the NAACP membership, who overwhelmingly voted for Neusom, sending a clear sign that they wanted to put the past behind them and get work done. Under Neusom's two-year tenure, the NAACP more than doubled its membership. Under the subsequent leadership of the Reverend Maurice Dawkins, pastor of the People's Independent Church, the NAACP continued to grow and launch aggressive new campaigns.

Particularly important for the NAACP's postwar growth, as the election of Dawkins suggested, was the expanded support of the city's black churches. Starting in 1955, the Los Angeles NAACP moved its monthly meetings from space it rented in the basement of the Golden State Mutual Life Insurance Company to the city's black churches. Few churches were more critical to the NAACP's growth than the Second Baptist Church of Los Angeles, one of the oldest and largest black churches in the city. Founded in 1885, the church grew quickly in the 1920s and 1930s under the tenure of its fifth pastor, Dr. Thomas Lee Griffith, the father of NAACP president Thomas L. Griffith Jr. The Reverend J. Raymond Henderson became the church's sixth pastor in 1941, serving for twenty-two years. Skillfully combining the prerogatives of spiritual guidance and community consciousness, Henderson brought his parishioners to the front lines of the city's civil rights battles. Although many political activists and social scientists of the 1960s contemptuously viewed religion as a deterrent to black civil rights activism, the opposite was true in the case of the Second Baptist Church.[62] In addition to Henderson's community-conscious leadership style, the church flourished because of the dramatic surge of assertive black Baptists who had recently migrated to Los Angeles. Thus, when Henderson launched an NAACP membership drive among his parishioners in 1956, he easily recruited almost six hundred new members.[63]

With strong ties to the church, the NAACP also extended its influence among the general black public through the use of well-orchestrated consumer boycotts. The most public of these was the 1957 campaign to desegregate the Anheuser-Busch brewery in the all-white Valley community of Van Nuys. After hearing rumors that blacks were not being hired, the NAACP sent a "test group" of whites and blacks alternately to the plant to inquire about job opportunities. While whites were encouraged to fill vacant positions, blacks were told that there were no openings.[64] The Los Angeles NAACP organized a Budweiser boycott in which they discouraged blacks from buying the beer and asked black-owned taverns and liquor store owners to stop selling it. As part of the "No Job, No Bud" campaign, teams of African American women visited local liquor stores to ensure that Budweiser signs were removed.[65] The West Coast regional branch of the NAACP threw its support behind the campaign, which spread to more than one hundred cities on the West Coast. In June of 1958, Anheuser-Busch finally agreed to seek job referrals from the Urban League, and the boycott was called off. Although African Americans still faced great difficulty securing housing in the surrounding community of Van Nuys, they were now at least part of the workforce.

In the years between World War II and the late 1950s, black protest in Los Angeles evolved from the sporadic movement of individuals to a series of confrontational protests led by the Communist Party to a sustained, communitywide civil rights movement spearheaded by the Los Angeles NAACP and drawing strength from the black church. It was in this later phase that African Americans scored the most decisive victories. The NAACP benefited as well, boosting its membership from a pitiful postwar low to a robust fifteen thousand by 1955. Through direct action protests and legal action, African Americans forced white Los Angeles to acknowledge their presence and recognize their demands.

Nevertheless, these increasingly effective campaigns against the legal scaffolding of segregation resolved only one set of concerns. Such campaigns did not address, nor could they have been expected to address, black isolation from municipal resources. African Americans in South Central could point, with great pride, to their successful battle to desegregate the fire department, but they still waited longer than white Angelenos for fire service in their neighborhoods. Blacks in Watts could now attend drive-in theaters, but the roads they drove on were dangerous and often lacked stop signs, traffic lights, or even basic street lighting. Black children gained increased access to public swimming pools, but they still ran the risk of drowning in the gaping potholes outside their homes. Without local black political power, the moral and legal victories of desegregation remained abstract.

The Postwar Battle for Black Political Representation

Between World War II and 1963, African Americans in Los Angeles moved from a position of almost complete political isolation to one of significant influence in both local and state politics. Historically ignored by both parties, many blacks in Los Angeles increasingly perceived their interests in frankly racial, rather than partisan, terms. Although generally inclined toward the Democratic Party since the Great Depression, African Americans did not give the party unconditional support. Rather, they demanded from candidates firm commitments to improve the quality of life of black citizens living in poor neighborhoods. As the black population of Los Angeles continued to expand rapidly in the 1950s, Democratic Party leaders quickly recognized the importance of making those commitments.

The determination and sheer size of Los Angeles's black population forced local and state political aspirants to talk publicly about race in ways that would have been unheard of even a decade earlier. Most important, many African Americans abandoned altogether the notion that white representatives could truly represent the interests of blacks. Thus, a new cadre of black political leaders and representatives emerged to articulate the demands of their long-underrepresented communities. As many contemporaries recognized, Southern California's new black leadership was both a product of and an inspiration for regional and national movements for African American civil rights.

Naturally, the African American search for political power started locally. But black influence in Los Angeles city government had always been minimal, and it remained so well after World War II. Efforts to change the situation were hampered by a unique feature of Los Angeles politics, the unusually large boundaries of city council districts. In striking contrast to cities such as New York and Chicago, both of which were divided by as many as fifty small ward boundaries, Los Angeles had only fifteen council districts. Before the war, the black population had been too small to significantly influence local politics. But as their numbers grew, African Americans were faced with another obstacle.

According to the city charter, the city council was required to reapportion council districts every four years based on the number of registered voters in geographic areas. Every reapportionment reduced the voting strength of black neighborhoods, provoking mounting criticism that the council intentionally gerrymandered districts to prevent the election of black representatives. Whether this was the council's intention is not clear, but that scarcely mattered, given the effects of redistricting. While Chicago and New York had produced black representatives in the 1920s and 1930s, and southern cities such as Richmond and Nashville elected black city council members during the 1940s,

Los Angeles remained stubbornly resistant to black representation until the 1960s.[66]

As the black population of Los Angeles grew, however, African Americans did benefit from another unique feature of local politics: district elections, which had become part of the city charter in 1925. District elections ensured that even if blacks failed to gain seats on the city council, district representatives would have to consider the concerns of their constituents. During the 1940s and early 1950s, a core group of nonblack Democrats in the Los Angeles city and county governments emerged as advocates of equal opportunity and improved conditions in minority neighborhoods. Young and ambitious, white council member Kenneth Hahn represented a portion of South Central on the city council from 1947 to 1952 and then moved on to the Los Angeles County Board of Supervisors, where he served until his death in 1997. A native of South Central, Hahn was one of the few white residents who never left his neighborhood. During his term on the city council, Hahn worked closely with *Sentinel* editor Leon Washington to identify specific problems faced by black residents of his district. As a supervisor, Hahn kept those issues in sight, consistently advocating rent control, urban renewal, publicly subsidized child care, and affirmative action hiring policies.[67] On the Board of Supervisors, Hahn found an ally in fellow supervisor John Anson Ford, a member of and staunch advocate for the Los Angeles County Commission on Human Relations. Although they met with bitter resistance, both Ford and Hahn pushed for the creation of fair employment practices committees at the city and county levels.

Also representing the interests of some black Angelenos was Mexican American World War II veteran, public health worker, and Community Service Organization organizer Edward Roybal. In 1949, Roybal ran for the Ninth district, which included parts of Boyle Heights, downtown, Chinatown and Little Tokyo, and Central Avenue. Although initially only 15 percent of his constituents were black, Roybal actively courted their votes. When African Americans asked Roybal why they should support him, he replied: "Our skin is also brown—our battle is the same. Our victory cannot but be a victory for you, too."[68] Roybal quickly received the endorsement of the *California Eagle* for his commitment to pass a municipal fair employment practices ordinance. He kept his promise to push for a municipal version of the wartime FEPC, called for the investigation of numerous incidents of alleged police brutality in the Mexican American and African American communities, and supported the NAACP's crusade to desegregate the fire department.[69] Roybal enjoyed increased popularity among black voters over his four terms, and, because of reapportionment, they came to represent just over half of his district.

Thus, from the Great Depression through the 1940s, the black strategy for gaining political power was to exercise influence within the Democratic Party through voting for, and lobbying, white—or, in the case of Roybal, Mexican American—representatives. With the important exception of state assembly member Augustus Hawkins, Los Angeles blacks had no other political representative in city, county, state, or federal government, a situation many came to view as simply intolerable. Appreciative of the efforts of Roybal, Hahn, Ford, and others, African Americans nonetheless felt that, without their own political representation, they would be doomed to second-class citizenship forever. Furthermore, Charlotta Bass's bold but unsuccessful 1945 campaign for the city council had whetted the appetite of the black community for greater local political participation.

Thus, in the early 1950s, a group of politically active African Americans met in what became known as the Democratic Minority Conference. The founding members of the organization included well-respected LAPD sergeant Thomas (Tom) Bradley; Vaino Spencer, one of Southwestern University's first black female graduates; attorney Leo Branton; and Gilbert Lindsay, a former janitor from Mississippi, who became Kenneth Hahn's deputy on the County Board of Supervisors. Members of the Democratic Minority Conference had grown weary of the Democratic Party's emphasis on "equal opportunity" and favored pushing instead for affirmative action. They called for communitywide support for black candidates, increased voter registration, and district reapportionment based on race. As one member stated:

We're beginning to feel that this attitude among white liberals is never going to get us anywhere and what we need is not opportunity but power. The only way we're going to get that is by drawing the district lines to give it to us. You're never going to have a Negro elected anywhere from a district that isn't all-Negro. We're just kidding ourselves if we think we can get it on any other basis.[70]

Members cultivated black political participation by canvassing neighborhoods and raising money through church bazaars, eventually building a membership of more than six hundred. They also worked in conjunction with the Committee for Representative Government, led by Leon Washington, which sought two congressional seats and four state assembly seats for black Los Angeles.[71]

Despite the new assertiveness with which African Americans approached local politics, they were still dogged by reapportionment. Most frustrating was the redistricting of the Seventh council district in 1957. The district, which included West Adams, part of South Central, and a sizable black population, nearly elected black council members in two city council elections. But when the council conducted its quadrennial reapportionment late in 1956, they decided to move the district to the rapidly expanding San Fernando Valley and redistribute the residents of the original district among three other districts.[72] This effectively prevented any black near-majorities in any city council districts, a major blow to members of the Democratic Minority Conference.

Politically active black citizens pushed forward with the help of the NAACP, which undertook expanded voter registration drives in Los Angeles after 1957. In 1959, five African American candidates from three districts ran in the city council election, although none won. In 1960, the city council approved a reapportionment that again split the black vote. Thus, as late as 1960, the editors of the *California Eagle* were not far off when they railed: "We're second class citizens in Los Angeles as far as representation in city government goes."[73]

But the 1961 mayoral election, which put Samuel Yorty in office, gave blacks new confidence that their votes mattered. Norris Poulson, a moderate Republican, had enjoyed steady support from African Americans during his two terms as mayor, largely because of his role in desegregating the fire department. In his bid for reelection in 1957, Poulson won more than 80 percent of the city's black vote.[74] But his failure to rein in the police department frustrated blacks, a fact that Poulson's opponent in the 1961 election happily exploited. Yorty promised that, if elected, he would "school" Police Chief Parker. Blacks broke with their traditional support of Poulson—and indeed with much of the Democratic Party, who considered the mercurial Yorty a pariah—and supported Yorty. Although the black press overstated the importance of the black vote in Yorty's election, African American support was indeed crucial.[75] This result engendered profound confidence among black voters, which in turn led to much wider voter registration and participation.

African Americans also benefited from the emerging liberal coalition in California state politics during the late 1950s and early 1960s. Changes in cross-filing rules, the rise of the California Democratic Council, and the election of liberal Democrat Edmund "Pat" Brown as governor in 1958 invigorated efforts to expand black representation.[76] With the state legislature now dominated by Democrats, the Republican reapportionment of 1951 was undone. An additional assembly seat was created for Los Angeles blacks, who quickly took advantage of this new development by electing African American Reverend F. Douglas Ferrell, a Republican, and West Indian Mervyn Dymally, a Democrat, in 1962.

Dymally's meteoric rise captured the enthusiasm and support of a great many African Americans. Having emigrated from Trinidad to Chicago in 1946 and then to Los Angeles in 1949, Dymally attended L.A. State College (now California State University, Los Angeles), graduated with a degree in education, and began teaching special education students and working at an electronics plant. Involved with the oil workers union in Trinidad and the teachers union and the United Auto Workers in Los Angeles, Dymally had a proven knack for political leadership. After joining the all-white Young Democrats in the mid-1950s, Dymally grew frustrated that there were simply "no young blacks in the Democratic Party." He was optimistic that he could "change the nature of discrimination through legislation."[77]

Through his association with the Democratic Minority Conference, Dymally made the acquaintance of Augustus Hawkins, who in turn urged Pat Brown to jumpstart Dymally's political career by appointing him to the State Disaster Office in Sacramento. Meanwhile, among blacks in Los Angeles, Dymally's outspoken critique of the Los Angeles Board of Education's segregated school districts earned him the reputation of being passionate and dedicated. This reputation was so strong that it propelled him into an assembly seat in 1962, even though he ran against Augustus Hawkins's brother, who many believed would easily win on his family name.[78]

Black political participation in Los Angeles was also invigorated by the determination and courage of the southern civil rights movement. For example, Dymally remembered that it was the Greensboro sit-ins of 1960 that inspired his political career, even though he was halfway across the county. Driving home on the Pasadena freeway after attending a Young Democrats meeting in 1960, Dymally heard about the sit-ins on the radio in his Plymouth: "I'm driving on the freeway . . . and I heard this news about the students sitting in in Greensboro, North Carolina. And I said to myself, 'What am I doing in Pasadena with all these white folks when there is a whole revolution taking place in the South? What can I do?'"[79] The Western Christian Leadership Conference, the western wing of Dr. Martin Luther King's Southern Christian Leadership Conference, counted on similar reactions from black Angelenos when it sponsored a Freedom Rally in Los Angeles to raise money for the southern Freedom Rides. Although organizers expected a crowd of twelve thousand to turn out at the Los Angeles Sports Arena to hear King speak, more than twenty-eight thousand attended. It was, as the Los Angeles Police Department put it, "the largest assembly of Negroes in Los Angeles within memory." [80]

Growing in numbers and strength, blacks in Los Angeles finally scored political victories in the city council elections of 1963, which changed the face of local politics in Los Angeles. Shortly before the elections, the council representative for the Ninth district vacated his post, leaving it open for an interim appointment by the council. The council selected Gilbert Lindsay, making him the city's first black officeholder. The popular police officer-turned-lawyer Tom Bradley won in the Tenth district, and newcomer Billy Mills won in the Eighth. Remarkably, three of the fifteen council districts now had African American representatives. No less impressive, the once staunchly white city of Compton elected its first black city council member, an automobile sales manager named Douglas Dollarhide, in the same year. [81]

Expanded political representation brought substantive gains for blacks. At the state level, the tireless lobbying of Augustus Hawkins and Byron Rumford, a black assembly representative from Berkeley, and the support of Governor Pat Brown produced a state Fair Employment Practice Commission in 1958. The state FEPC, which handled approximately seven hundred cases of discrimination annually, was a major triumph for African Americans in California and Los Angeles. [82] In 1946, California voters had overwhelmingly rejected Proposition 11, an early measure that would have created a state FEPC; and in 1947, the Los Angeles City Council had soundly defeated an ordinance creating a municipal FEPC like those already in place in San Francisco and Bakersfield. With Governor Brown's support, Hawkins and Rumford also pushed through the famous and highly controversial Rumford Fair Housing Act in 1963, prohibiting racial discrimination by real estate brokers.

After Hawkins went to Congress to pursue education, labor, and employment reforms for his Southern California district, Dymally and Ferrell perpetuated Hawkins's liberal legacy in the state legislature. Dymally introduced the popular Child Care Center Construction Bill, headed the Education and Social Welfare Committee, and ushered through the "Horizon Bill," which provided state resources for technical education in poor areas. [83] Dymally and Ferrell also introduced legislation, the first of its kind in the nation, requiring that African American history be taught as part of the history curriculum in California's public schools.

At the local level, which was perhaps most important for average African Americans, Los Angeles's new black council members pushed for important neighborhood improvements. Mills almost single-handedly improved neighborhood safety in his district, installing street lamps on residential streets and in alleyways. Generally, Lindsay, Bradley, and Mills substantially improved basic city services in their districts, demanding equal access to municipal resources traditionally denied to poorer neighborhoods. Finally, the three black council members forced the city council to acknowledge and discuss the growing civil rights movement and the status of black people in America. For example, Bradley introduced a passing motion of support for the fifty-seven Los Angeles students who went to Mississippi for the Freedom Summer of 1964. Although purely symbolic, motions such as these likely pushed Los Angeles's civic leaders into greater awareness of racial disparities in their own city.[84]

In many respects, African American gains in local and state politics were much more meaningful than those brought about by more famous federal landmarks of the civil rights movement. With no de jure segregation and few racial demagogues, Los Angeles erected fewer easy targets for the federal government's civil rights mandates. For example, Eisenhower's Civil Rights Act of 1957, banning racial discrimination at the polls, did little for blacks in Los Angeles, where the vote had never been denied. But few events demonstrated more the vast disparity between federal race policy and meaningful racial change than the battle to integrate Los Angeles's sharply segregated public school system. Although many contemporaries saw the Supreme Court's 1954 *Brown v. Board of Education* decision as at least a partial cure to America's race problem, Los Angeles proved profoundly resistant to this new medicine. In fact, while many southern schools were becoming less segregated, Los Angeles's were only becoming more so.

Bringing *Brown* to Southern California: The Battle for School Desegregation

The historic 1954 Supreme Court decision in *Brown v. Board of Education* permanently and abruptly transformed southern race relations. In virtually all of the South, and much of the Midwest, advocates of legalized racial segregation now found themselves on the defensive. In fact, as some scholars have`argued, white backlash, rather than black gains, may have been the most important transformation engendered by the *Brown* decision.[85] Certainly the crisis in Little Rock, where Arkansas governor Orval Faubus ordered the National Guard to defy the federal government by blocking the integration of Central High School in 1957, exemplified this trend.

But for black students in segregated communities, the effects of the decision were more personal: they could no longer be denied an equal education. Moreover, the Supreme Court of the United States had legitimized African Americans' long quest for equality. Accordingly, African Americans in Los Angeles celebrated the *Brown* decision as a moral and symbolic victory. But in Los Angeles and other western cities, where school segregation was the product of racial geography, willful neglect, and racial gerrymandering, the substantive impact of *Brown* was insignificant. *Brown*'s failure in Los Angeles ensured that the racial desegregation of schools would be the top priority of the emerging civil rights movement.

The official policy of the Los Angeles Board of Education had been one of color-blindness, a fact that the board frequently cited in its own defense when the push for desegregation emerged in the 1950s. But what the board's official policy failed to do was easily accomplished by other means. As scholars and ACLU activists John and LaRee Caughey wrote, "Los Angeles' segregated schooling, far from being temporary, has become an ingrained, continuing element long since locked into the operational procedure of the school district."[86]

Foremost among such procedures was the highly conspicuous racial gerrymandering of the school district. Although the board usually assigned students to schools based on residential proximity, it waived these rules in racially mixed areas, allowing white students to attend white schools even when they lived farther away. This policy, combined with the sharply segregated racial geography of the city, created racial segregation as complete as any in the pre-*Brown* South. In fact, a survey of integration in public schools across the country clearly demonstrated that Los Angeles schools in particular, and California schools in general, were more segregated those in Louisiana, Alabama, North Carolina, Virginia, and South Carolina.[87] Any casual passerby in Los Angeles could easily determine which schools were white and which schools were predominantly black or predominantly Mexican.

Yet, when the Los Angeles NAACP began probing the Los Angeles Board of Education in 1953, it met with strident denials of segregation. The burden of proof, the board argued, fell on the NAACP. But because the board collected no regular data on the racial distribution of schools, the NAACP was faced with the time-consuming task of proving the obvious fact of segregation. Fortunately for civil rights advocates, the Pasadena school district, whose policies otherwise mirrored those of the Los Angeles Board of Education, had begun collecting racial data on its students in 1946.[88] A suburb of Los Angeles with substantial but highly segregated black and Mexican communities, Pasadena quickly became the hub of Southern California's desegregation movement.

Pasadena's predominantly minority Garfield, Cleveland, and Lincoln elementary schools had grown more segregated over time; by 1957, Cleveland's black students represented 82 percent of the student body.[89] As in Los Angeles, the Pasadena Board of Education argued that those disparities were the result of residential patterns and not the product of any affirmative board decisions. In reality, white students were given transfers easily, while black requests for transfers, in the words of the president of the board, "would probably be refused."[90]

The Pasadena board threw down the gauntlet in 1953 when it adopted a measure to spend fifteen thousand dollars building additional classrooms in the all-white Arroyo Seco School, while Garfield, the nearby minority school, had vacant classrooms.[91] The Pasadena NAACP filed a suit to restrain the Pasadena School Board from developing the new classrooms and to force the board to modify its system of discriminatory transfers. But before the case was resolved, the U.S. Supreme Court handed down the *Brown* decision. After consulting with the Los Angeles County counsel, the Pasadena Board of Education recognized that it would have a difficult time defending its inherently discriminatory practices in court. Thus, in June 1954, the board agreed to change those policies most conducive to racial segregation. It agreed to deny all requests for transfer except in the case of a proven physical hardship and canceled plans to construct new classrooms at Arroyo Seco until enrollment at Garfield reached capacity.[92]

But the Pasadena board delayed action until the NAACP, with little recourse, filed a suit with the California Supreme Court. In its 1963 decision, *Jackson v. Pasadena City School District*, the California Supreme Court ruled that school boards had an obligation to take affirmative steps to eradicate racial segregation, regardless of its causes.[93] Hailed in Southern California as a civil rights victory, the *Jackson* decision nonetheless failed to specify a deadline for racial desegregation or suggest strategies through which it might be achieved.

The Los Angeles Board of Education virtually ignored both the

FIGURE 9. African American students attempt to transfer to an all-white
Huntington Park school, out of their home district, in September 1962, in an
effort to put pressure on the Los Angeles Board of Education to integrate.
Courtesy of the Los Angeles Public Library.

Brown and *Jackson* decisions. In 1961, the Southern California ACLU,
under the leadership of Eason Monroe, began pressuring the board to
admit that district schools were racially segregated and to implement
some schedule for reform. After delaying for almost a year, the board established an Ad Hoc Committee on Equal Educational Opportunities
in June 1962, charged with investigating the problem and making recommendations to the board. But African Americans wasted no time
waiting for the committee's findings. When school opened again in
September 1962, black parents tested the board's claims by sending their
children to enroll in white schools. Organized by the NAACP, a group
of black and Japanese parents living near Baldwin Hills sent their children to enroll in the all-white Baldwin Hills Elementary School. When
they were refused, the NAACP began picketing the school. Several days
later, a group of black students tried to enroll at Huntington Park High
School and were also rebuffed (see figure 9). Within a week, fifty black

transfer students were accepted to the Baldwin Hills Elementary School, and the NAACP called off the picketing.[94]

While black parents pursued direct action protests at the schools, the NAACP and the ACLU continued to reason with the board, pointing to the most egregious examples of racially segregated schools in the southeastern portion of the school district, Jordan High School and South Gate High School. Though multiracial through the 1930s, Jordan had become increasingly black through the 1940s; by the 1950s, its student body was approximately 98 percent African American. As the school became more racially isolated, it was far less appealing to experienced teachers, and its academic standards declined precipitously. Dropout rates at the school reached an alarming 25 percent by the late 1950s. Meanwhile, South Gate High School, a strong high school located in the city of South Gate but part of the Los Angeles Unified School District, had only five black students out of a student population of eighteen hundred.[95] Less than two miles apart, these schools represented the worst effects of racial segregation.

Most galling to integrationists, many South Gate students lived closer to Jordan, and vice versa. The NAACP and the ACLU urged the board to rezone the southeastern portion, using commuting distance as the sole criterion for enrollment. This would have required black enrollment in South Gate and white enrollment in Jordan. When residents of the white working-class suburb of South Gate heard about the plan to rezone the district, they organized a highly effective campaign of resistance, circulating petitions throughout their area opposing boundary changes. South Gate residents threatened not only to refuse to send their children to Jordan High School but also to break away from the school district. Their grassroots campaign had the imprimatur of the South Gate City Council, which unanimously opposed any rezoning of the district.[96] After the reaction of the South Gate residents, the Los Angeles Board of Education quickly dropped the short-lived plan to rezone the southeastern portion of the school district.

Continuously frustrated by the board's intransigence and inspired by the southern civil rights movement, African Americans in Los Angeles struck an increasingly militant stance in 1963. As he had two years earlier, Martin Luther King Jr. again visited Los Angeles, this time drawing a crowd of more than thirty-five thousand at Wrigley Field Baseball Stadium on Forty-Second Place and Avalon in May of 1963.[97] And, as he had two years before, King inspired blacks to fight for freedom "whether you're in Birmingham or Los Angeles."

Particularly inspired was Marnesba Tackett, a recent African American migrant to Los Angeles and a veteran of civil rights struggles. Raised in Kansas City, Tackett became an active member of both the NAACP and the YWCA and participated in sit-ins and protests in the 1930s and 1940s. Migrating with her husband to Los Angeles in 1952, Tackett picked up where she left off, remembering that "one of the first things that I did after getting a job was look up the NAACP office."[98] Appalled by the segregation and overcrowding in Los Angeles schools, Tackett quickly ran for and was selected chair of the NAACP's education committee. Forming the Committee to Better Schools, she soon joined the ACLU in its protest of the board's intransigence. Already determined to improve Los Angeles schools, Tackett was further inspired when she asked King what blacks in Los Angeles could do for blacks in Birmingham. He answered, as Tackett recalled, "The most important thing that you can do is set Los Angeles free."[99]

Shortly after King's visit, NAACP president Christopher Taylor invited members of the NAACP, the ACLU, CORE, labor unions, and black leaders Tom Bradley, Douglas Dollarhide, F. Douglas Ferrell, Loren Miller, and Gilbert Lindsay to organize under the banner of the United Civil Rights Committee. While the organization would tackle discrimination in all areas of black life, it focused most of its energy on desegregating schools. Tackett was unanimously selected to head the education committee. Under her guidance, the UCRC briefly became the most vocal and assertive organization for black equality in the history of Los Angeles.

The most dramatic display of UCRC's public profile was the Freedom March of 1963, organized by Taylor and Tackett. In May 1963, NAACP spokesperson, pastor of the People's Independent Church, and former NAACP president Reverend Maurice Dawkins publicly announced UCRC's intention to march. The front page of the *Los Angeles Times* carried the story under the headline, "L.A. Declared Target for Total Integration." "We are not just asking for a small specific adjustment," Dawkins told the *Times*, "but a total community integration."[100] The UCRC boldly told Angelenos: "It is necessary for us to show Los Angeles and the world, in the spirit of non-violence, we mean what we say."[101]

The planned protest upset many black and white allies of the civil rights movement, most notably Kenneth Hahn, who felt that the march would only alienate potential white support for civil rights. Tackett remembered Hahn arguing that "we don't have to have Birmingham-type

FIGURE 10. The United Civil Rights Committee organized more than a thousand citizens in June 1963 to protest the Los Angeles Board of Education's refusal to take affirmative steps to end school segregation. Protesters marched from the First African Episcopal Church to the Board of Education offices. Courtesy of the Los Angeles Public Library.

demonstrations here."[102] Frank Chuman of the County Commission on Human Relations believed that the plan to march "manifests an impatience by these leaders that borders on emotion and ill-considered judgment."[103] Even some African Americans contacted UCRC to urge the group to call off the march, but Christopher Taylor boldly responded, "The Uncle Toms are no longer in the saddle."[104] For Taylor, Tackett, and well over one thousand others, immediate and direct protest was the only way to confront the board's obduracy.

Thus, on Monday, 24 June 1963, the UCRC led the largest march for black civil rights in the history of Los Angeles (see figure 10). Marching from the First African Episcopal Church, through the heart of the downtown business district, and finally to the Los Angeles Board of Education, marchers observed all traffic rules and fulfilled their commitment to nonviolence. This was the first in a series of marches that continued through the summer. In August, UCRC marchers encountered

FIGURE 11. Anti-integrationists calling themselves the Committee Against Integration and Intermarriage meet United Civil Rights Committee marchers at the Board of Education in August 1963. Courtesy of the Los Angeles Public Library.

a well-organized counter-protest by a group of white citizens identifying themselves as the Committee Against Integration and Intermarriage (see figure 11). Other scattered white protesters carried signs reading "White Rights," but no violence erupted.

Meanwhile, the western regional office of CORE, established in 1962, had initiated a series of its own campaigns in the city. Staffed largely by white college students and, in Los Angeles, activists from Hollywood, CORE launched a series of aggressive strikes at racial discrimination in the white working-class industrial suburb of Torrance in the summer of 1962. Like South Gate and dozens of other white Los Angeles suburbs, Torrance had long barred blacks from residence.

FIGURE 12. The Congress of Racial Equality protests the segregated Don
Wilson Housing Tracts in Torrance in 1963. Courtesy of the Los Angeles
Public Library.

Starting in 1962 and gathering steam in the volatile summer of 1963,
CORE picketed tract housing developer Don Wilson, whose South-
wood Riviera Royale tract in Torrance and another tract in Compton
brazenly discriminated against potential black homeowners (see figure 12). As the threat to desegregate Jordan High had done in South
Gate, the CORE protests punctured Torrance's longstanding insulation
from Southern California's race problem. Also, as in the case of South
Gate, white Torrance residents quickly mobilized to protect their perceived interests. CORE protesters were often met by racist white protesters, including the American Nazi Party and the Committee Against
Intermarriage and Integration.[105] More typical were the three hundred
Torrance residents who crowded into a Torrance City Council meeting
in June 1963, demanding that the council close all roads leading into the
city on weekends to prevent people who "have no business being there"
from entering.[106]

    CORE dramatically entered the school desegregation cause by stag-
ing a hunger strike at the Los Angeles Board of Education. But this

dedicated action, and the countless other protests organized by CORE, the UCRC, and the NAACP, produced little change. In August of 1963, the ACLU filed a class action lawsuit against the Los Angeles Unified School District with the California Supreme Court, beginning more than two decades of litigation to desegregate Los Angeles schools. After a brief flurry of interest, the case lay essentially dormant until the ACLU devised a new legal strategy and reintroduced an expanded suit, *Crawford v. Board of Education of the City of Los Angeles,* in 1968. Although Judge Alfred Gitelson ruled favorably, calling for an end to de facto segregation, the ensuing debacle over busing left the mechanics of desegregation unresolved. If the defining characteristic of America's race problem was the racial segregation of schools, then Los Angeles represented America's race problem at its worst. This fact undoubtedly seared the consciousness of the thousands of African Americans who continued to come to Los Angeles, hoping to escape southern racism.

Assessing Los Angeles's Civil Rights Movement

In the twenty years following World War II, African Americans in Los Angeles County fought in new ways and on new fronts to achieve total social, political, and economic equality with whites. And by almost any standard, they made critically important gains. The NAACP, with the support of the mayor, desegregated the Los Angeles Fire Department. Through consumer boycotts and picketing, African Americans forced countless banks, stores, and even some larger industrial firms such as the Budweiser brewery, to hire them. In local and state politics, blacks moved from a position of complete isolation to one of significant influence. At the state level, growing black influence culminated in the state Fair Employment Practice Commission (1958) and the Rumford Fair Housing Act (1963). Locally, black representation resulted in significant improvements in the infrastructure of black neighborhoods.

But many critical demands of the civil rights movement had not been met. Although police brutality had declined somewhat since the 1940s, it continued to run rampant, generating tremendous anger in the black community. And as blacks in Los Angeles watched television news coverage of the desegregation of public schools in the South, their own children were less and less likely to attend integrated schools.

More broadly, postwar African American freedom struggles in Los Angeles engendered a new public consciousness of race. UCRC marches, CORE sit-ins, and black representatives in local politics brought race in general, and African Americans in particular, to the forefront of public life in Los Angeles. Some whites, notably young CORE volunteers, had responded to this new consciousness by embracing the struggle for civil rights themselves. Never before had black equality had so many supporters in Los Angeles.

But the new public consciousness of race also, and perhaps more often, had the opposite effect: it ignited bitter hostility and resistance from a great many whites. Now forced to affirmatively defend practices of segregation, many whites organized with equal passion to retain racial separation. As homeowners, whites began to organize to keep blacks out of Torrance. As parents, South Gate's white residents organized to prevent school desegregation. And as voters, whites demonstrated their utter refusal to integrate neighborhoods. In 1964, 65 percent of state voters and 70 percent of Los Angeles County voters supported Proposition 14, a proposed amendment to the California Constitution undermining the Rumford Fair Housing Act of 1963.[107] Although declared unconstitutional by the California Supreme Court in 1966 and the U.S. Supreme Court in 1967, Proposition 14 clearly demonstrated the deepening hostility among white voters to racial integration in housing. In 1964, many African Americans wondered, and many whites feared, what it would take to truly desegregate California.

CHAPTER 6

Black Community Transformation in the 1960s and 1970s

Contextualizing the Watts Riot

For both black and white Los Angeles, few moments were more terrifying or more memorable than the six consecutive days in August 1965 when African Americans—mostly young men—rampaged through the streets of Watts and South Central, looting and burning retail stores, beating passing motorists, and attacking the firefighters and police officers who had been sent to quell the disturbance (see figure 13). The grim results—thirty-four deaths (twenty-eight of those who died were black), more than one thousand injuries, four thousand arrests, and $40 million in property damage—sent chills down the spines of whites and blacks across the country.

Having weathered racial disturbances in New York City, Rochester, Jersey City, Paterson and Elizabeth in New Jersey, and Philadelphia in 1964, Americans had become familiar with racial violence in cities. But the Watts riot shocked blacks and whites alike not only because it was the most destructive racial explosion since the Detroit riots of 1943 but also because it took place in Los Angeles, still perceived by many as a relatively favorable city for blacks. As Mayor Sam Yorty had only recently told the U.S. Civil Rights Commission: "I think we have the best race relations in our city of any large city in the United States."[1] Perhaps the most enduring and important legacy of the Watts riot was that it violently and permanently obliterated that popular myth, almost one hundred years in the making.

The Watts riot of 1965 had many immediate and important effects on

FIGURE 13. Firefighters attempt to put out a fire at a small shopping complex in Watts while police stand guard during the 1965 riot. Courtesy of the Los Angeles Public Library.

black Los Angeles. It encouraged many of South Central's remaining white residents to abandon their efforts at "neighborhood preservation" and simply move out. It was also transformative for the rising group of well-employed black families who sought to flee the rising crime and poverty, and the declining schools, of South Central. In contrast, for young black participants, the very destructiveness of the riot proved to be an affirmation of their growing numerical strength and their power to shape the racial psychology of white Los Angeles by making people afraid. Perhaps most tangibly, the Watts riot brought belated attention and much-needed resources from city, state, and federal governments. The riot did what more than a year of political wrangling had failed to do: it finally brought the War on Poverty to Los Angeles. And, in the broadest sense, the Watts riot forced white Los Angeles to publicly face the long history of racial inequality in the city.

Although these were all important developments, the Watts riot was not the only, or even the most important, event in black Los Angeles during those years. It was one of the ironic legacies of the riot, in fact, that the enormity of the event obscured, to contemporary observers and subsequent scholars alike, the many more profound and enduring political and economic transformations reshaping black Los Angeles in the 1960s.

First, and most obvious to the Great Migration generation, was the increased ideological fragmentation of the black community. Specifically, the children of this generation questioned the political strategies and goals of their parents. Impatient with peaceful protest and increasingly skeptical about the possibility—and even the desirability—of racial integration, these young African Americans struck out on a new course, one often frowned on by their elders. Second, while the events in Watts brought much-needed resources to black Los Angeles, they also fueled the existing groundswell of white social and economic conservatism. Beginning in the late 1950s, soaring property taxes in Los Angeles County, coupled with the perceived excesses of the War on Poverty during the 1960s, fueled widespread support for tax cuts. This growing fiscal conservatism, combined with white voters' virulent opposition to busing, would have significant effects on black Los Angeles. Finally—and of much greater long-term importance than the Watts riot, black ideological fragmentation, or white backlash— were the widening economic disparities among African Americans themselves, produced by regional, national, and global economic restructuring.

Most catastrophic was the sharp decline in blue-collar manufacturing jobs, the jobs that had been the foundation of black prosperity in the postwar years. Beginning slowly in the 1960s, many of South Central's manufacturing firms had begun relocating to outlying suburban areas; by the end of the 1970s, many would disappear altogether in the face of international economic competition. While blue-collar black workers were devastated by this transformation, another group of black workers—better educated and disproportionately female—found exciting new opportunities in Los Angeles's expanding white-collar workforce. For them, the most important development of the 1960s was not the Watts riot but the new opportunities to escape the deepening poverty and despair of South Central.

Although few at the time could have predicted the long-term effects of these developments, in retrospect, they would deeply affect black Los Angeles long after the fires of the Watts riot had been extinguished.

The Children of the Great Migration
Generation and the Watts Riot

By the early 1960s, many African Americans in Los Angeles, particularly those of the Great Migration generation, could look with pride at the strides they had made toward racial equality in their lifetimes. In the twenty years following World War II, blacks in Los Angeles moved from a position of restricted marginality to one of tempered inclusion in many aspects of urban life. Despite the bitter persistence of segregation in Los Angeles, by 1960 blacks performed a wide range of jobs, lived in a variety of neighborhoods, participated in electoral politics, and inhabited public space to a degree virtually unimaginable before the war. From the perspective of migrants who had moved from areas where opportunities were far more circumscribed than they had ever been in Los Angeles, these gains were even more impressive. How then, so many wondered, could African Americans in Los Angeles riot?

Asking the same question, the McCone Commission—the body assigned by Governor Edmund G. "Pat" Brown to determine the cause of the Watts riot—was particularly bemused, noting that "[a] Negro in Los Angeles has long been able to sit where he wants in a bus or a movie house, to shop where he wishes, to vote, and to use public facilities without discrimination. The opportunity to succeed is probably unequaled in any other major American city."[2] During the McCone Commission proceedings, the ubiquitous and insightful Loren Miller offered a simple answer to the question: "I think that when the Los Angeles Negro compares his living and decides his way of life . . . is unfortunate, he compares it with Los Angeles, not with Harlem, not with Philadelphia, not with Kansas City."[3]

This was true for many black Angelenos, even migrants, but it was particularly true for the children of the Great Migration, who had been born or raised in Los Angeles. They compared their opportunities not to what blacks in other cities had, nor to the opportunities their parents had, but rather to the opportunities enjoyed by their white peers in Los Angeles. This increasingly prevalent perception engendered new challenges to the methods, and sometimes even the goals, of the civil rights movement of the 1940s and 1950s.

Young African Americans, like their parents, were frustrated with segregation in any aspect of daily life. But few issues aroused more anger among the young people of black Los Angeles than harassment by the police. Beginning in the early 1960s, African American youths increasingly confronted real and perceived police harassment not with protests or sit-ins but with physical resistance and reprisal. White officers soon found that routine harassment and even justified arrests could incite black outrage.

For example, in 1961, a Memorial Day picnic in Griffith Park erupted into a small race riot. When a seventeen-year-old African American boy was arrested for riding a merry-go-round without a ticket, more than two hundred young black men attending the picnic confronted police. When the police refused to release the boy, the crowd grew agitated, and seventy-five police officers were called in. A melee followed, in which blacks attacked the police with rocks, baseball bats, and bottles, sending five officers to the hospital.[4] In another incident several months later, when LAPD officers attempted to handcuff two young black men suspected of a theft in Venice, a black bystander shouted, "Dirty cops!" which incited a growing crowd of African American spectators. After forty-five additional police officers arrived, an hour-long riot ensued, in which three officers were injured and several police car windshields were smashed by flying rocks. The five African Americans charged with starting the riot were all between eighteen and twenty-two years old, and one was the son of a prominent and well-respected Venice pastor.[5]

This new aggressiveness also found expression in more organized forms, most notably the Nation of Islam. Although always a fringe group within black America, the Nation of Islam did appeal to a small but loyal group of young African Americans in Los Angeles after it opened Mosque No. 27 in 1957.[6] The Nation of Islam did not officially endorse violence, but its members were frequently involved in violent encounters. For example, when private security guards at a Safeway store on Western Boulevard tried to prevent black Muslims from selling their national newspaper, *Muhammad Speaks,* in front of the store, six Muslims (five of them under the age of twenty-five) attacked the guards, stomping and beating them. When the arrested youths were questioned, one simply said that he was tired of being "pushed around."[7]

But these sporadic incidents of violence by Muslims paled in comparison to the campaign of repression waged against the Nation of Islam by the LAPD. In addition to a sustained campaign of LAPD surveillance focusing on the activities of Muslims, law enforcement agencies throughout Southern California were put on high alert. For example, the training manual for the San Diego Police Department contained the following description:

The nucleus of the Nation of Islam is comprised of 20 to 30 year old men called, "the Fruit of Islam." These men are selected for their physical prowess and are adept for their aggressive tactics and judo. They are psychotic in their dedication and hatred of Caucasians and are comparable to the Mau Mau or Kamikaze in their dedication and fanaticism. It has been reported that many temples have gun clubs in which this militant group is trained in weapons.[8]

The logic of this paranoia was tragically borne out in April 1962, when LAPD officers fired on unarmed black Muslims during a scuffle outside Mosque No. 27. The attack, which left one Muslim dead, another paralyzed, and five others wounded, also hardened the resolve of some black youths to exact revenge on the police and whites in general. As one member of the mosque remembered, after the shooting, "we were ready to kill. . . . many brothers had guns in their pockets, others were sharpening knives."[9] Some members of the mosque were so outraged that they formed a group called the "band of angels," which cruised downtown's skid row beating up and occasionally killing drunken and homeless whites.[10]

Thus, to anyone paying attention, the Watts riot of 1965 should not have been a surprise. It started, just as the "mini-riots" in Griffith Park and Venice had, with an encounter between a law enforcement officer and a young black man. Twenty-one-year-old Marquette Frye, who had migrated to Los Angeles with his mother in 1957, was an unemployed Fremont High School dropout with a juvenile record—the epitome, in many respects, of the failed promise of Los Angeles and certainly of its public education system. On a hot summer night in August 1965, Frye was pulled over by the California Highway Patrol on suspicion of drunk driving outside his mother's home. Frye's mother immediately came outside to berate him for his behavior. As she became agitated, a crowd gathered, and the CHP officer called for backup. When CHP and LAPD officers arrived, Frye physically resisted arrest, prompting the arresting officer to draw his weapon. Frye's mother jumped on the back of the arresting officer, and a melee erupted. Although officers managed to get the Fryes into squad cars, the growing crowd seethed at the rumor that the officers had assaulted Frye's mother. The crowd surged toward the fleeing patrol cars, and by the next morning a vast, violent, and uncontrollable riot was in full swing. For six terrifying days, black rioters and white police officers and National Guard troops battled in an area that ranged over forty-six square miles. Arsonists destroyed 261 buildings, mostly stores.[11]

During and after the riot, African American community leaders and average black citizens reiterated the message that most blacks did not condone or support the rioting, a claim substantiated by later estimates that about ten thousand blacks (less than 2 percent of Southern California's black population) participated.[12] Although the actual number of participants was relatively small, the ideological implications of their participation were great. Sparked and sustained by black anger at white America, the Watts riot also reflected the deepening political divide between the Great Migration generation and their children. Though casual observers assumed that the young rioters were recent arrivals from the South, the greatest numbers either had been born in Los Angeles or had moved to the city with their parents before 1960.[13] Those rioting were not disappointed newcomers but rather young black men who had grown up disappointed, not only with the persistence of discrimination but also with their black leaders.

Few moments better epitomized the growing chasm between black leadership and youth than Mervyn Dymally's interaction with a group of young rioters. Dymally, a state assembly representative and always a crusader for black rights in Los Angeles, immediately went to the epicenter of the riot to encourage young participants to leave the area. When he tried to dissuade the group from throwing rocks at passing police cars, one young man challenged him: "Who you with?" Dymally earnestly replied, "I'm with you, man." The incredulous young rioter turned to Dymally, extended a hand holding a large stone, and replied: "Then here's a rock, baby. Throw it." When Dymally refused, the rioter responded: "Hell! You're with the Man."[14]

If the Watts riot laid bare the obvious generational disputes in the politics of black Los Angeles, it also further revealed real economic class differences in the black community. As chapter 3 described, expanding opportunities in blue-collar and white-collar occupations on the one hand and rising unemployment and underemployment on the other had caused growing disparities in the economic life of African Americans. Expanding residential opportunities, described in chapter 4, allowed those black workers who benefited from job expansion to slowly move away from South Central to the fringes of the area, in Compton, Leimert Park/Crenshaw, and West Adams. The implications of those growing disparities were apparent during the Watts riot. For example, when rioters in Watts and Willowbrook moved toward Compton, they were met with fierce resistance from both white and black homeowners. Leroy Conley, a black man who headed the Business Men's Association in Compton, organized a group of black and white Compton residents armed with shotguns. "We were all working together," Conley recalled. "There wasn't any black or white."[15]

But class disparity among African Americans was not simply a relic from the 1950s. Rather, it deepened through the 1960s and well beyond. Moreover, it was only one symptom of a much larger and more complex set of developments affecting Southern California. The mid-1960s marked the beginning of the end of one phase of economic growth in the region and the simultaneous emergence of another. After two decades of rapid growth, the postwar industrial manufacturing boom had begun to slow in Los Angeles County. Many large factories employing numerous unionized, skilled, and semiskilled workers either closed in the face of increasing global competition or relocated to surrounding Orange, San Bernardino, and Riverside Counties in order to expand their operations and lower their tax burdens. Like their counterparts in Detroit and the Northeast, where deindustrialization had begun in the 1950s, blacks in Los Angeles were devastated by these developments.[16]

In Southern California, however, the challenges of the post-boom years were even more complex than in the northeastern "rust belt." Rather than simply undergoing a process of deindustrialization, the Southern California economy experienced what has been appropriately described as a process of "selective deindustrialization" and "selective reindustrialization," creating sustained overall job growth.[17] Thus, as some job opportunities disappeared, many more new ones emerged. But, because of persistent discrimination in more distant suburban housing markets, the continuing inadequacy of training and education for many blacks in South Central, poor private and public transportation, and rising competition from newer immigrant groups, African Americans made far less headway in this new phase of the economy than they had in the immediate postwar years. Unfortunately, however, the new and emerging sources of racial inequality remained largely invisible to liberals in the 1960s and 1970s, most of whom were, somewhat myopically, still seeking to eliminate the relics of past racial inequality.

The War on Poverty, Civil Rights, and Los Angeles's Fading Blue Collar

African Americans in Los Angeles and across the country were cautiously optimistic about the August 1964 passage of the Economic Opportunity Act, the centerpiece of President Lyndon Johnson's War on Poverty. "The passage of the 'war on poverty' bill is a long step forward in sociological progress," the *Los Angeles Sentinel* opined, "but we must make sure that some of its benefits come to communities like ours where its objectives are vitally needed."[18]

Yet even this cautious optimism quickly turned to bitter cynicism when the projected $20 million in anti-poverty funds earmarked for Los Angeles were withheld for more than a year because of a political struggle between the mayor and representatives from the black community. Replicated to a lesser degree in other cities, the struggle in Los Angeles centered on the most ambiguous and controversial component of the Office of Economic Opportunity's (OEO) proposal, Community Action Programs (CAPS). Emerging from the liberal consensus that the poor were better qualified to assess their economic needs than were remote federal officials, the OEO sought to disburse its funds for alleviating urban poverty through local community service organizations.

Shortly after the passage of the Economic Opportunity Act, the Youth Opportunities Board, a local organization created in 1962 in response to the National Delinquency and Manpower Training Act, submitted a detailed proposal to the OEO requesting funding. Led by five representatives from city and county government and the Los Angeles Board of Education, and backed by Mayor Yorty, the Youth Opportunities Board outlined an ambitious agenda that included, among other projects, a work training program for city and county government employment, general vocational guidance, an adult education program, and a communication skills program.[19]

But before the ink was dry on the funding proposal, a group of politically active African Americans, organized as the Equal Opportunities Federation, challenged the right of the Youth Opportunities Board to disburse federal funds. Backed by Augustus Hawkins, Governor Brown, and other high-profile liberals, the Equal Opportunities Federation argued that it was better qualified to represent the interests of the poor. Critics of the Youth Opportunities Board further argued that it was at best an officious and paternalistic screening agency and at worst simply a mechanism for the mayor to retain control over federal money.[20]

While other cities began to receive generous anti-poverty funds, Los Angeles languished as the two sides debated. By June 1965, almost a year after the passage of the Economic Opportunity Act, the conflict reached its nadir when Yorty attended the U.S. Conference of Mayors and proposed a resolution condemning the OEO and its director, Sargent Shriver. Yorty lambasted Shriver for "fostering class struggle" and complained that "mayors all over the United States are being harassed by agitation promoted by Sargent Shriver's speeches urging those he calls the poor, in quotes, to insist upon taking control of local programs."[21]

It took the Watts riot to break the deadlock over the War on Poverty in Los Angeles. Many riot participants had seen the battle over OEO funds as the last straw. One young white CORE activist told the *Los Angeles Sentinel:* "This is the best thing that could happen. We've been asking, pleading for better housing, better facilities and by burning these buildings down we can show Mayor Yorty and his friends that they can't sit on that anti-poverty money and not let us have it."[22] Shortly after the riot, under great pressure from African Americans and the OEO, a compromise was reached, in the form of the Economic and Youth Opportunities Agency of Greater Los Angeles (EYOA). The most significant change was that seven of the EYOA's twenty-five directors would be chosen by the poor in annual community elections. Although no more than about nine thousand poor citizens were ever involved in the process, it nonetheless represented significant community participation in what was essentially a municipal government entity.[23]

Once in place, the EYOA sponsored a number of important projects in South Central. In addition to youth education projects, including Head Start, perhaps the most ambitious and potentially transformative EYOA program was the Neighborhood Adult Participation Project (NAPP). NAPP was particularly effective at placing its beneficiaries, mostly women, into on-the-job training positions in clerical fields in both the public and the private sectors. In 1966, EYOA reported that, through NAPP and other programs, it had provided more than thirty thousand permanent and part-time jobs.[24]

Despite some successes, the War on Poverty in Los Angeles and nationwide failed. In Los Angeles, the stewardship of federal funds continued to be a highly charged issue that drove no small amount of political patronage and manipulation. To complicate this problem, conflict erupted between blacks and Mexicans. The latter group believed—correctly—that the War on Poverty disproportionately benefited blacks, despite the obvious problem of poverty in Mexican areas of the city.[25] More broadly, the War on Poverty came under attack in California and the rest of the nation in the early 1970s. EYOA became so fiscally unsound that the OEO finally forced it to shut down in 1972. The OEO itself closed its doors in 1974. Given the herculean task facing the War on Poverty, it should come as no surprise that it did not eradicate urban poverty. But many had hoped that these efforts would at least stop or slow the malignant growth of such privation. In fact, just the opposite was true: unemployment and poverty among African Americans in Los Angeles actually increased through the 1960s. The great tragedy of the War on Poverty is not that it failed to eradicate poverty and unemployment among the black population but that it failed to recognize the new, as well as the old, causes.

Undoubtedly influenced by two decades of uninterrupted postwar economic prosperity, the framers of the landmark social legislation of the 1960s shared an unshakable faith in the economic health of the United States. They believed that by improving the daily lives of the poor through after-school, vocational, and family planning programs, the OEO and CAPS would make poor citizens more employable, the key to eradicating poverty. Title VII of the Civil Rights Act of 1964, which gave employees the right to sue employers who engaged in discriminatory practices, implicitly framed white racism as the great barrier to black economic progress. The eradication of white racism, many believed, would allow blacks to share in the country's economic prosperity.

The U.S. Department of Labor's "Moynihan report," which, despite its infamy, deeply influenced the course of the federal anti-poverty movement, took a somewhat different tack, arguing that a compromised black family structure lay at the root of racial inequality. But that structure had been caused by years of racial discrimination in education and employment. Although the report shied away from explicit policy recommendations, it followed that aggressive anti-discrimination efforts and even affirmative action programs would cure what ailed black families. Like the War on Poverty and the Civil Rights Act of 1964, the Moynihan report sought to "bring the Negro American to full and equal sharing in the responsibilities and rewards of citizenship."[26]

Yet, what remained unrecognized was that the nature of that citizenship was quickly changing. As the EYOA launched its educational and vocational programs, and the Equal Employment Opportunities Commission (the EEOC, created by the Civil Rights Act of 1964) held hearings in Los Angeles, few noticed that the economic geography of the city was subtly shifting. Although many blamed the 1965 Watts riot for industrial flight from black Los Angeles, there was evidence as early as 1963 that manufacturing firms were leaving South Central and the Alameda industrial corridor for distant suburban areas. Following a trend set by aircraft, aerospace, and electronics firms in prior decades, manufacturers of electrical machinery, apparel, metals, and food and petroleum products increasingly sought to lower their tax burden, expand their plant size, and connect to new markets by leaving the central city. Between mid-1963 and mid-1964, twenty-eight industrial manufacturing firms left South Central and parts of East Los Angeles, including four metal shops, eight furniture factories, one electrical machinery factory, one food processing plant, four textile plants, and two oil refineries.[27]

A 1964 survey of unemployed black workers in South Central revealed the difficulties imposed by these industrial relocations. The vast majority of those surveyed had recently been blue-collar workers. Now unemployed, almost 63 percent reported that they had sought work outside South Central. But the job search proved difficult for these workers, 58 percent of whom did not own automobiles. And those who did have cars were discouraged in their search because they were often prohibited from living in the communities surrounding newly suburbanized industries.[28]

The relocation of basic manufacturing industries in the 1960s was just the first phase in a long period of economic restructuring in Southern California, but it had a critical effect on black Los Angeles. After climbing steadily for two decades, the proportion of the black male workforce employed as operatives in manufacturing firms began to fall in the 1960s, and the absolute employment of black men in manufacturing dropped in the early 1970s. While some industries suburbanized, dislocating their formerly urban workforce, many others began to decline altogether. Undoubtedly, the most salient feature of the economy in the 1970s was corporate disinvestment in the large-scale production capacity of the nation. Deindustrialization—caused by increased global competition; aging, inefficient, and expensive capital stock; and corporate management's desire to save labor costs by relocating to foreign countries—sharply narrowed opportunities for America's industrial workers.[29]

Following the national trend, Los Angeles's steel industry began to shrink in the 1960s, followed by the automobile and tire industries in the 1970s and early 1980s. A wave of large plant closures rocked the industrial corridor in the 1970s: Chrysler (Commerce) in 1971; B.F. Goodrich (Commerce) in 1975; Uniroyal (Commerce) in 1978; U.S. Steel (Commerce) in 1979; Norris Industries (South Gate) in 1979; Ford Motors (Pico Rivera) in 1980; Firestone (South Gate) in 1980; Goodyear

(South Central) in 1980; Bethlehem Steel (Vernon) in 1982; General Motors (South Gate) in 1982.[30] By one estimate, more than seventy thousand jobs disappeared from the area between 1978 and 1982 alone.[31] Exacerbating the crisis of job loss was the continued influx of African Americans to Southern California. During the 1960s, the last decade of heavy black migration to Los Angeles, the African American population grew by more than 50 percent. Even in good times, the manufacturing economy of South Los Angeles could scarcely have absorbed this booming population.

The Great Migration generation was hit hardest by industrial relocation and decline. In most auto, steel, and rubber plants, workers needed to have twenty years of service or to be sixty-two years old in order to collect pensions. Thus, blacks, most of whom had entered the industry in the early 1950s, saw their retirement hopes dashed. Black and white workers between the ages of forty-five and sixty found their hard-earned pensions frozen and retraining very difficult. National surveys reported that 65 percent of industrial workers in that age group were still not working after a year, and some would likely never find work.[32]

The personal consequences of industrial plant closures for black male employees could be frustrating at best and devastating at worst. When the Chrysler plant left the city of Commerce in 1971, eighteen hundred workers were laid off. Arvella Grigsby, a Texas migrant whose husband had worked at the Chrysler plant, recognized that her husband had few options. The company offered to relocate displaced Southern California workers to Michigan near Chrysler's Canadian plant, but the relocation appealed to very few. "When Chrysler closed down," Grigsby recalled, "they would pay your way if you wanted to go, but he didn't want to go back there and take the kids out of school." Instead, her husband accepted a much lower-paying job as a cook with a catering company.[33]

Many others were not as fortunate. Otis W. Muse, fifty-four, had worked at the Goodyear plant for twenty-eight years before it closed. His wife recalled that it had been impossible for him to find work at another factory. Most devastating, she felt that "all of this . . . caused him to feel less than a man, than he had always been." She believed that this stress contributed to Otis's fatal heart attack less than one year after the plant closure.[34]

The economic dislocation of the Great Migration generation also had severe implications for its children. For an already disillusioned minority of these children, watching their parents lose hard-won jobs confirmed the fruitlessness of playing by the rules. Woodward Rideaux, president of the Watts branch of the NAACP and a dislocated auto-worker himself, told a California Senate committee on plant closures: "When we look at this plant closure . . . we have to look at it as a package. We have it so bad in some high schools . . . they don't show up to school because they don't see no use working and going to school. . . . many of them are sitting around drinking alcohol." [35]

The crime rate throughout black Los Angeles skyrocketed as young African Americans, particularly young men, sought financial stability outside the legitimate labor force. Although the infamous concept of the "tangle of pathology" described in the Moynihan report was widely shunned by civil rights advocates because it appeared to undermine their claim of a growing community power base among urban blacks, the rising crime rate in Watts and South Central seemed only to confirm the hypothesis. In fact, the conception of the negative behavioral and psychological impact of ghetto life decried in the report was not new. Many social scientists had long recognized the problem of what William Julius Wilson has recently described as "ghetto-related behavior." [36] But in the superheated atmosphere of the mid-1960s, the notion of behavioral problems among blacks—even when presented in a sympathetic light, as they were in the Moynihan report—was wildly unpopular.

The personal, economic, and psychological consequences of black Los Angeles's fading blue collar were clearly evident in the physical landscape of the city. In Watts, where poverty had always been endemic, declining manufacturing work merely intensified old problems. But in the city of Compton, once the pride of Southern California's blue-collar African American middle class, the transformation was devastating. With more than one-third of its population employed in manufacturing industries, Compton was probably affected more than any other black area in Southern California. [37] Although the unemployment rate in Compton remained much lower than in neighboring Watts and Willowbrook, it crept from 8.7 percent to 10 percent for black men between 1960 and 1970. Complicating the effects of this slowly rising unemployment was the unusually high proportion of young people in Compton: by the late 1960s, 56 percent of the male population and 52 percent of females were under the age of twenty. [38]

Since a large proportion of the city was either in school or unemployed, Compton experienced a steady decline in its tax base, which further eroded the infrastructure of the city. The rising crime rate discouraged potential businesses, including retail stores, from operating in Compton. One reporter from the *New York Times* observed that black "residents noticed changes: Stores are closing, the streets are dirtier, the merchandise is shoddier." Consequently, the children of Compton felt very differently about the city than their parents had when they moved there in the 1950s. One black teenager felt that "the kids should have something they can be proud of. Now they just hang their heads when they mention Compton."[39] A 1967 survey by the EYOA found that Compton had one of the highest rates of youth poverty in the county.[40] The election of black city council member Douglas Dollarhide to the mayor's office in 1969 temporarily brought hope to the city's residents. And Dollarhide made good on his promise to seek expanded employment opportunities in Compton by bringing a 540-acre industrial park to the city in 1971. But tenants were slow to move into the increasingly depressed area, and the industrial park employed scarcely more than a handful of the city's dislocated blue-collar workers.

In one of the tragic ironies of postwar African American history, the decline in industrial employment began just as the civil rights movement was finally making headway in America's largest industries. As Woodward Rideaux put it, "We have sought for many years to get the mass of minorities into the industrial [plants]—major industries as such, and we were able to win a victory . . . and got many into the employment ... [but] then there come no plants. The plants is closing."[41]

Starting in the late 1960s, both automobile and steel manufacturers had begun to implement—albeit unevenly—affirmative action hiring policies. A decade after the passage of the Civil Rights Act of 1964, the EEOC, leaders of the steel industry, and the United Steelworkers of America finally developed a systematic approach to implementing and enforcing Title VII of the act—the clause barring discrimination in employment. A consent decree covering the steel industry was signed in April 1974. Many hoped that the consent decree—which forced discriminatory employers to hire minorities on a quota basis and offer financial restitution for past grievances—would become the primary tool for creating racial equality in American industry. But it was often an awkward and inefficient tool, upsetting black workers by offering paltry cash rewards for years of discrimination and angering white workers by undermining the many legitimate nondiscriminatory foundations of job seniority. At Bethlehem Steel in Los Angeles, the most vocal dissenters were black workers, infuriated by the two hundred dollars in back pay they were offered for their years of service under discriminatory rules.[42]

Before the 1974 consent decree, dozens of African American workers at the Bethlehem Steel plant in Vernon had utilized Title VII of the Civil Rights Act in their battle against discrimination. Clevron Tucker, who had worked as a truck driver for the company since 1951, found himself assigned to broken-down trucks and paid less than both white and Mexican American workers. He filed suit against the company and the union in 1971. Similarly, Bethlehem truck mechanic Jim Haley sued the company in 1972, claiming discrimination in promotion, wages, and work assignments. The most outspoken critic of the discriminatory policies of both the company and the union was black welder Charles Bratton, who began working for Bethlehem Steel in 1950. Bratton, elected as the first black president of USWA Local 1845 in 1973, had been consistently passed over for a promotion to supervisor, solely, he believed, because of his race. He filed suits against both the company and the union in 1967 and 1969. Bratton, Tucker, Haley, and many others were dissatisfied with the two-hundred-dollar settlement offered in the consent decree of 1974 and collectively sued the company in 1980.[43] In a stark example of the hollowness of civil rights victories in American industry, Bratton and his fellow black workers finally received favorable settlements in 1983, just one year after they had permanently lost their jobs when the Bethlehem plant closed down.

But if black industrial workers were hit hard by the closure of automobile, steel, and tire plants, Southern California itself was far more resilient. While the city's older, semiskilled, blue-collar, and heavily unionized manufacturing industries declined, rapid growth occurred in both unskilled and highly skilled manufacturing industries. Thus, in manufacturing, the greatest growth in the 1970s and 1980s occurred simultaneously in the notoriously low-paying, nonunion apparel and garment industries and in the aerospace and electronics industries, which increasingly depended on well-educated and highly skilled workers. As chapter 3 described, inadequate education and training kept many African Americans out of high-technology industries long after the racial barriers had fallen. And the continued suburbanization of the electronics industries in the 1970s and 1980s—by then located not only in the San Fernando Valley but also in distant Orange, Riverside, and San Bernardino Counties—intensified familiar transportation problems. Meanwhile, dislocated blue-collar workers, both whites and blacks, rarely considered seeking work in the rapidly expanding apparel industry. Few could stomach the notion of trading in years of unionized, relatively high-wage work for nonunion, low-paying jobs.

Yet, even if African Americans had sought positions in Southern California's new manufacturing economy, they would have found it difficult to gain a foothold. The new economy—characterized by dispersed, smaller, and notoriously unsafe plants—catered particularly to recent immigrants from Latin America and Asia. Employers actively recruited immigrants, both legal and illegal, in the belief that new immigrants were more likely to accept sweatshop conditions and were more responsive to employer control. Their efforts were aided by the passage of the Hart-Cellar Immigration Act of 1965, ironically inspired by the black civil rights movement. Under the 1965 act, quotas for legal immigrants were relaxed for Asian countries, Mexico, and the rest of Latin America. But even more critical to Southern California's new manufacturing economy were illegal immigrants. One study of the region's apparel industry estimated that by the 1980s as much as 80 percent of the workforce was undocumented. Indicative of the conditions in which these immigrants worked, more than 80 percent of the plants fell below legal health and safety standards. Even if blacks had wanted to work under these conditions, extensive immigrant recruitment networks kept a steady supply of workers at the employers' behest.[44]

For young unskilled black men seeking employment, the city's ever-vibrant service sector continued to provide opportunities. But employment in the service sector, as always, was a poor substitute for the vanishing unionized blue-collar jobs of their fathers and mothers. For the blue-collar population of black Los Angeles, the 1960s marked the end of an era. Of far more enduring importance than the Watts riot, the fading of the blue collar shattered the dreams of postwar prosperity that had influenced so many black migrants' lives. And the dual curse of continued in-migration and declining employment fueled a bitter and deepening disillusionment among young African Americans. Some channeled this frustration into constructive political activity. In addition to the Nation of Islam, the Black Panthers, founded in Oakland in 1967, drew a small but loyal group of African Americans to their ranks. But for many others, no constructive outlet existed. Consequently, the economic problems of South Central contributed significantly to crime, drug addiction, rising rates of out-of-wedlock births, and the creation of a substantial—and semipermanent—underclass of African Americans.

From within South Central, black community leaders struggled to stop the rising tide of poverty and unemployment. By far the most ambitious and successful was autoworker Ted Watkins. Born in Meridian, Mississippi, in 1923, Watkins migrated to Los Angeles in 1938, settled in Watts, attended Jefferson High, and had just begun training in metal finishing and auto body repair when he was called to fight in World War II. Shortly after returning, Watkins found work at the Ford plant in Pico Rivera, a suburban city about eight miles east of South Central, and became an active member of the United Auto Workers, representing his union on the Los Angeles CIO Council. Also involved with numerous community organizations in Watts, Watkins sought to apply the principles of union activity to his own neighborhood, creating in Watts "an economic base which the area lacked and would require in order to become a healthy, self-sustaining segment of the city of Los Angeles."[45] With the support of fellow union members (both blacks and whites), seven international unions, and staff members at the Institute of Industrial Relations at the University of California, Los Angeles, Watkins founded the Watts Labor Community Action Committee (WLCAC) in 1965, shortly before the Watts riot.

One of WLCAC's first campaigns was to get the county to build a hospital to serve residents of Watts, Willowbrook, and Compton. WLCAC coordinated more than eighty organizations and recruited hundreds of volunteers to put the proposal for a new hospital on the ballot in 1966. The measure passed, construction began in 1968, and the doors of the hospital opened in 1972 as the Martin Luther King Jr./ Drew Medical Center on South Wilmington Avenue at 120th Street.

Recognizing that unemployment was perhaps the greatest problem in Watts and South Central, WLCAC established several innovative employment training and placement programs with the support of AFL-CIO unions and grants from the Department of Labor. In 1966, WLCAC launched the Community Conservation Corps, a New Deal–inspired educational, job training, and placement program serving seventeen hundred black youths between the ages of seven and twenty-one (see figure 14).[46] WLCAC acquired twenty vacant lots in Watts, putting these youths to work building parks, a senior citizens center, classrooms, and a farm complete with a poultry ranch. The organization leased and operated a Mobil service station on 103rd and Central, where it trained young people in auto repair in addition to selling gas. African American workers and union members would often volunteer their time to teach various trades to young black people in Watts and to serve as positive role models. The effect of these programs was often palpable. For example, one young black man in a WLCAC wood-shop class told a reporter for the *Los Angeles Times:* "Before I got into this program I was stayin' in trouble. Now I'm learning cabinet work and I figure I'll be able to get a job."[47]

FIGURE 14. Black youths stand in line in 1967 to fill out applications for employment in the Watts Community Conservation Corps, a program sponsored by the Department of Labor and the Watts Labor Community Action Committee. WLCAC director Ted Watkins can be seen in the foreground, passing out applications. Courtesy of the Los Angeles Public Library.

Leading the crusade to improve education in South Central was Odessa Cox, who had migrated to Los Angeles with her husband, Raymond, in 1944.[48] Born in Whatley, Alabama, but raised in Bessemer, Odessa Cox received an early education in racial discrimination and methods to combat it. During the late 1930s, her father worked at the Tennessee Coal, Iron and Railroad Company (TCI) in Bessemer. Frustrated by rampant racial discrimination in the steel industry, he became a volunteer organizer for the CIO, earning a reputation as a rabble-rouser among local whites. After his home was raided by the Klan and his family threatened, he moved on to other jobs, but his pugnacity rubbed off on young Odessa. After graduating from high school in 1940, Odessa met Ray Cox, one of her father's recruits from TCI, and the two were married in 1941.

Both Odessa—who worked as a cook in a motel—and her husband chafed at Bessemer's racial restrictions and were determined to start

FIGURE 15. Alabama migrants Odessa and Raymond Cox at their Watts business, Utopia Cleaners, ca. 1955. Odessa Cox founded the South-Central Junior College Committee in 1950, which lobbied the Los Angeles Board of Education and the County Board of Supervisors for a junior college for seventeen years. Only after the Watts riot of 1965 did the board agree to build the college. In 1967, Los Angeles Southwest College was opened in several bungalows on Imperial and Western. Courtesy of the Los Angeles Public Library.

anew outside the South. Following the advice of close friends in Los Angeles, the Coxes moved west. Once in Los Angeles, the couple moved into the Jordan Downs housing project in Watts, and Ray found work as a longshoreman in San Pedro. But when he heard about Local 13 president L. B. Thomas's promise to make the union "lily white" again after the war, he told Odessa, "We better start looking around for something more permanent."[49]

Having some experience working at a dry cleaning establishment in Bessemer, Ray suggested that the couple start their own dry cleaning business. In 1945, they opened Utopia Cleaners at 1820 Ninety-Seventh Street in Watts (see figure 15). Initially, Utopia only pressed and altered clothes, but in 1950 the Coxes bought their own cleaning plant and dramatically improved their business, not closing their doors until Ray's death in 1994. The Coxes were a migrant success story, owning their own home and business and eventually sending all three of their daughters to college.

Unlike some of her peers, however, Odessa Cox did not leave South Central. Rather, she stayed and launched what would become one of the most successful campaigns in the community's history. From the time she first settled in Watts, Odessa had been active in local community organizations. In 1950, she founded the South-Central Junior College Committee, a group determined to bring a junior college to the black community. A business owner and mother of three, Cox nonetheless tirelessly lobbied the Los Angeles Board of Education and the County Board of Supervisors for seventeen years to build a junior college.

It took the Watts riot to convince the county that it should commit to building the school. In 1967, the first bungalows were erected on a 75-acre site on Imperial and Western, and Los Angeles Southwest College was born. The first permanent structure was built in 1977. Since then, the junior college has developed both academic and vocational programs geared to the needs of the community. The majority of the faculty is black, and the community college hosts programs designed to appeal to prospective African American students, including a black film festival and frequent performances by the Watts Prophets, a group of black poets/rappers from South Central. Cox continued to play an influential role in the direction of Los Angeles Southwest College until her death in 2001.

Both Cox and Watkins were remarkable community organizers and waged herculean campaigns to improve life for African Americans in South Central. Yet, the backdrop to their successes was an increasingly bleak one. Through the late 1960s and 1970s, both unemployment and crime rose steeply in many South Central neighborhoods. While WLCAC continued to provide important services for South Central, the critical link between industrial employment, unions, and the black community had faded considerably by the late 1970s. But perhaps most frustrating to black community leaders was the continuing out-migration of blacks from South Central. Watkins's slogan, "Don't move, improve," was rarely heeded by those African Americans who could afford to leave.

African American Mobility and New Class Status: Baldwin Hills

Although a sizable segment of the black population was traumatized by the decline in heavy manufacturing, other African Americans benefited from the rapid growth in different sectors, particularly office work, retail, and finance. The proportion of black men employed in white-collar positions rose from 16 percent in 1950 to 28 percent in 1970. More impressive was the proportion of black women in white-collar occupations, which rose from 17 percent to 50 percent during the same years.[50] Indeed, the expanding number of black workers in white-collar occupations was the engine driving the continuous black flight from South Central. Just as the rising proportion of black workers in blue-collar jobs had transformed the racial geography of Los Angeles during the 1940s and 1950s, so too did the rising proportion of white-collar African Americans during the 1960s and 1970s.

As the economic disparity among blacks continued to grow in the post-boom era, and as white resistance became less tolerable both socially and legally in Los Angeles, the racial geography of the city came to more closely reflect the economic diversity of the black community. One *New York Times* reporter visiting Compton in 1972 grimly noted: "As the town approached a black majority something else happened. The affluent blacks who moved here began to move on too."[51] As they had in the 1940s and early 1950s, well-employed blacks continued moving west. By the late 1950s and early 1960s, blacks had pushed west and south of West Adams into Leimert Park and the exclusive area of Baldwin Hills, which quickly became the heart of affluent black Los Angeles, a position it still holds today.

A five-square-mile area of unincorporated hillside west of Leimert Park/Crenshaw and south of West Adams, Baldwin Hills boasted large homes and expansive views. Largely undeveloped until the 1940s, hundreds of houses and apartment complexes were built there in the 1950s. As they had in Compton, blacks moved into new and large homes, with an average of four to six bedrooms per household.[52] African Americans in Baldwin Hills were generally much better educated than their South Central counterparts, a fact that translated into greater job opportunities in the post-boom economy. Accordingly, just over 71 percent of all employed African Americans in Baldwin Hills were white-collar workers.[53] Many Baldwin Hills residents were typical of those who fled South Central after the Watts riot; according to the 1970 census, 57 percent of blacks in Baldwin Hills had lived in the central city in 1965.[54]

In addition to superior housing, residents of Baldwin Hills and the nearby Leimert Park and Crenshaw areas also enjoyed many more conveniences as consumers. While many Watts and Willowbrook residents were forced to buy groceries at overpriced liquor stores, Baldwin Hills residents had other options. The Crenshaw Shopping Center—opened in 1947, as one of the first planned suburban malls in the United States—was the most popular shopping area for local residents.[55] And, during the 1960s, the Baldwin Hills Center and the Ladera Center also opened, offering residents even greater selection and convenience. Central to this improved consumer selection, and middle-class life in general, was the greater mobility of Baldwin Hills residents relative to blacks in the central city. Whereas 57 percent of Baldwin Hills households had one car, and 37 percent had two or more cars, a survey of Watts residents found that 57 percent did not own a car.[56]

Perhaps the greatest advantage to residing in Baldwin Hills was the superior quality of the area's public schools. In 1971, the Los Angeles Department of City Planning described Baldwin Hills public schools as the "the best schools of any city area inhabited primarily by black people" and "on par with those in West Los Angeles and the San Fernando Valley."[57] In addition to boasting low dropout rates and small class sizes relative to public schools in Watts and South Central, public schools in Baldwin Hills were also more racially integrated. For example, at a time when the vast majority of black students in Los Angeles attended schools that were more than 80 percent black, Baldwin Hills Elementary and Coliseum Elementary—both in Baldwin Hills—were only 38 percent and 31 percent black, respectively. Local high schools serving the area, including Dorsey and Hamilton, had dropout rates below the citywide average and well below the average for heavily black schools in the city.[58]

Upwardly mobile African Americans worked hard to protect their new neighborhoods from the same deterioration that had occurred in former middle-class black neighborhoods like Compton. Shortly before the Watts riot, black homeowners in the Crenshaw/Leimert Park area founded Crenshaw Neighbors, an organization committed to retaining the racially integrated character of their neighborhood by preventing white flight. Multiracial but predominantly black, Crenshaw Neighbors met with school administrators and white parents in an effort to prevent racial conflict in the area's schools and worked with local apartment owners and managers to prevent rapid tenant turnover and property deterioration. Concerned with "stabilizing" integrated neighborhoods, Crenshaw Neighbors explicitly rejected militancy and protest. In its quarterly magazine, *The Integrator,* Crenshaw Neighbors chastised bigots for their resistance to peaceful integration but also warned against the presence of "militant liberals," arguing that they were a potential "nuisance in an integrated area" because their protests and promotion of civil disobedience "scares the daylights out of probable candidates for integration."[59]

Farther south in the integrated pocket of Inglewood known as Morningside Park, Morningside Park Neighbors made similar efforts to preserve the character of their community. Remarkably, the organization's membership—which was as high as thirteen hundred at its peak in the late 1960s—was predominantly white. Concerned that the community would soon become all-black, Morningside Park Neighbors argued to Inglewood's white community that by completely desegregating schools and neighborhoods they could prevent any area of the city from becoming exclusively black, thereby reducing the likelihood of wholesale white flight.[60]

Crenshaw Neighbors and Morningside Park Neighbors may have eased racial tension in their respective communities; indeed, there were remarkably few "racial incidents" in these communities during the 1960s and 1970s. Nonetheless, these organizations were not able to "stabilize" neighborhoods for very long; by the mid-1970s, each had become heavily black. At the time of the 1980 census, Morningside Park was 88 percent black, and the Crenshaw/Leimert Park area was 86 percent black.[61]

Nonetheless, the migration of middle-class African Americans out of Watts, South Central, Compton, and West Adams into other, more affluent communities was a cheerful indicator of both increasing black prosperity and the declining power of racial discrimination in the housing market. But the meaning of this transformation to African Americans in poor neighborhoods was more ambiguous. Many ghetto dwellers perceived the out-migration of affluent blacks as a betrayal. One Baldwin Hills resident complained that young blacks "have gotten the impression that struggling to get to a place like Baldwin Hills is bad" or that its residents were snobs. "What they should be made to understand," she continued "is that we are no different from them, except we and our husbands worked hard so that we could have something for ourselves and our children."[62]

Other blacks did not see out-migration per se as a betrayal but believed that affluence brought with it responsibilities to the rest of the black community. Freita Shaw Johnson of Watts articulated this position during the McCone Commission hearings in 1965: "Baldwin Hills, and the people who are in View Park, are going to have to lend a hand to people in South Los Angeles, because we are all colored people."[63]

Black *Los Angeles Times* journalist J. K. Obatala sympathized with critics of the out-migrating middle class but recognized that most blacks, if given the opportunity, would leave the ghetto: "Buried somewhere in the minds of most Afro-Americans are the ruins of a secret utopia, a fossilized dreamland that, if unearthed, would probably look very much like Baldwin Hills."[64]

Beyond Baldwin Hills, a small but growing number of well-employed African Americans sought housing in Southern California's outlying suburbs. Blacks benefited from Title VIII of the 1968 Civil Rights Act, which prohibited racial discrimination in the sale, rental, or financing of property, ostensibly hammering the final nail into the coffin of racial segregation in housing.[65] Adjacent to South Central, the formerly restricted suburbs of Inglewood, Carson, and Gardena witnessed an influx of black residents beginning in the 1960s. Farther away from South Central, blacks found homes in previously restricted San Fernando Valley communities such as Northridge and Sylmar and in the distant suburb of Pomona, at the far eastern edge of Los Angeles County. Most remarkably, some African Americans found homes in Orange County, where concerted exclusion had kept the entire county's black population under a thousand in 1950.[66] By 1970, more than 12 percent of Los Angeles County's black population lived in suburban communities.[67]

Even as the 1970s began, however, race still powerfully shaped suburban housing opportunities for blacks. Audits and reports of the U.S. Department of Housing and Urban Development revealed that many African Americans continued to face "unfavorable treatment" by realtors, lenders, and landlords and that their applications for mortgages were denied much more often than the applications of whites.[68] Undoubtedly, these practices discouraged a number of African Americans from moving to outlying suburbs, even when they could afford to.

The Racialization of Politics in Southern California

For both rich and poor black Los Angeles, Tom Bradley's election as mayor in 1973 was a tremendous victory. Gaining strength from the alliance he had formed with the city's liberal Jewish community in his failed bid for mayor in 1969, Bradley returned to defeat Yorty in 1973. Having been completely locked out of local politics until a decade earlier, African Americans derived great psychological satisfaction from the knowledge that one of their own was now the mayor of a city of almost three million.

And there were hopeful signs that Bradley, who campaigned as a liberal reformer, could make concrete improvements in city hall. As Raphael Sonenshein has explained, Bradley appointed numerous African Americans to his administration, implemented successful affirmative action programs in city hiring, and attempted to rein in the LAPD by appointing aggressive civil rights advocates to the police commission. Bradley forced the LAPD to eliminate use of the highly controversial chokehold and limited the department's rampant intelligence-gathering program. Ultimately, however, police reforms under the Bradley administration were quite modest compared to those established in other cities: Los Angeles still lacked a civilian review board, and the number of police shootings barely changed at all under Bradley's tenure. More troubling for liberal critics was Bradley's deference to downtown business interests in his assignment of urban redevelopment funds. In his unswerving commitment to make Los Angeles a "World Class City," Bradley diverted resources toward downtown redevelopment and away from projects aimed at expanding the affordable housing stock in the city or improving infrastructure in blighted neighborhoods.[69]

Though much of the emerging liberal criticism of the Bradley administration was legitimate, the oft-quoted claim that Bradley "killed South Central" was pure hyperbole. The greatest blow to South Central—blue-collar job loss—had its origins in regional, national, and global economic restructuring, transformations far beyond the reach of city hall. Nonetheless, in his failure to create or direct creative policy responses to the economic decline in South Central, Bradley undoubtedly alienated many formerly supportive African Americans.

For African Americans in California, one of the most troubling developments of the post-boom era was the rising tide of anti-liberalism among whites. As early as the 1950s, white homeowners and homeowners' associations throughout Los Angeles County began protesting sharply rising property taxes.[70] This frustration with taxes had already significantly eroded support for liberal governor Pat Brown by the early 1960s. As many black leaders had feared, the Watts riot of 1965 further intensified this groundswell of white conservatism. For liberals and moderates, those six days in August undermined the emerging consensus that redirecting federal resources toward the nation's poorest communities would alleviate racial inequality and black frustration, a notion long rejected by conservatives.[71]

Ronald Reagan's defeat of Governor Brown in California's 1966 gubernatorial election clearly reflected growing white conservatism. Reagan, who had consistently opposed the Rumford Fair Housing Act of 1963, campaigned in 1966 almost exclusively on an anti-tax platform, suggesting that many government services were "just goodies dreamed up for our supposed betterment."[72] In the same year, South Gate voters—typically Democrats—elected anti-busing Republican Floyd Wakefield to the state assembly.

But the most powerful and enduring expression of the new California conservatism came more than a decade later with the passage of Proposition 13 in 1978. Proposition 13, which effectively pitted taxpayers against the beneficiaries of tax-funded programs, passed by an overwhelming margin of 65 percent to 35 percent. Although its proponents carefully avoided racial rhetoric, both the motivation and the support for the initiative had clear racial origins and effects. Surveys found that African Americans were the only social group to consistently oppose tax-cutting propositions, and Proposition 13 in particular.[73] As the disproportionate beneficiaries of welfare, public housing, and public employment, blacks lost the most during California's tax revolt.

Equally frustrating for African Americans in Los Angeles, the rising tide of conservatism in California further crippled the school desegregation effort. Although Los Angeles Superior Court Judge Alfred Gitelson ruled in 1970 that the city's schools were clearly and illegally segregated on the basis of race, the California Supreme Court did not hand down its decision ordering the Los Angeles Unified School District (LAUSD) to desegregate until 1976. Meanwhile, black students were becoming ever more segregated; by the early 1970s, 87 percent of black students in Los Angeles were in schools whose students were 80 to 100 percent minorities, and 8 percent were in schools that were 100 percent minority.[74] The situation became even more difficult as California voters and state legislators tried repeatedly to derail the desegregation project. South Gate assembly representative Floyd Wakefield proposed several laws ruling out busing as a solution. In a 1972 referendum—later declared unconstitutional—voters approved Proposition 21, stating that no child could be assigned to a school on the basis of race.

Finally, in 1978, two years after the California Supreme Court had ordered the school district to "bring about 'reasonably feasible' desegregation of its schools," the LAUSD unveiled a multifaceted desegregation plan combining voluntary and mandatory transfers. Affecting approximately eighty-five thousand students, the plan called for the mandatory reassignment of fifty-four thousand students, some of whom were sent to ten "mid-site" schools halfway between the San Fernando

Valley and the central city. Others could voluntarily select one of forty-five magnet schools that attracted interracial enrollments through specialized educational offerings.[75]

The Los Angeles school desegregation plan, perhaps the largest in the nation, went into effect on Tuesday, 12 September 1978. Although no violence accompanied the desegregation, white resistance, particularly in the San Fernando Valley, reached a fever pitch. Some white Valley parents organized protest organizations, such as Bustop and United Parents Against Forced Busing, to boycott schools. Some sent their children to local private and parochial schools, while others pulled their children from school altogether. Shortly before the start of the school year, Catholic and Protestant school principals in the Valley complained that their applicant pool had more than doubled. One mother even offered to pay for the construction of an additional classroom if Our Lady of the Valley Catholic school in Canoga Park, already filled to capacity, admitted her child. On the first day of school, another Valley mother, Corrine Jay, attempted to prevent a busload of black students from arriving at their new Woodland Hills school by swerving her brown station wagon in front of the crowded bus and slowing to ten miles per hour on the busy 101 freeway. Though few white Valley parents were so reckless, many shared Jay's sentiment. During the first year of desegregation alone, an estimated ten thousand white students dropped out of LAUSD schools because of their parents' opposition to busing.[76]

Although desegregation clearly accelerated white flight from the LAUSD, that process had been well under way before 1978. The district's white enrollment fell 15 percent in 1978, but it had already declined by 20 percent between 1966 and 1977, and it would continue to steadily decline through the 1980s and 1990s.[77] In short, by the time the LAUSD was legally compelled to desegregate its schools two decades after *Brown,* there were no mechanisms—including busing—that would have stemmed the tide of growing racial isolation. As in the case of Title VII in American industry, the solutions to racial inequality came far too late and were, in any case, probably far too little.

The 1960s and the African American Community in Transition

For black Los Angeles, the 1960s ushered in a series of abrupt shifts. For a crucial segment of the Great Migration generation, the events of the decade undermined its economic stability and challenged its core values. Having fought for, trained for, and gained steady, unionized jobs in industrial manufacturing, many blacks were surprised by the rapid disappearance of these jobs and were ill prepared to seek work in a newer economy that demanded workers at the extremes of the labor market: highly skilled workers on the one hand, and low-skilled sweatshop labor on the other. And in part because their continuing fight for integration had been rewarded with concrete gains in employment and housing, older African Americans were also troubled by the countervailing trend among black youth toward radicalism and violence, of which the Watts riot was the most explosive manifestation.

Tom Bradley's success was heartening for the Great Migration generation, a sort of vindication for those African Americans who believed that through hard work and determination—and, when necessary, principled protest—blacks could achieve anything. But the era also witnessed the erosion of the Brown-era liberal coalition in state politics and the emergence of a distinctly anti-liberal political climate in California. Meanwhile, the trend toward black out-migration from South Central, which had begun in the 1950s, accelerated in the 1960s. Propelled by African American economic gains in white-collar occupations, this out-migration allowed a segment of black Los Angeles to experience the long-sought-after standard of middle-class life for which Southern California was famous. After the 1968 Civil Rights Act, these African Americans also found housing in distant suburbs where black residences would have been unheard of in the 1940s and 1950s.

As it always had been, the story of black Los Angeles continued to be one of simultaneous prosperity and poverty, progress and decline, hope and frustration. But by the 1960s, the disparity between these extremes had become much wider, and the stakes much higher.

Epilogue

> The stories were true for the most part but the truth wasn't
> like the dream.
>> Easy Rawlins, in Walter Mosley's *Devil in a Blue Dress,* 1990

In 1998, seventy-three-year-old Sylvester Gibbs sat at the Watts Senior Citizens Center on East Century Boulevard, reflecting on the decision he had made fifty years earlier to leave Mississippi and move to Los Angeles.

After serving in the Navy during World War II, Gibbs returned to his native Lauderdale, Mississippi, a changed man. Emboldened by his military service and now twenty-one years old, Gibbs wanted to be treated like a man. He began resisting the rules of racial etiquette, refusing, for example, to call white men "sir." "The bad part about this," Gibbs remembered, "was that the white folks, when they can't be the chief and you the little Indian, they'll do something to you." Sensing that Mississippi could no longer safely contain his ambition, Gibbs determined to join his brother, who had moved to Los Angeles during the war and worked as a longshoreman on Terminal Island.

On 1 May 1948, the twenty-three-year-old veteran and his fiancée packed their Chevrolet and drove straight from Mississippi to Los Angeles. Although Gibbs "came out with a chip on my shoulder," he quickly warmed to Los Angeles: "When I came out here, I said this is for me, I'm not going anyplace else. This is certainly better than Mississippi." "In California," Gibbs recalled, "you ain't got these white folks feeling superior over the blacks—well, they may feel that, but they can't go around showing it." The strict rules of racial etiquette were missing. In Los Angeles, "you don't go around saying 'sir.' If he don't say 'sir' to you, you don't have to say 'sir' to him." "Out here," Gibbs concluded, "everybody just called their name."

Gibbs worked as a crane operator for almost forty years. For most of that time, he worked at Hugo Neu-Proler, the nation's largest scrap steel recycling plant, located on Terminal Island. With their combined salaries, Gibbs and his wife bought a brand-new home in Compton in 1952. And when he retired in the 1980s, the company bought him a gold watch and a twenty-two-day vacation in Europe with his wife. For Sylvester Gibbs and his wife, migration to Los Angeles provided opportunities they would likely never have had in their native Mississippi. Though life was not always easy, and Gibbs always chafed at racism, he felt that he and his family had been given a fair chance in California and that they had lived a good life.[1]

But for others, racism was not a matter of degree: either it existed or it did not. For one Oklahoma native who migrated to Los Angeles during the war at the age of seventeen, Los Angeles was a complete disappointment.[2] She recalled, "I didn't like it then," adding, "and I still don't like it." In particular, she could never forget what her husband had to endure. On one of his first trips as a trucker for a local manufacturing firm, he stopped at a service station on Alameda to gas up and buy lunch. He filled his tank and bought his food but was then told he could not eat there. Leaving the service station, he looked back to see a sign reading: "No colored trade solicited." For this woman, these and other incidents laid bare the utter falseness of the city's reputation for racial tolerance. Los Angeles "wasn't that different from Oklahoma. . . . In Oklahoma, you knew. You was raised up that way and you didn't expect anything else. But out here, it was supposed to be different." One of the few positive memories she had was that "the wages was better here" and job opportunities more plentiful. She herself found steady clerical employment and continued to work long after her husband died in 1973. But these moderate gains were never enough to offset the bitter scourge of racism. Acknowledging in 1998 that "we do have a lot that have made it," she felt, nonetheless, that for most blacks, life in Los Angeles was about "making the best of a bad situation."

These markedly different impressions underscore the difficulty of trying to identify one unified African American experience in postwar Los Angeles, let alone in urban America. African American communities have always been diverse in their values, their politics, and their economies. Yet, despite differences, the almost five million African Americans who migrated from the South to northern and western metropolises between World War II and the 1960s shared a common hope for a better life. Moreover, they shared similar conceptions of what the ingredients of this better life would be: they wanted freedom from the fear of Southern racial violence; they wanted to be treated with respect, dignity, and equality in public; they wanted the opportunity to find employment commensurate with their experience and to receive payment equal to that of white co-workers; they wanted to buy their own homes and live in safe neighborhoods; and they wanted their children to receive the same education as white children and become adults in a world where the color of a person's skin was of no consequence.

In their search for this better life, blacks often found urban America to be uneven terrain, bitterly reminiscent of the old South one moment, brilliantly bursting with opportunity the next. Like Gibbs, thousands of African Americans secured stable, unionized, blue-collar employment and purchased their own homes in the postwar decades. Many black women—and later their children—secured white-collar employment, which helped to open up even greater housing opportunities farther outside South Central. Since the 1970s, African Americans who hold white-collar jobs have enjoyed a rising standard of living. According to David M. Grant and colleagues, real earnings for black men increased faster than earnings for white, Asian, or Latino men between 1969 and 1989, although in 1989 African American men still made only 72 cents on the dollar compared with whites, 77 cents on the dollar compared with Asians, and 96 cents on the dollar compared with Latinos. More impressive was the 61 percent growth in black women's real earnings over the same period. Black women's earnings reached parity with white women's earnings in 1979 and exceeded the earnings of Latinas by 22 percent in 1989.[3]

As the incomes of black workers have increased, so too has the geographic mobility of Southern California's black population. While some upwardly mobile blacks stayed on in South Central, an increasing number moved out of the area, out of the city, and even out of the county. During the 1980s, for example, the black population of San Bernardino County increased 132 percent, rising from 47,220 to 109,575.[4] Analyses of the 2000 census reveal that almost one-quarter of the black population of South Central left during the 1990s, while the black populations of Orange, Ventura, Riverside, San Bernardino, and Imperial Counties continued to grow.[5] To be sure, access to distant suburbs did not always guarantee the suburban dream, as numerous racial incidents in Azusa, Lancaster, Palmdale, and Santa Clarita during the mid-1990s clearly demonstrated.[6] But continuing suburbanization has provided a growing stratum of the black population with better housing and educational opportunities than their grandparents, or even their parents, could have attained.

Yet, despite these favorable developments, more disturbing ones have also been evident. The mid-1980s represented the nadir of South Central's already tumultuous history. Fueled primarily by the wave of plant closures, black unemployment and poverty rates rose throughout the decade. An analysis of income distribution in black Los Angeles between 1970 and 1990 revealed the polarizing effects of the decline in low-skilled and semiskilled employment among blacks. David M. Grant and colleagues found that between 1970 and 1990 the number of blacks in the poorest quintile and the wealthiest quintile increased significantly, while the number of blacks in the middle three quintiles decreased by as much as 30 percent.[7]

Nor were the effects of this rising unemployment purely economic. In *When Work Disappears*, William Julius Wilson explored the psychological effects of young people growing up "in an environment that lacks the idea of work as the central experience of adult life." Arguing that the "institutional ghetto" was replaced by a "jobless ghetto" in the 1970s and 1980s, Wilson identified the emergence of "ghetto-related behavior," evidently one of the causes of the unacceptably high rates of drug abuse, criminal activity, and teen pregnancy in the nation's black ghettos.[8] Though, strictly speaking, not a new phenomenon, "ghetto-related behavior" reached crisis levels during the 1980s.[9] Having lost the expectation that they would be part of the normal labor force, many black youths turned to the illegitimate labor force, a dangerous decision after the early 1980s, when crack cocaine first hit the streets of Los Angeles and quickly spread to other major metropolitan areas. In addition to creating thousands of addicts, the crack trade brought an unprecedented wave of violence to South Central and drove thousands of young black people into gangs. As South Central became a virtual war zone, the crack explosion also worsened the already troubled relationship between the community and the Los Angeles Police Department.[10]

Described as a "tinderbox ready to explode," South Central did just that in 1992, following the acquittal of four police officers whose savage beating of intoxicated black motorist Rodney King had been captured on videotape. But the riot of 1992 differed in important ways from the

Watts riot of 1965. Far more destructive and violent than the events of 1965, the 1992 riot—during which sixteen thousand people were arrested—left a sickening toll of fifty-two dead, 2,383 injured, and nearly $1 billion in property damage.[11] And while the targets of the Watts riot of 1965 had been clearly defined—white store owners perceived to be exploiting the poverty and isolation of South Central residents—they were far less obvious in 1992. Many Korean liquor store owners—products of the explosion of immigration in the 1980s—lost their businesses, as did white and black shopkeepers.[12] Most senselessly, Ted Watkins's Watts Labor Community Action Committee complex—which had risen from the ashes of 1965—was burned to the ground, at a loss of $4.2 million, the largest single loss in the city.

In addition, the 1992 riot occurred in a very different South Central. The startling arrest statistics—which showed that more Latinos were arrested than blacks—revealed the extent to which South Central was becoming a Latino, rather than a black, neighborhood. Beginning in the 1980s, this trend accelerated during the subsequent decade, when the Latino population of South Central increased by approximately seventy-eight thousand, whereas the black population decreased by almost seventy thousand. Remarkably, the census of 2000 revealed that the Latino population of South Central (58 percent) finally outnumbered the black population (40 percent).[13]

This dramatic demographic shift marks a sharp reversal of the century-long trend toward black dominance in South Central. Although this shift is partially a function of the expanded housing opportunities for blacks outside South Central—ostensibly a favorable development—black residents of the community view the transformation with considerable trepidation and often resentment. Having been forced by law into segregated communities during the first half of the twentieth century, blacks made the best of their predicament by investing their time, energy, and earnings to improve their neighborhoods, their schools, and their institutions. Many within South Central have retained an unshakable sense of proprietorship over the community, long after the disappearance of de jure housing segregation and long after many of their black neighbors have left. For black residents like Leroy Shepard, the Latin Americanization of South Central has been a bitter pill to swallow. When Shepard migrated to Los Angeles in 1962, he "didn't mind that white folks left. It just gave us more houses." But as blacks have moved out in and more Latinos have moved in, Shepard feels a growing resentment, noting that "it won't be too long before the place is all Mexican." Recognizing that "black people are saying the same thing about Mexicans that the whites said about us," Shepard nonetheless admitted: "Sometimes we get mad at those doggone Mexicans."[14]

If sharing neighborhoods with Latin American newcomers presents challenges for South Central's remaining black residents, sharing historically black institutions may be even more difficult. For example, at St. Philip's Episcopal Church on Twenty-Eighth and Stanford Avenue—founded in 1907 as the second black Episcopal church west of the Mississippi—some longtime black parishioners bemoan the rising presence of Latinos. Sylvia McLymont, the choir director of the church and a St. Philip's parishioner since 1947, noticed that in the mid-1980s, "all of a sudden, it seemed like we were invaded."[15] But with a 30 percent Latino membership by 1999, St. Philip's Episcopal Church and its black parishioners have simply had to accept that times are changing.

Nor have historically black schools been immune to the challenges of Latin American immigration. Odessa Cox's Los Angeles Southwest College has had the largest percentage of black students of any college or university on the West Coast. Although the neighborhood surrounding the Southwest campus on Imperial and Western has become increasingly Latino in the past decade, and although Latinos now make up 20 percent of the student body, some Southwest administrators are reluctant to change the curriculum, fearing that it would derail the school's historic mission to educate blacks in South Central.[16] As the Latin American population explosion continues, dilemmas such as these will undoubtedly become more common in Los Angeles, other sunbelt cities, and urban America in general.

Finally, the Latin Americanization of South Central, coupled with increased Asian immigration citywide, has created new challenges to traditional black politics in Los Angeles. As Raphael Sonenshein explains, the political clout wielded by blacks during the Bradley years has steadily eroded over the past decade. Not only has the coalition between white liberals and African Americans in the city suffered in the wake of the 1992 riot and the infamous O. J. Simpson case, but blacks are also losing their place as the most politically important minority. Although blacks are still politically more organized than Latinos or Asians, there are a growing number of conflicting interests among blacks, Latinos, Asian Americans, and white liberals that threaten black hegemony in the realm of minority politics.[17] As immigration continues, California's African Americans will clearly have to forge creative new political alliances, not an easy task for a group that fought so long to elect its own representatives to address specific community needs.

However, viewed within the larger sweep of twentieth-century history, South Central's demise as a predominantly black community may be as auspicious as it is troublesome. Although it is a frustrating development to many of South Central's longtime African American residents, it will also present their children with an opportunity that they themselves never had: the opportunity to grow up in a racially mixed community. Today, in fact, many pockets of South Central resemble the mixed neighborhoods of pre–World War II Los Angeles, described in chapter 1. No longer forced by law into these neighborhoods, no longer forced to compete only for the few bad jobs available to them before World War II, the predominantly black and Latino youths of these communities now have the potential to develop a level of interracial understanding that could render the apparent challenges of their new coexistence insignificant.

More important, the gradual disappearance of black South Central also suggests that the longstanding "opportunity gap" between blacks and whites is indeed closing. More and more African Americans in California and nationwide are achieving comfortable standards of living in integrated communities and sending their children to integrated schools. Recent figures from the National Urban League show declining unemployment and poverty rates and rising homeownership and white-collar employment rates among blacks nationwide.[18]

But if the importance of race in America is indeed declining, the continued concentration of poverty, joblessness, and crime in many urban black communities proves that it still plays a powerful role in shaping the opportunities and destinies of African Americans. Today's city limits are surely not what they once were. But they still exist, and those who desire complete racial equality in the United States should think seriously about where these limits have come from and what their future may be.

Maps

The Historical Geography of African American Los Angeles

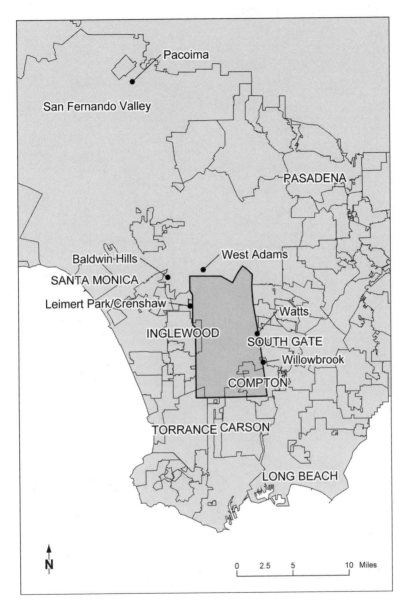

MAP I. South Central and the greater Los Angeles area. Darker shading
indicates South Central. The names of incorporated cities appear in capital
letters. Maps 1–8 created by Michael Bufalino, Center for Geographic Information Science Research, Cal Poly, Pomona. Based on data from Philip
J. Ethington, Anne Marie Kooistra, and Edward De Young, *Los Angeles
County Union Census Tract Data Series, 1940–1990, Version 1.01* (Los Angeles: University of Southern California, 2000).

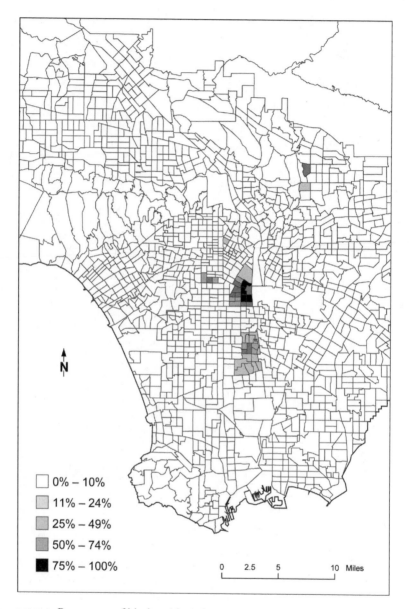

MAP 2. Percentage of black residents by census tract, 1940.

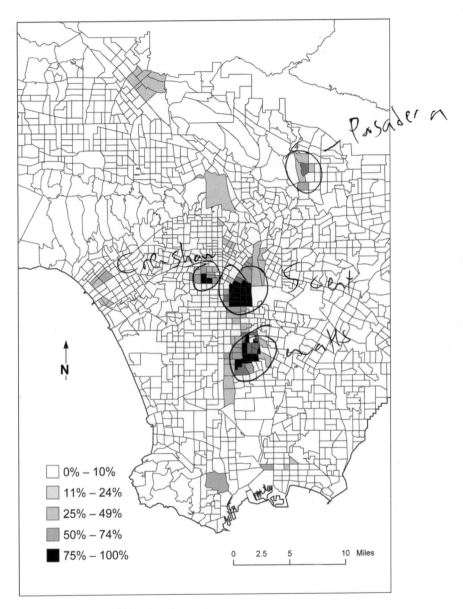

MAP 3. Percentage of black residents by census tract, 1950.

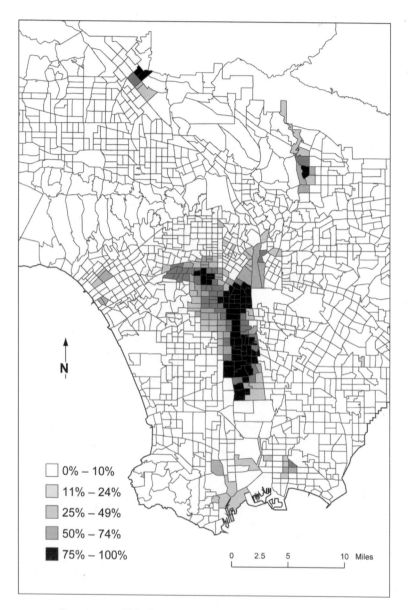

MAP 4. Percentage of black residents by census tract, 1960.

0% – 10%
11% – 24%
25% – 49%
50% – 74%
75% – 100%

N

0   2.5   5   10 Miles

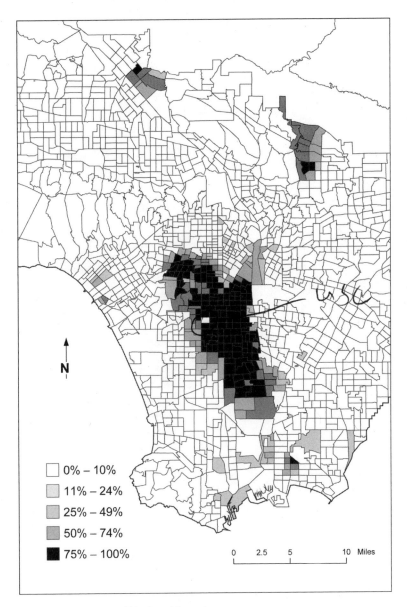

Legend:
- 0% – 10%
- 11% – 24%
- 25% – 49%
- 50% – 74%
- 75% – 100%

0   2.5   5   10   Miles

MAP 5. Percentage of black residents by census tract, 1970.

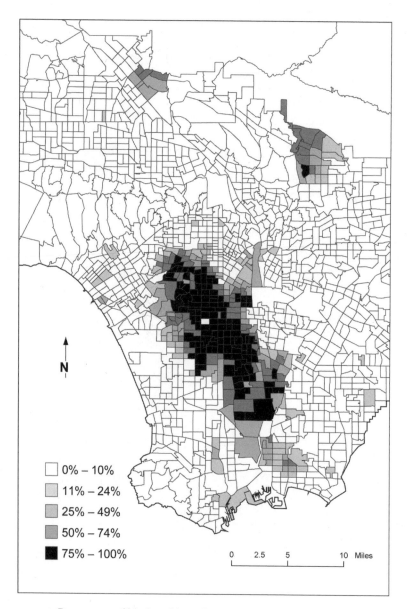

MAP 6. Percentage of black residents by census tract, 1980.

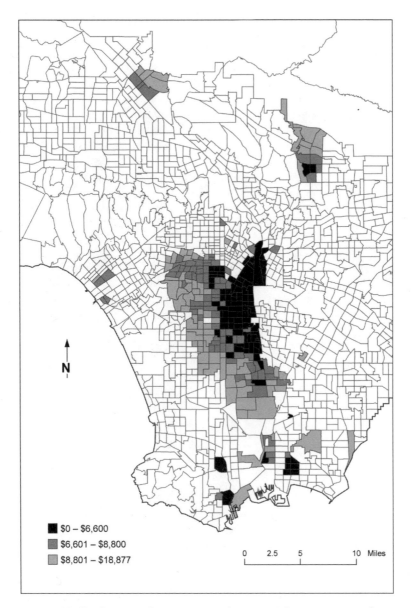

MAP 7. Median income of census tracts where more than 10 percent of residents were black, 1970.

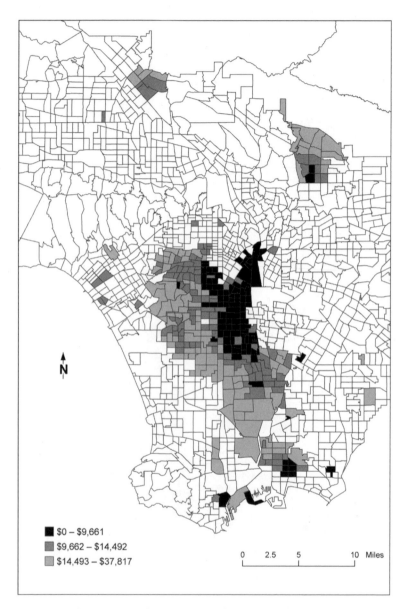

$\blacksquare$ $0 - $9,661

$\blacksquare$ $9,662 - $14,492

$\blacksquare$ $14,493 - $37,817

0   2.5   5   10 Miles

MAP 8. Median income of census tracts where more than 10 percent of residents were black, 1980.

Notes

Introduction

1. The interview with Mary Trimble appeared in the *Daily People's World,* 31 March 1950.

2. U.S. Bureau of the Census, *Historical Statistics of the United States, Colonial Times to 1970* (Washington, D.C.: GPO, 1975), 1:95.

3. In some cities, in fact, a growing proportion of dissatisfied African Americans actually began migrating back to the South. For information on slowing black in-migration and increased black out-migration, see James H. Johnson Jr. and Curtis C. Roseman, "Increasing Black Outmigration from Los Angeles: The Role of Household Dynamics and Kinship Systems," *Annals of the Association of American Geographers* 80 (June 1990):205–222; Curtis C. Roseman and Seong Woo Lee, "Linked and Independent African American Migration from Los Angeles," *Professional Geographer* 50 (May 1998):204–214; Carol Stack, *Call to Home: African Americans Reclaim the Rural South* (New York: Basic Books, 1996).

4. A number of excellent studies have explored the impact of this migration. See Nicholas Lemann, *The Promised Land: The Great Black Migration and How It Changed America* (New York: Knopf, 1991); Albert S. Broussard, *Black San Francisco: The Struggle for Racial Equality in the West, 1900–1954* (Lawrence: University Press of Kansas, 1993); Marilynn S. Johnson, *The Second Gold Rush: Oakland and the East Bay in World War II* (Berkeley: University of California Press, 1993); Quintard Taylor, *The Forging of a Black Community: Seattle's Central District, From 1870 Through the Civil Rights Era* (Seattle: University of Washington Press, 1994); Gretchen Lemke-Santangelo, *Abiding Courage: African American Migrant Women and the East Bay Community* (Chapel Hill: University of North Carolina Press, 1996); Quintard Taylor, *In Search of the Racial Frontier: African Americans in the American West, 1528–1990* (New York: Norton, 1998); Shirley Ann Wilson Moore, *To Place Our Deeds: The African Ameri-

can Community in Richmond, California, 1910–1963 (Berkeley: University of California Press, 2000).

5. The growth rate of the black population in Los Angeles from 1940 to 1970 was 1,096 percent. Black growth rates for other large northern and western cities are as follows: Newark, 661 percent; Detroit, 407 percent; Chicago, 342 percent; New York, 310 percent; Cleveland, 293 percent; Kansas City, 263 percent; St. Louis, 248 percent; Philadelphia, 198 percent; Baltimore, 195 percent; Washington, D.C., 187 percent; Pittsburgh, 174 percent; Cincinnati, 174 percent; Indianapolis, 169 percent. Data drawn from the following U.S. Bureau of the Census publications (all published in Washington, D.C., by the GPO): *Sixteenth Census of the United States: 1940, Population*, vol. 2, *Characteristics of the Population*, pts. 1–7 (1943); *Census of Population: 1950*, vol. 2, *Characteristics of the Population*, pts. 5, 9, 14, 22, 25, 30, 32, 35, 38 (1952); *Census of Population, 1960*, vol. 1, *Characteristics of the Population*, pts. 6, 10, 15, 23, 24, 34, 37, 40 (1963); *Census of Population, 1970*, vol. 1, *Characteristics of the Population*, pts. 6, 10, 15, 24, 27, 32, 34, 37 (1971); *1980 Census of Population*, vol. 1, *Characteristics of the Population*, chap. C, *General Social and Economic Characteristics*, pts. 6, 15, 16, 24, 32–34, 37, 40 (1983); Jesse McKinnon, *The Black Population: 2000* (2001), 7.

6. See, for example, Richard M. Dalfiume, "The 'Forgotten Years' of the Negro Revolution," *Journal of American History* 55 (June 1968):90–106; Dale L. Hiestand, *Economic Growth and Employment Opportunities for Minorities* (New York: Columbia University Press, 1964). For an opposing view, see Karen Tucker Anderson, "Last Hired, First Fired: Black Women Workers During World War II," *Journal of American History* 69 (June 1982):82–97.

7. For an excellent description of this process, see Johnson, *Second Gold Rush*, 60–82.

8. Gunnar Myrdal, *An American Dilemma: The Negro Problem and Modern Democracy* (New York: Harper and Brothers, 1944), 997; St. Clair Drake and Horace R. Cayton, *Black Metropolis: A Study of Negro Life in a Northern City* (1945; rev. ed., Chicago: University of Chicago Press, 1993), 782.

9. "Los Angeles Biennial Report of the Executive Director," 1 March 1943, p. 12, box 19, National Urban League Papers, Library of Congress, Washington, D.C.

10. See, for example, Robert Korstad and Nelson Lichtenstein, "Opportunities Found and Lost: Labor, Radicals, and the Early Civil Rights Movement," *Journal of American History* 75 (December 1988):786–811. The implications of the case studies by Korstad and Lichtenstein are more fully developed in Michael Goldfield, *The Color of Politics: Race and the Mainsprings of American Politics* (New York: The New Press, 1997).

11. Governor's Commission on the Los Angeles Riots, *Violence in the City— An End or a Beginning? A Report* (Los Angeles, 1965), 3.

12. *Report of the National Advisory Commission on Civil Disorders, 1968* (Kerner Commission) (New York: Bantam Books, 1968); Governor's Commission on the Los Angeles Riots, *Violence in the City;* U.S. Department of Labor,

Office of Policy Planning and Research, *The Negro Family: The Case for National Action* (Washington, D.C.: GPO, 1965).

13. One of the earliest articulations of the concept of the "underclass" can be found in E. Franklin Frazier, *The Negro Family in the United States* (Chicago: University of Chicago Press, 1939); see also Lee Rainwater and William L. Yancey, *The Moynihan Report and the Politics of Controversy* (Cambridge: MIT Press, 1967); Ken Auletta, *The Underclass* (New York: Random House, 1982); Christopher Jencks and Paul E. Peterson, eds., *The Urban Underclass* (Washington, D.C.: Brookings Institution, 1991). For an excellent overview of this debate, see Michael B. Katz, "The Urban 'Underclass' as a Metaphor of Social Transformation," in *The "Underclass" Debate: Views from History*, ed. Michael B. Katz (Princeton: Princeton University Press, 1993), 3–23. The most influential and historically minded work on the underclass has been William Julius Wilson, *The Declining Significance of Race: Blacks and Changing American Institutions* (Chicago: University of Chicago Press, 1978).

14. See, for example, Ronald Formisano, *Boston Against Busing: Race, Class, and Ethnicity in the 1960s and 1970s* (Chapel Hill: University of North Carolina Press, 1991); Jonathan Rieder, *Canarsie: The Jews and Italians of Brooklyn Against Liberalism* (Cambridge: Harvard University Press, 1985); Jim Sleeper, *The Closest of Strangers: Liberalism and the Politics of Race in New York* (New York: Norton, 1990); Thomas Byrne Edsall and Mary D. Edsall, *Chain Reaction: The Impact of Race, Rights, and Taxes on American Politics* (New York: Norton, 1991).

15. Douglas S. Massey and Nancy A. Denton, *American Apartheid: Segregation and the Making of the Underclass* (Cambridge: Harvard University Press, 1993); Arnold R. Hirsch, *Making the Second Ghetto: Race and Housing in Chicago, 1940–1960* (Chicago: University of Chicago Press, 1998); Gregory D. Squires et al., *Chicago: Race, Class, and the Response to Urban Decline* (Philadelphia: Temple University Press, 1987); William J. Wilson, "The Urban Underclass in Advanced Industrial Society," in *The New Urban Reality*, ed. Paul E. Peterson (Washington, D.C.: Brookings Institution, 1985), 129–160; William J. Wilson, *The Truly Disadvantaged: The Inner City, the Underclass, and Public Policy* (Chicago: University of Chicago Press, 1987). For analyses of specific aspects of racial inequality in postwar urban America, see Gary Orfield, "Ghettoization and Its Alternatives," in Peterson, *New Urban Reality*, 161–193; John F. Bauman, *Public Housing, Race, and Renewal: Urban Planning in Philadelphia, 1920–1974* (Philadelphia: Temple University Press, 1987); John D. Kasarda, "Urban Change and Minority Opportunities," in Peterson, *New Urban Reality*, 33–67; John D. Kasarda, "The Jobs-Skills Mismatch," *New Perspectives Quarterly* 7 (Fall 1990):34–37. For a superb overview of approaches to postwar black urban history, see Kenneth L. Kusmer, "African Americans in the City Since World War II: From the Industrial to the Post-Industrial Era," *Journal of Urban History* 21 (May 1995):458–504.

16. Thomas J. Sugrue, *The Origins of the Urban Crisis: Race and Inequality in Postwar Detroit* (Princeton: Princeton University Press, 1996). For an im-

portant case study of these issues in the steel industry, see Judith Stein, *Running Steel, Running America: Race, Economic Policy, and the Decline of Liberalism* (Chapel Hill: University of North Carolina Press, 1998). For Stein's comments on Sugrue's work, see Judith Stein, "Opening and Closing Doors," *Labor History* 39 (February 1998):52–57.

17. For a provocative alternative to the black "rust belt" narrative, see Raymond Mohl, "Miami: The Ethnic Cauldron," in *Sunbelt Cities: Politics and Growth Since World War II*, ed. Richard M. Bernard and Bradley R. Rice (Austin: University of Texas Press, 1983), 58–91. Postwar Miami resembled Los Angeles in its diversified economy (with thriving trade, finance, service, tourism, and manufacturing sectors), its large and rapidly growing suburbs, its climate, and its extensive new Latin American immigration. These "sunbelt" characteristics exercised a profound influence over blacks in Miami, as they did in Los Angeles. For example, Mohl finds evidence that competition from Cuban immigrants undercut economic opportunities for both low-skilled black workers and black entrepreneurs ("Miami," 62–64, 87). For an investigation of black progress in multiracial Seattle, see Taylor, *Forging of a Black Community*.

18. Here and throughout, I use the term "Mexican" to refer both to Mexican immigrants and to Mexican Americans. When speaking about either group specifically, I use the term "Mexican immigrants" or "Mexican Americans." For scholarship on the multiracial character of the city, particularly before World War II, see Lawrence B. de Graaf, "Negro Migration to Los Angeles, 1930–1950" (Ph.D. diss., University of California, Los Angeles, 1962); Lawrence B. de Graaf, "The City of Black Angels: Emergence of the Los Angeles Ghetto, 1890–1930," *Pacific Historical Review* 39 (August 1970):323–352; Brian Masaru Hayashi, *"For the Sake of Our Japanese Brethren": Assimilation, Nationalism, and Protestantism Among the Japanese of Los Angeles, 1895–1942* (Stanford: Stanford University Press, 1995); Kevin Allen Leonard, "Years of Hope, Days of Fear: The Impact of World War II on Race Relations in Los Angeles" (Ph.D. diss., University of California, Davis, 1992); John Modell, *The Economics and Politics of Racial Accommodation: The Japanese of Los Angeles, 1900–1942* (Urbana: University of Illinois Press, 1977); Douglas Monroy, *Rebirth: Mexican Los Angeles from the Great Migration to the Great Depression* (Berkeley: University of California Press, 1999); George J. Sánchez, *Becoming Mexican American: Ethnicity, Culture, and Identity in Chicano Los Angeles, 1900–1945* (New York: Oxford University Press, 1993); Max Vorspan and Lloyd P. Gartner, *History of the Jews in Los Angeles* (San Marino, Calif.: Huntington Library, 1970); Mark H. Wild, "A Rumored Congregation: Cross-Cultural Interaction in the Immigrant Neighborhoods of Early Twentieth Century Los Angeles" (Ph.D. diss., University of California, San Diego, 2001).

19. The best overview of this economic restructuring is found in Edward W. Soja, *Postmodern Geographies: The Reassertion of Space in Critical Social Theory* (London: Verso, 1989), 190–221. See also Edward Soja, Rebecca Morales, and Goetz Wolff, "Urban Restructuring: An Analysis of Social and Spatial Change in Los Angeles," *Economic Geography* 59 (1983):195–230.

20. Wilson, *Declining Significance of Race.*

21. Mike Davis, *City of Quartz: Excavating the Future in Los Angeles* (New York: Vintage Books, 1992). For a brief history of this idea, see Carl Abbott, *The Metropolitan Frontier: Cities in the Modern American West* (Tucson: University of Arizona Press, 1993), 123–128, 222–223.

22. See, for example, Abbott, *Metropolitan Frontier;* Gerald D. Nash, *The American West in the Twentieth Century: A Short History of an Urban Oasis* (Englewood Cliffs, N.J.: Prentice-Hall, 1973); Rob Kling, Spencer Olin, and Mark Poster, eds., *Postsuburban California: The Transformation of Orange County Since World War II* (Berkeley: University of California Press, 1991); Bernard and Rice, *Sunbelt Cities; New York Times,* 19 November 1997.

23. *New York Times,* 7 May 2001.

24. Joel Garreau, *Edge City: Life on the New Urban Frontier* (New York: Anchor Books, 1992), 3.

25. Clora Bryant et al., eds., *Central Avenue Sounds: Jazz in Los Angeles* (Berkeley: University of California Press, 1998); Jacqueline Cogdell DjeDje and Eddie Meadows, eds., *California Soul: Music of African Americans in the West* (Berkeley: University of California Press, 1998); Bette Yarbrough Cox, *Central Avenue: Its Rise and Fall, 1890–c. 1955, Including the Musical Renaissance of Black Los Angeles* (Los Angeles: BEEM Publications, 1996). For an interesting foray into black religion in Los Angeles, see Thomas Kilgore and Jini Kilgore Ross, *A Servant's Journey: The Life and Work of Thomas Kilgore* (Valley Forge, Penn.: Judson Press, 1998).

Chapter 1. African Americans in Prewar Los Angeles

Epigraph: The author wishes to thank Crisis Publishing Co., Inc., publisher of the magazine of the National Association for the Advancement of Colored People, for the use of the quotation from W. E. B. Du Bois that opens this chapter, first published in the July 1913 issue of *The Crisis.*

1. Lonnie G. Bunche III, "'The Greatest State for the Negro:' Jefferson L. Edmonds, Black Propagandist of the California Dream," in *Seeking El Dorado: African Americans in California,* ed. Lawrence B. de Graaf, Kevin Mulroy, and Quintard Taylor (Seattle: University of Washington Press, 2001), 129, 135–136, 140.

2. The lynching statistic is taken from Joel Williamson, *A Rage for Order: Black-White Relations in the American South Since Emancipation* (New York: Oxford University Press, 1986), 85.

3. See, for example, Peter Gottlieb, *Making Their Own Way: Southern Blacks' Migration to Pittsburgh, 1916–30* (Urbana: University of Illinois Press, 1987); James R. Grossman, *Land of Hope: Chicago, Black Southerners, and the Great Migration* (Chicago: University of Chicago Press, 1989); Joe William Trotter Jr., ed., *The Great Migration in Historical Perspective: New Dimensions of Race, Class, and Gender* (Bloomington: Indiana University Press, 1991); Nicholas Le-

mann, *The Promised Land: The Great Black Migration and How It Changed America* (New York: Knopf, 1991).

4. Gilbert Osofsky, *Harlem: The Making of a Ghetto — Negro New York, 1890–1930* (New York: Harper and Row, 1968), 11.

5. See, for example, Leonard Pitt, *The Decline of the Californios: A Social History of the Spanish-Speaking Californians, 1846–1890* (Berkeley: University of California Press, 1966); Douglas Monroy, *Thrown Among Strangers: From Indians to Mexicans on the Landscape of Southern California, 1769–1900* (Berkeley: University of California Press, 1990).

6. Robert M. Fogelson, *The Fragmented Metropolis: Los Angeles, 1850–1930* (1967; reprint, with new preface and foreword, Berkeley: University of California Press, 1993), 85–93.

7. Ibid., 72–75.

8. Clark Davis, *Company Men: White-Collar Life and Corporate Cultures in Los Angeles, 1892–1941* (Baltimore: Johns Hopkins University Press, 2000), 74.

9. Douglas Monroy, *Rebirth: Mexican Los Angeles from the Great Migration to the Great Depression* (Berkeley: University of California Press, 1999), 96–106; Charles Wollenberg, "Working on El Traque: The Pacific Electric Strike of 1903," *Pacific Historical Review* 42 (August 1973): 358–369.

10. Monroy, *Rebirth*, 89.

11. Davis, *Company Men*, 72.

12. George J. Sánchez, *Becoming Mexican American: Ethnicity, Culture, and Identity in Chicano Los Angeles, 1900–1945* (New York: Oxford University Press, 1993), 258–259, 253–254.

13. See, for example, Arna Bontemps, *God Sends Sunday* (1931; reprint, New York: AMS Press, 1972), 118.

14. Don L. Hofsommer, *The Southern Pacific, 1901–1985* (College Station: Texas A&M University Press, 1986), 5, 161–163.

15. Augustus F. Hawkins, "Black Leadership in Los Angeles," interview by Clyde Woods, oral history transcript, 1995, Oral History Program, Department of Special Collections, Young Research Library, University of California, Los Angeles, 15, 13–14.

16. Lawrence B. de Graaf and Quintard Taylor, "Introduction: African Americans in California History, California in African American History," in de Graaf, Mulroy, and Taylor, *Seeking El Dorado*, 13–14.

17. Lawrence B. de Graaf, "The City of Black Angels: Emergence of the Los Angeles Ghetto, 1890–1930," *Pacific Historical Review* 39 (August 1970): 323–352.

18. *California Eagle*, 24 November 1933.

19. Edmonds is quoted in Lonnie G. Bunche, "A Past Not Necessarily Prologue," in *Twentieth Century Los Angeles: Power, Promotion, and Social Conflict*, ed. Norman M. Klein and Martin J. Schiesl (Claremont, Calif.: Regina Books, 1990), 102–103.

20. U.S. Bureau of the Census, *Negro Population in the United States, 1790–1915* (New York: Arno Press, 1968), 477, 480.

21. J. Max Bond, "The Negro in Los Angeles" (Ph.D. diss., University of Southern California, 1936), 26–35.

22. Charlotta Bass, *Forty Years: Memoirs from the Pages of a Newspaper* (Los Angeles: California Eagle Press, 1960), 14.

23. First AME Church, Los Angeles, "History of the First AME Church," typescript, ca. 1992; de Graaf and Taylor, "Introduction," 19.

24. Douglas Flamming, "African-Americans and the Politics of Race in Progressive-Era Los Angeles," in *California Progressivism Revisited*, ed. William Deverell and Tom Sitton (Berkeley: University of California Press, 1994), 221.

25. *Los Angeles Times,* 12 February 1909.

26. Bond, "The Negro in Los Angeles," 35.

27. D. O. McGovney, "Racial Residential Segregation by State Court Enforcement of Restrictive Agreement, Covenants, or Conditions in Deeds Is Unconstitutional," *California Law Review* 33 (1945):8.

28. Bass, *Forty Years,* 53–60.

29. David M. Katzman, *Before the Ghetto: Black Detroit in the Nineteenth Century* (Urbana: University of Illinois Press, 1973); Kenneth L. Kusmer, *A Ghetto Takes Shape: Black Cleveland, 1870–1930* (Urbana: University of Illinois Press, 1976); Thomas L. Philpott, *The Slum and the Ghetto: Neighborhood Deterioration and Middle-Class Reform, Chicago, 1880–1930* (New York: Oxford University Press, 1978); Joe William Trotter Jr., *Black Milwaukee: The Making of an Industrial Proletariat, 1915–1945* (Urbana: University of Illinois Press, 1985).

30. See, for example, Commission of Immigration and Housing of California, *A Community Survey Made in Los Angeles City* (San Francisco, 1917). On Boyle Heights, see Sánchez, *Becoming Mexican American,* 74–78. For a fascinating analysis of Los Angeles's multiracial/multiethnic neighborhoods, see Mark H. Wild, "A Rumored Congregation: Cross-Cultural Interaction in the Immigrant Neighborhoods of Early Twentieth Century Los Angeles" (Ph.D. diss., University of California, San Diego, 2001).

31. Karl Holton, "Report for Deterioration Zone Committee, 1940," ca. 1940, box 2, folder 14, Los Angeles Urban League Papers, Department of Special Collections, Young Research Library, University of California, Los Angeles (hereafter cited as LAUL Papers).

32. Watts Writers' Workshop, *From the Ashes: Voices of Watts,* ed. Budd Schulberg (New York: New American Library, 1967), 213.

33. *Liberator,* 23 May 1913; cited in Bunche, "A Past Not Necessarily Prologue," 103.

34. Bunche, "A Past Not Necessarily Prologue," 115.

35. Johnny Otis, *Upside Your Head! Rhythm and Blues on Central Avenue* (Hanover, N.H.: University Press of New England, 1993), 21.

36. Bontemps, *God Sends Sunday,* 118.

37. U.S. Bureau of the Census, *Sixteenth Census of the United States: 1940, Population and Housing: Statistics for Census Tracts, Los Angeles–Long Beach, California* (Washington, D.C.: GPO, 1942), 4–6.

38. Judith Rosenberg Raftery, *Land of Fair Promise: Politics and Reform*

in Los Angeles Schools, 1885–1941 (Stanford: Stanford University Press, 1992), 192, III.

39. Grossman, *Land of Hope,* 254.

40. Ersey O'Brien, interview by author, Los Angeles, 22 April 1998.

41. Charles Mingus, *Beneath the Underdog: His World as Composed by Mingus* (1971; reprint, New York: Penguin Books, 1982), 50.

42. Ibid., 23.

43. Helen Bruce, "Occupations for Negro Women in Los Angeles," 28 May 1933, box 203, folder 2, LAUL Papers.

44. Charles S. Johnson, "Negro Workers in Los Angeles Industries," *Opportunity,* August 1928, 234.

45. *Liberator,* 21 April 1911; cited in Bunche, "A Past Not Necessarily Prologue," 104.

46. "The Race Problem at Swimming Pools," *American City* 47 (August 1932):76–77.

47. Bass, *Forty Years,* 56.

48. Andrew Murray and Chester Murray, interview by author, Los Angeles, 22 October 1997; O'Brien, interview.

49. U.S. Bureau of the Census, *Fifteenth Census of the United States: 1930* (Washington, D.C.: GPO, 1933); specifically, see *Population,* vol. 4, 25–34, 198–202; *Population,* vol. 3, pt. 1, 88–97, and pt. 2, 311–318.

50. See Greg Hise, "Industry and Imaginative Geographies," 30–31; and Mike Davis, "Sunshine and the Open Shop: Ford and Darwin in 1920s Los Angeles," 97, 117; both in *Metropolis in the Making: Los Angeles in the 1920s,* ed. Tom Sitton and William Deverell (Berkeley: University of California Press, 2001).

51. Los Angeles County Chamber of Commerce, *General Industrial Report of Los Angeles County: Advantages of Los Angeles* (Los Angeles: Chamber of Commerce, 1927).

52. Louis B. Perry and Richard S. Perry, *A History of the Los Angeles Labor Movement, 1911–1941* (Berkeley: University of California Press, 1963), vii, 269–270, 440.

53. Los Angeles County Chamber of Commerce, *Facts About Industrial Los Angeles: Nature's Workshop* (Los Angeles: Chamber of Commerce, 1927).

54. *California Eagle,* 30 October 1931.

55. Johnson, "Negro Workers in Los Angeles Industries," 234–235.

56. Charles Johnson, "Industrial Survey of the Negro Population of Los Angeles, California, Made by the Department of Research and Investigations of the National Urban League" (Los Angeles: Urban League, 1926), 20, 23, 28, 32, 55.

57. "Half a Million Workers," *Fortune* 23, March 1941, 98.

58. Johnson, "Industrial Survey of the Negro Population of Los Angeles," 34.

59. William Smith, "The Negro in Hollywood," ca. 1937, report for the Los Angeles Urban League, box 1, folder 32, LAUL Papers.

60. Johnson, "Industrial Survey of the Negro Population of Los Angeles," 20, 23, 28, 32, 55, 70a.

61. James M. Ervin, "The Participation of the Negro in the Community Life of Los Angeles" (M.A. thesis, University of Southern California, 1931), 18.

62. O'Brien, interview.

63. Leonard Leader, *Los Angeles and the Great Depression* (New York: Garland, 1991), 6, 11, 14.

64. Ibid., 169, 173.

65. See, for example, August Meier and Elliot Rudwick, *Black Detroit and the Rise of the UAW* (New York: Oxford University Press, 1979); Robert Korstad and Nelson Lichtenstein, "Opportunities Found and Lost: Labor, Radicals, and the Early Civil Rights Movement," *Journal of American History* 75 (December 1988):786–811; Lizabeth Cohen, *Making a New Deal: Industrial Workers in Chicago, 1919–1939* (New York: Cambridge University Press, 1990); Robin D. G. Kelley, *Hammer and Hoe: Alabama Communists During the Great Depression* (Chapel Hill: University of North Carolina Press, 1990); Rick Halpern and Roger Horowitz, *Meatpackers: An Oral History of Black Packinghouse Workers and Their Struggle for Racial and Economic Equality* (New York: Twayne, 1996); Rick Halpern, *Down on the Killing Floor: Black and White Workers in Chicago's Packinghouses, 1904–1954* (Urbana: University of Illinois Press, 1997).

66. See *Labor Herald,* 3 April 1942, 7 August 1942; John H. M. Laslett and Mary Tyler, *The ILGWU in Los Angeles, 1907–1988* (Inglewood, Calif.: Ten Star Press, 1989), 37–52; Sánchez, *Becoming Mexican American,* 249, 250; Mario T. García, *Memories of Chicano History: The Life and Narrative of Bert Corona* (Berkeley: University of California Press, 1994), 104–105; Luis Leobardo Arroyo, "Chicano Participation in Organized Labor: The CIO in Los Angeles, 1938–1950. An Extended Research Note," *Aztlan* 6 (1975):291.

67. See *California Eagle,* 2 July 1937; Eric Arnesen, *Brotherhoods of Color: Black Railroad Workers and the Struggle for Equality* (Cambridge: Harvard University Press, 2001), 170.

68. For information on integrated union membership, see Johnson, "Industrial Survey of the Negro Population of Los Angeles," 70–72. For information on redcaps, see Alice Burger, "Negro Labor Unions in the Transportation Industry in Los Angeles," 1938, box 2, folder 14, LAUL Papers; and *California Eagle,* 15 September 1933. On porters, see Charles Upton to C. L. Dellums, 9 August 1939; and Bernie Cook to C. L. Dellums, 9 October 1939; both found in box 5, file "Los Angeles, 1939" (incoming letters), Cottrell Laurence Dellums Papers, Bancroft Library, University of California, Berkeley.

69. See Douglas Flamming, "Becoming Democrats: Liberal Politics and the African American Community in Los Angeles, 1930–1965," in de Graaf, Mulroy, and Taylor, *Seeking El Dorado,* 290, 291; Olen Cole Jr., "Black Youth in the National Youth Administration in California, 1935–1943," *Southern California Quarterly* 73 (1991):385–402; *California Eagle,* 15 December 1933; O'Brien, interview.

70. See Bond, "The Negro in Los Angeles," 93, 94, 183.

71. *California Eagle,* 16 November 1934.

72. Ruth Washington, "Black Leadership in Los Angeles," interview by Ran-

ford B. Hopkins, oral history transcript, 1984, Oral History Program, Department of Special Collections, Young Research Library, University of California, Los Angeles, 56–57.

73. *Los Angeles Sentinel,* 26 January 1934.

74. California Communist Party, "Two Decades of Progress: Communist Party, Los Angeles County, 1919–1939," ca. 1940, box 58, "Los Angeles" folder, Dorothy Ray Healey Papers, Department of Special Collections, University Library, California State University, Long Beach; Dorothy Ray Healey and Maurice Isserman, *California Red: A Life in the American Communist Party* (Urbana: University of Illinois Press, 1993), 41.

75. For biographical information, see Pettis Perry, *Pettis Perry . . . Speaks to the Court: Opening Statement to the Court and Jury in the Case of the Sixteen Smith Act Victims in the Trial at Foley Square, New York* (New York: New Century, 1952); see ibid., 5–6, for Perry's comment about his work on the Scottsboro case. See also Dorothy Healey, telephone interview by author, 22 February 1998.

76. In 1933, the John Reed club, an interracial political/artistic club named after the left-wing journalist and Communist Party functionary, who died in 1920, wrote a series of plays depicting the experiences of the Scottsboro Boys. Members of the club performed these plays weekly and set up a space where fellow artists could display their paintings, also depictions of the Scottsboro tragedy. When the red squad heard about the event, police stormed one of the performances. Despite the chaos, the red squad quite systematically destroyed all the paintings. A red squad member—one of the many who were not police officers at all but merely "concerned citizens"—justified the destruction of the paintings because he personally found them to be "coarse, uncouth, destructive, [and] anti-social." See *California Eagle,* 21 July 1933.

77. E. Frederick Anderson, *The Development of Leadership and Organization Building in the Black Community of Los Angeles from 1900 Through World War II* (Saratoga, Calif.: Century Twenty One Publishing, 1980), 87.

78. de Graaf and Taylor, "Introduction," 31.

79. Flamming, "Becoming Democrats," 286–287.

80. "Assembly Bills," box 99, folder 1, Augustus Hawkins Papers, Department of Special Collections, Young Research Library, University of California, Los Angeles.

81. *California Eagle,* 10 November 1960.

82. Bass, *Forty Years,* 111.

Chapter 2. The Great Migration and the Changing Face of Los Angeles

Epigraph: The quotation is from *Southern California: An Island on the Land,* by Carey McWilliams (1946); used by permission of Harold Ober Associates.

1. According to census statistics concerning black in-migrants to Los Ange-

les County in 1950, approximately 30.6 percent of migrants were in their twenties, 18.6 percent were one to thirteen years old, 16.8 percent were in their thirties, 15 percent were in their forties, 10.8 percent were fourteen to nineteen years old, and 8.5 percent were fifty-five and over. See U.S. Bureau of the Census, *Census of Population: 1950*, vol. 4, *Special Reports*, pt. 4, chap. B, *Population Mobility, States, and State Economic Areas* (Washington, D.C.: GPO, 1956), 294.

2. For an interesting look at the implications of black male/white female interaction, see Kevin Boyle, "The Kiss: Racial and Gender Conflict in a 1950s Automobile Factory," *Journal of American History* 84 (September 1997):496–523.

3. Los Angeles Board of Harbor Commissioners, *Annual Report of the Board of Harbor Commissioners of the City of Los Angeles, California, Fiscal Year July 1, 1946 to June 30, 1947* (Los Angeles, 1947), 18–20; "Confidential Report of Conditions in Los Angeles," 1943, Reports of Regional Offices, Region VII, Committee for Congested War Production Areas, Records, National Archives II, College Park, Md.

4. U.S. Bureau of the Census, *Historical Statistics of the United States, Colonial Times to 1970* (Washington, D.C.: GPO, 1975), 1:95; Marcus E. Jones, *Black Migration in the United States with Emphasis on Selected Central Cities* (Saratoga, Calif.: Century Twenty One Publishing, 1980), 35, 37.

5. Migration figures are based on the Integrated Public Use Microdata Series (IPUMS) from 1950, 1960, and 1970, developed by the University of Minnesota's Historical Census Project; see Steven Ruggles, Matthew Sobek, et al., *Integrated Public Use Microdata Series: Version 2.0* (Minneapolis: Historical Census Project, University of Minnesota, 1997). The term "metropolitan area" refers to a county or group of contiguous counties that contained at least one city of at least fifty thousand residents and where more than two-thirds of the workforce was engaged in nonagricultural occupations. See also U.S. Bureau of the Census, *U.S. Census of Population: 1950, Special Reports: Population Mobility—Farm-Nonfarm Movers: 1949 Residence of the Population by Age, Marital Status, Education, Employment Status, Occupation, Family Income, Etc.* (Washington, D.C.: GPO, 1957), 200, 235.

6. The statistics cited in the text are an average of state of birth figures for migrants between 1930 and 1970. Data for 1940 to 1970 is based on Ruggles, Sobek, et al., *Integrated Public Use Microdata Series;* data for 1930 is based on U.S. Bureau of the Census, *Negroes in the United States, 1920–1932* (Washington, D.C.: GPO, 1935), 37–39.

7. See Gretchen Lemke-Santangelo, *Abiding Courage: African American Migrant Women and the East Bay Community* (Chapel Hill: University of North Carolina, 1996); Shirley Anne Wilson Moore, *To Place Our Deeds: The African American Community in Richmond, California, 1910–1963* (Berkeley: University of California Press, 2000); Bette Yarbrough Cox, *Central Avenue: Its Rise and Fall, 1890–c. 1955, Including the Musical Renaissance of Black Los Angeles* (Los Angeles: BEEM Publications, 1996); Jacqueline Cogdell DjeDje and Eddie Meadows, eds., *California Soul: Music of African Americans in the West* (Berkeley: University of California Press, 1998); Marilynn S. Johnson, *The Sec-*

ond Gold Rush: Oakland and the East Bay in World War II (Berkeley: University of California Press, 1993).

8. Bailey Thomson and Patricia L. Meador, *Shreveport: A Photographic Remembrance, 1873–1949* (Baton Rouge: Louisiana State University Press, 1987); Adam Fairclough, *Race and Democracy: The Civil Rights Struggle in Louisiana, 1915–1972* (Athens: University of Georgia Press, 1995), 8.

9. Letter to NAACP Director, 6 December 1937, branch files, group II, box c83, National Association for the Advancement of Colored People, Records, Library of Congress, Washington, D.C. (hereafter cited as NAACP Papers); Reverend M. McElroy Flynn, Shreveport, Louisiana, to William Pickens, Oklahoma, 8 March 1940, branch files, group II, box c73, NAACP Papers.

10. Robin D. G. Kelley, "'We Are Not What We Seem': Rethinking Black Working-Class Opposition in the Jim Crow South," *Journal of American History* 80 (June 1993):75–112.

11. "Some Observations of Little Tokyo," 6 July 1943, Charles Bratt Papers, Southern California Library for Social Studies and Research, Los Angeles.

12. Eric Arnesen, *Waterfront Workers of New Orleans: Race, Class, and Politics, 1863–1923* (New York: Oxford University Press, 1991), 189, 202, 223.

13. Bruce Nelson, "Class and Race in the Crescent City: The ILWU, from San Francisco to New Orleans," in *The CIO's Left-Led Unions,* ed. Steve Rosswurm (New Brunswick, N.J.: Rutgers University Press, 1992), 26, 37.

14. O'Neil Cannon, interview by author, Los Angeles, 10 March 1998. Here and throughout, the term " white-collar workers" refers to those employed in professional, managerial, sales, and clerical occupations, as defined by the U.S. Bureau of the Census.

15. Merl Reed, "The FEPC, the Black Worker, and the Southern Shipyards," *South Atlantic Quarterly* 74 (Autumn 1975):452, 462.

16. *Chicago Defender,* 12 August 1944.

17. Lorenzo J. Greene, "Sidelights on Houston Negroes as Seen by an Associate of Dr. Carter G. Woodson in 1930," in *Black Dixie: Afro-Texan History and Culture in Houston,* ed. Howard Beeth and Cary D. Wintz (College Station: Texas A&M University Press, 1992), 151.

18. Charles Johnson, *Source Material for Patterns of Segregation, Houston, TX* (New York: International Microfilm Press), reel 7.

19. U.S. Bureau of the Census, *Negroes in the United States, 1920–1932,* 277.

20. U.S. Bureau of the Census, *Fifteenth Census of the United States: 1930, Population,* vol. 4 (Washington, D.C.: GPO, 1933), 1593–1596.

21. Greene, "Sidelights on Houston Negroes," 139.

22. Johnson, "Patterns of Segregation and Discrimination, Houston, Texas," *Source Material,* 1–2.

23. Donald Jones to Walter White, 9 April 1943, branch files, box c193, NAACP Papers.

24. "Proposed Program for Houston Branch NAACP," 8 April 1943, branch files, box c193, NAACP Papers.

25. Lulu White to Walter White, 31 July 1943, branch files, box c193, NAACP Papers.

26. *Houston Informer*, 23 January 1943.

27. Reed, "FEPC," 452, 462.

28. *Houston Informer*, 19 December 1942.

29. Ibid., 19 September 1942.

30. Ibid., 23 January 1943.

31. "California Calls," *The Crisis*, May 1942, 153–157.

32. Dorothy W. Baruch, "Sleep Comes Hards," *The Nation*, 27 January 1945, 95–96.

33. *Daily People's World*, 15 June 1944.

34. "Pilgrim House Progress, 1947," box 76, folder ee (7), John Anson Ford Papers, Huntington Library, San Marino, California (hereafter cited as JAF Collection).

35. Andrew Murray and Chester Murray, interview by author, Los Angeles, 22 October 1997.

36. Cannon, interview.

37. Cox, *Central Avenue*, 139.

38. *Daily People's World*, 12 November 1943.

39. John Anson Ford to State Board of Equalization, 14 September 1944, box 76, folder ee (9), JAF Collection.

40. Newspaper clipping from *Eastside Journal*, 3 November 1943, box 76, folder ee (8), JAF Collection.

41. "Little Tokyo Committee, October 8, 1943," box 104, National Urban League Papers, Library of Congress, Washington, D.C. (hereafter cited as NUL Papers).

42. Ford to State Board of Equalization, 14 September 1944, JAF Collection.

43. Elmo William Hollbrook to Governor Earl Warren, 11 May 1947, folder 364:3677, Earl Warren Papers, California State Archives, Sacramento (hereafter cited as EW Papers).

44. William C. Ardery to Governor Earl Warren, 17 July 1946, folder 364:3677, EW Papers.

45. U.S. Department of Justice, Federal Bureau of Investigation, *Uniform Crime Reports* (Washington, D.C.: GPO); see vol. 14, no. 2 (1943), 75; vol. 15, no. 2 (1944), 76; vol. 16, no. 2 (1945), 98; vol. 18, no. 2 (1947), 100; vol. 19, no. 2 (1948), 99; vol. 20, no. 2 (1949), 102; vol. 21, no. 2 (1950), 97.

46. Ardery to Warren, 17 July 1946, EW Papers.

47. Edwina R. Robbins to Governor Earl Warren, 10 January 1944, folder 3640–3677, EW Papers.

48. Alice R. to Governor Earl Warren, ca. 1943, folder 364:3677, EW Papers.

49. Mauricio Mazon, *The Zoot-Suit Riots: The Psychology of Symbolic Annihilation* (Austin: University of Texas Press, 1984), 95–97.

50. Kevin Allen Leonard, "'In the Interests of All Races': African Americans and Interracial Cooperation in Los Angeles During and After World War II," in *Seeking El Dorado: African Americans in California*, ed. Lawrence B. de Graaf,

Kevin Mulroy, and Quintard Taylor (Seattle: University of Washington Press, 2001), 324. See also Kevin Allen Leonard, "Years of Hope, Days of Fear: The Impact of World War II on Race Relations in Los Angeles" (Ph.D. diss., University of California, Davis, 1992).

51. Mazon, *Zoot-Suit Riots*, 78–79; *California Eagle,* 10 June 1943.

52. Thanks to Tom Sitton for drawing my attention to these quotes and this interview transcript. See Loren Miller, interview by Lawrence B. de Graaf, oral history transcript, 3 March and 29 April 1967, Oral History Program, California State University, Fullerton, 36, 44.

53. Cannon, interview.

54. Murray and Murray, interview; Cannon, interview.

55. *California Eagle,* 14 May 1942, 9 July 1942.

56. Roberta Washington to Governor Earl Warren, 21 August 1946, folder 364:3676, EW Papers; "Little Tokyo Committee," NUL Papers.

57. *Chicago Defender,* 23 September 1944.

58. Charlotta Bass, *Forty Years: Memoirs from the Pages of a Newspaper* (Los Angeles: California Eagle Press, 1960), 132.

59. Oliver Carlson, "The Negro Moves West," *Fortnight,* 6 October 1954, 24.

60. *California Eagle,* 16 July 1942.

61. "Los Angeles Urban League, Biennial Report of the Executive Director," 1943, box 104, NUL Papers.

62. Fletcher Bowron to County Board of Supervisors, 6 March 1945, box 76, folder ee (1945), JAF Collection.

63. "Housing Conference in Mayor's Office, 1943," box 76, folder ee (8), JAF Collection..

64. "Report of the 1949 Pilgrim House Vacation Project," box 76, folder ee (9), JAF Collection.

65. Ford to State Board of Equalization, 14 September 1944, JAF Collection.

66. *California Eagle,* 15 November 1945.

67. Chester Himes, *The Quality of Hurt: The Early Years,* vol. 1 of *The Autobiography of Chester Himes* (1972; reprint, New York: Paragon House, 1990), 74.

68. Ibid., 74–75.

69. Chester Himes, *If He Hollers, Let Him Go* (Garden City, N.Y.: Doubleday, Doran, 1945); Chester Himes, *Lonely Crusade* (1947; reprint, New York: Thunder's Mouth Press, 1975).

70. *California Eagle,* 11 December 1941.

71. St. Clair Drake and Horace R. Cayton, *Black Metropolis: A Study of Negro Life in a Northern City* (1945; rev. ed., Chicago: University of Chicago Press, 1993), 755, 767.

Chapter 3. The Window of Opportunity: Black Work in Industrial Los Angeles, 1941–1964

1. The survey is cited in Lawrence B. de Graaf and Quintard Taylor, "Introduction: African Americans in California History, California in African Ameri-

can History," in *Seeking El Dorado: African Americans in California,* ed. Lawrence B. de Graaf, Kevin Mulroy, and Quintard Taylor (Seattle: University of Washington Press, 2001), 33.

2. Southern California Research Council, *The Next Fifteen Years, 1955–1970: The Los Angeles Metropolitan Area* (Los Angeles: SCRC, 1955), 20; Los Angeles Chamber of Commerce, "Business Trends in Southern California, 1963," box 45, Fletcher Bowron Papers, Huntington Library, San Marino, California.

3. In the view of many labor historians, however, the benefits of the era were not without cost. The rise in union membership was accompanied by the bureaucratization of the labor movement. America's largest companies negotiated nationwide contracts with industrial unions in an effort to avoid a repetition of the massive wartime strike waves. The institutionalization of collective bargaining on the national level and organized labor's willingness to enter into "no-strike" contracts alienated many workers, who increasingly felt that union leaders had more in common with business leaders than with the workers they had been chosen to represent. The Taft-Hartley Act of 1947 further limited local union autonomy and rank-and-file militancy by restricting union rights during national emergencies and prohibiting sympathy strikes and other forms of industrial solidarity. Perhaps most restrictive were the anti-communist purges within the CIO, which effectively imposed political orthodoxy on union members. See, for example, Steve Rosswurm, ed., *The CIO's Left-Led Unions* (New Brunswick, N.J.: Rutgers University Press, 1992); George Lipsitz, *Rainbow at Midnight: Labor and Culture in the 1940s* (Urbana: University of Illinois Press, 1994); Martin Glaberman, "Walter Reuther and the Decline of the American Labor Movement," *International Journal of Politics, Culture, and Society* 11 (Fall 1997):73–99.

4. U.S. Bureau of the Census, *Historical Statistics of the United States, Colonial Times to 1970* (Washington, D.C.: GPO, 1975), 1:178.

5. Los Angeles County Chamber of Commerce, *Notes on Business Trends Within Southern California* (Los Angeles: Chamber of Commerce, 1963).

6. U.S. Bureau of the Census, *Historical Statistics of the United States, Colonial Times to 1970,* 1:224.

7. Manufacturing employment in the Los Angeles–Long Beach area skyrocketed from approximately 209,000 workers in 1940 to just over 1 million by 1977, and the number of manufacturing establishments grew from approximately 5,700 to more than 28,000 during the same period; see U.S. Bureau of the Census, *County and City Data Book Consolidated File, County Data, 1947–1977* (Ann Arbor, Mich.: Inter-University Consortium for Political and Social Research, 1980).

8. *Life,* 13 July 1953, 23–29; cited in Greg Hise, *Magnetic Los Angeles: Planning the Twentieth-Century Metropolis* (Baltimore: Johns Hopkins University Press, 1997), 1.

9. *The Crisis,* January 1942.

10. Keith E. Collins, *Black Los Angeles: The Maturing of the Ghetto, 1940–1950* (Saratoga, Calif.: Century Twenty One Publishing, 1980), 63.

11. Merl Reed, *Seedtime for the Modern Civil Rights Movement: The Presi-*

dent's Committee on Fair Employment Practice, 1941–1946 (Baton Rouge: Louisiana State University Press, 1991), 63, 65.

12. *California Eagle,* 16 July 1942.

13. Ibid., 10 June 1943.

14. Herbert Hill, *Black Labor and the American Legal System: Race, Work, and the Law* (1977; reprint, Madison: University of Wisconsin Press, 1985), 313.

15. Kevin A. Leonard, "Federal Power and Racial Politics in Los Angeles During World War II," in *Power and Place in the North American West,* ed. Richard White and John M. Findlay (Seattle: University of Washington Press, 1999), 95.

16. California CIO Council, *Proceedings: Eighth Annual Convention, December 5–9, 1945, San Francisco* (San Francisco: California CIO Council, 1945), 112. See also California CIO Council, *Proceedings: Seventh Annual Convention, August 31-September 3, 1944, Los Angeles* (San Francisco: California CIO Council, 1944), 24–25.

17. *California Eagle,* 12 November 1942.

18. Ibid., 11 April 1946.

19. Walter E. Williams, "ILWU, Local 13," interview by Robert Marshall and Tony Salcido, oral history transcript, 1990, ILWU Local 13 Oral History Project, Urban Archives Center, California State University, Northridge, 27–28.

20. Ibid., 4.

21. There is no consensus about the CIO's record on race. One group of scholars, while acknowledging the organization's shortcomings, generally views the CIO's treatment of African Americans in a favorable light. See, for example, Lizabeth Cohen, *Making a New Deal: Industrial Workers in Chicago, 1919–1939* (New York: Cambridge University Press, 1990); Rick Halpern, *Down on the Killing Floor: Black and White Workers in Chicago's Packinghouses, 1904–1954* (Urbana: University of Illinois Press, 1997); Robert Korstad and Nelson Lichtenstein, "Opportunities Found and Lost: Labor, Radicals, and the Early Civil Rights Movement," *Journal of American History* 75 (December 1988):786–811. Others, however, argue that the CIO's primary role in matters of race was as a defender of white privilege. Most outspoken among this group has been Herbert Hill, a scholar and former labor secretary for the NAACP; see Hill, "Racism Within Organized Labor: A Report of Five Years of the AFL-CIO, 1955–1960," *Journal of Negro Education* 30 (Spring 1961):109–118; and Hill, "Race, Ethnicity, and Organized Labor: The Opposition to Affirmative Action," *New Politics* 1 (1987):33.

22. California CIO Council, *Proceedings: Sixth Annual Convention, October 21–24, 1943, Fresno* (San Francisco: California CIO Council, 1943), 127.

23. *Daily People's World,* 20 November 1943.

24. "Hearings Before the President's Committee on Fair Employment Practice, Western Pipe and Steel Company, Consolidated Steel Corporation (Shipbuilding Division), California Shipbuilding Corporation, Kaiser Corporation, Inc., and Subordinate Lodge 92 and Auxiliary Lodge A-35 of the International Brotherhood of Boiler Makers, Iron Ship Builders and Helpers of America, AFL; Summary, Findings, and Directives in Los Angeles Hearings, Novem-

ber 19 and 20, 1943," *Selected Documents from Records of the Committee on Fair Employment Practice* (Glen Rock, N.J.: Microfilming Corporation of America, 1971) (hereafter cited as FEPC Records), Region 12, reel 103.

25. For information on the AFL's racial policies in other war production centers, see, for instance, Bruce Nelson, "Organized Labor and the Struggle for Black Equality in Mobile During World War II," *Journal of American History* 80 (December 1993):952–988.

26. Hill, *Black Labor,* 186; Reed, *Seedtime,* 267–269.

27. "Resolution Defining Policy with Regard to Colored Members," *Boilermakers Journal* 56 (March 1944):73.

28. Lester Rubin, *The Negro in the Shipbuilding Industry,* Racial Policies of American Industry, Report no. 17, Wharton School of Finance and Commerce (Philadelphia: University of Pennsylvania Press, 1970), 49–50.

29. Walter Williams to FEPC, 14 June 1943, FEPC Records, reel 13.

30. "Testimony of Thomas Madison Doram . . . In and Before the Committee on Fair Employment Practices," 18 November 1943, FEPC Records, reel 106.

31. "Complainants Interviewed on October 14 and 15," 1943, FEPC Records, reel 105.

32. *California Eagle,* 24 February 1943.

33. Ibid., 16 March 1944.

34. Ibid.

35. Chas. J. MacGowan to Western Pipe and Steel, Los Angeles, 15 December 1943, FEPC Records, reel 13.

36. *California Eagle,* 6 January 1944.

37. *James v. Marinship Corp.* (1945), 25 Cal. 2d 726; Charles Wollenberg, "*James vs. Marinship:* Trouble on the New Black Frontier," *California History* 60, no. 3 (Spring 1981):278–279; Hill, *Black Labor,* 204–205.

38. *California Eagle,* 4 January 1945.

39. Ibid., 8 February 1945.

40. Raymond Thompson, Judge of the Superior Court, "The decree should afford the defendants the following alternatives . . . ," 4 June 1945, FEPC Records, reel 103.

41. See Rubin, *The Negro in the Shipbuilding Industry.*

42. On the history of the port at San Pedro, see Robert M. Fogelson, *The Fragmented Metropolis: Los Angeles, 1850–1930* (1967; reprint, with new preface and foreword, Berkeley: University of California Press, 1993), chapter 6.

43. Corky Wilson is quoted in Harvey Schwartz, ed., "Violence, Struggle, and Victory: San Pedro in '34," *Dispatcher,* December 1994, 6.

44. George W. Love, "ILWU, Local 13," interview by Tony Salcido, oral history transcript, 1989, ILWU Local 13 Oral History Project, Urban Archives Center, California State University, Northridge.

45. See "Membership Committee Minutes, 1936–37"; "Membership Committee Minutes, 1937–1941"; and "Membership Committee Minutes, 1941–1942," box 35, pt. 1, International Longshoremen's and Warehousemen's

Union, Local 13, AFL-CIO, Collection, Urban Archives Center, Oviatt Library, California State University, Northridge (hereafter cited as ILWU Local 13 Collection).

46. See, for example, *Dispatcher*, 18 December 1942.

47. Lester Rubin, *The Negro in the Longshore Industry*, Racial Policies of American Industry, Report no. 29, Wharton School of Finance and Commerce (Philadelphia: University of Pennsylvania Press, 1974).

48. Bruce Nelson, "The 'Lords of the Docks' Reconsidered: Race Relations Among West Coast Longshoremen, 1933–1961," in *Waterfront Workers: New Perspectives on Race and Class*, ed. Calvin Winslow (Urbana: University of Illinois Press, 1998), 165.

49. Williams, interview, 2–5.

50. Ibid., 2.

51. Willie McGee, "ILWU, Local 13," interview by Tony Salcido, oral history transcript, 1990, ILWU Local 13 Oral History Project, Urban Archives Center, California State University, Northridge, 11–13.

52. "Regular Meeting Minutes, 18 February 1943," series I: Executive Board and Regular Meeting Minutes, box 3, folder 6, ILWU Local 13 Collection.

53. Bruce Nelson, *Workers on the Waterfront: Seamen, Longshoremen, and Unionism in the 1930s* (Urbana: University of Illinois Press, 1988), 265.

54. For an excellent analysis of the limits of egalitarianism within the ILWU's hiring hall, see Nancy L. Quam-Wickham, "Who Controls the Hiring Hall? The Struggle for Job Control in the ILWU During World War II," in *The CIO's Left-Led Unions*, ed. Steve Rosswurm (New Brunswick, N.J.: Rutgers University Press, 1992), 47–67.

55. "Phoney ID Cards," in "Unemployed 500" folder, box 5, "unprocessed," pt. 3, ILWU Local 13 Collection.

56. Harold Irving Roth to Local Executive Board, ILWU 13, 28 October 1950, "Unemployed 500" folder, box 5, "unprocessed," pt. 3, ILWU Local 13 Collection.

57. Henry Gaitan is quoted in Harvey Schwartz, ed., "A Long Struggle for Equality: The Mexican American Longshoremen of Local 13, 1934–1975," *Dispatcher*, April 1999, 7.

58. Quam-Wickham, "Who Controls the Hiring Hall?" 62.

59. U.S. Bureau of the Census, *Census of Population, 1960*, vol. 1, *Characteristics of the Population*, pt. 6, *California* (Washington, D.C.: GPO, 1963), 706.

60. Author's calculations based on the following documents from the U.S. Bureau of the Census: *Sixteenth Census of the United States: 1940, Population*, vol. 3, *The Labor Force*, pt. 2, *Alabama-Indiana* (Washington, D.C.: GPO, 1943), 244–250; *Census of Population: 1950*, vol. 2, *Characteristics of the Population*, pt. 5, *California* (Washington, D.C.: GPO, 1952), 350–351; *Census of Population, 1960*, vol. 1, *Characteristics of the Population*, pt. 6, *California* (Washington, D.C.: GPO, 1963), 705–707.

61. Scott Greer, "The Participation of Ethnic Minorities in the Labor

Unions of Los Angeles County" (Ph.D. diss., University of California, Los Angeles, 1952), 127.

62. Myrna Donahoe, "Workers' Response to Plant Closures: The Cases of Steel and Auto in Southeast Los Angeles, 1935–1986" (Ph.D. diss., University of California, Irvine, 1987), 111–117.

63. "Los Angeles Urban League Biennial Report," 1943, box 19, National Urban League Papers, Library of Congress, Washington, D.C. (hereafter cited as NUL Papers).

64. Donahoe, "Workers' Response to Plant Closures," 185.

65. For discussion of the role of the Steel Workers Organizing Committee (the precursor to the USWA) in the South, see Robert J. Norrell, "Caste in Steel: Jim Crow Careers in Birmingham, Alabama," *Journal of American History* 73 (December 1986): 669–694; Robin D. G. Kelley, *Hammer and Hoe: Alabama Communists During the Great Depression* (Chapel Hill: University of North Carolina Press, 1990).

66. See "Civil Rights Committee Minutes," box 3, folders 23–26, United Steelworkers of America, Los Angeles, District 38 Papers, Special Collections Division, Pennsylvania State University, University Park, Penn.

67. Donahoe, "Workers' Response to Plant Closures," 185.

68. Los Angeles County Chamber of Commerce, *Industrial Establishments in Los Angeles County Employing 25 or More Persons* (Los Angeles: Chamber of Commerce, 1952).

69. U.S. Bureau of the Census, *Census of Population, 1960*, vol. 1, *Characteristics of the Population*, pt. 6, *California*, 706.

70. U.S. Equal Employment Opportunity Commission, *Job Patterns for Minorities and Women in Private Industry, 1966*, Equal Employment Opportunity Report no. 1 (Washington, D.C.: GPO, 1966), D133–D134. According to census tract figures compiled by Ethington and colleagues, the ratio of Mexicans to blacks in Los Angeles County rose from 1.27:1 in 1960 to 1.7:1 in 1970. Thus, a fair estimate for the middle of the decade would be a ratio of approximately 1.5:1. Therefore, the unequal ratio of Mexicans to blacks—which far exceeded this general population ratio in most industries—cannot be attributed only to the larger size of the Mexican population. See Philip J. Ethington, Anne Marie Kooistra, and Edward De Young, *Los Angeles County Union Census Tract Data Series, 1940–1990, Version 1.01* (Los Angeles: University of Southern California, 2000).

71. For information about the history of ILWU Local 26, I benefited greatly from a conversation (20 February 2001) with Luisa Gratz, president of the local from 1967 to the present.

72. Sylvester Gibbs, interview by author, Los Angeles, 2 June 1998.

73. Southern California Research Council, *The Next Fifteen Years*.

74. *California Eagle*, 11 July 1946.

75. See Becky Nicolaides, *My Blue Heaven: Life and Politics in the Working-Class Suburbs of Los Angeles, 1920–1965* (Chicago: University of Chicago Press, 2002).

76. "Final Report on the Campaign for a Los Angeles Equal Opportunity Ordinance by the Council for Equality in Employment," ca. 1949, box 31, folder 6c (7), John Anson Ford Papers, Huntington Library, San Marino, California (hereafter cited as JAF Collection), n.p.

77. August Meier and Elliot Rudwick, *Black Detroit and the Rise of the UAW* (New York: Oxford University Press, 1979), 52–53. Some scholars suggest that the UAW's legacy of racial tolerance and, particularly, the favorable historical accounts of Walter Reuther are overstated; see, for instance, Glaberman, "Walter Reuther."

78. Nicolaides, *My Blue Heaven,* 252–255.

79. Herbert Northrup, *The Negro in the Rubber Tire Industry,* Racial Policies of American Industry, Report no. 6, Wharton School of Finance and Commerce (Philadelphia: University of Pennsylvania Press, 1969), 88, 54.

80. Ibid., 2.

81. Ibid., 430.

82. Ersey O'Brien, interview by author, Los Angeles, 22 April 1998.

83. See the table titled "Wage and Salary Workers in Manufacturing," in *The Researcher* 11, no. 5 (August-September 1957). (*The Researcher* is published bimonthly by the Los Angeles County Chamber of Commerce.)

84. National Negro Congress, Los Angeles Council, *Jim Crow in National Defense* (Los Angeles: National Negro Congress, 1940), 13.

85. James Wilburn, "Social and Economic Aspects of the Aircraft Industry in Metropolitan Los Angeles During World War II" (Ph.D. diss., University of California, Los Angeles, 1971), 169.

86. U.S. Fair Employment Practices Committee, "Public Hearing in the Matter of Complaints of Discrimination in Employment in Defense Industries," Los Angeles, 20 October 1941, :73, FEPC Records.

87. "Los Angeles Urban League, Biennial Report of the Executive Director," 1943, box 104, NUL Papers.

88. "Los Angeles Urban League Biennial Report," 1943, box 19, NUL Papers.

89. "Los Angeles Urban League, Biennial Report of the Executive Director," 1943, NUL Papers.

90. From the *Lockheed-Vega Star,* 21 November 1941; cited in Wilburn, "Social and Economic Aspects of the Aircraft Industry," 179.

91. *American Aeronaut,* 23 July 1943.

92. "Final Report on the Campaign for a Los Angeles Equal Opportunity Ordinance by the Council for Equality in Employment," ca. 1949, box 31, folder 6c (7), JAF Collection.

93. Wyndham Mortimer, *Organize: My Life as a Union Man!* ed. Leo Fenster (Boston: Beacon Press, 1971), 166.

94. *California Eagle,* 9 October 1941.

95. Herbert Northrup, *The Negro in the Aerospace Industry,* Racial Policies of American Industry, Report no. 2, Wharton School of Finance and Commerce (Philadelphia: University of Pennsylvania Press, 1968), 65.

96. Southern California Research Council, *Help Wanted: Manpower Outlook for the Los Angeles Area in the 1960s* (Los Angeles: SCRC, 1957), 22.

97. Northrup, *The Negro in the Aerospace Industry*, 141.

98. "The Negro Wage Earner and Apprenticeship Training Programs" (New York: NAACP, 1960), box 51, folder 185.2, NAACP West Coast Region Papers, Bancroft Library, Berkeley, California.

99. Greg Hise, "Home Building and Industrial Decentralization in Los Angeles: The Roots of the Postwar Urban Region," *Journal of Urban History* 19 (February 1993): 98, 117.

100. "Report on Adequacy of Services and Facilities in the Los Angeles, California, Area," Reports of Regional Offices, Region VII, Committee for Congested War Production Areas, Records, National Archives II, College Park, Md.

101. U.S. Commission on Civil Rights, *Hearings Held in Los Angeles and San Francisco, January 25–28, 1960* (Washington, D.C.: GPO, 1960), 335.

102. Ibid., 241–242.

103. Author's calculations based on the following documents from the U.S. Bureau of the Census: *Sixteenth Census of the United States: 1940, Population*, vol. 3, *The Labor Force*, pt. 2, *Alabama-Indiana*, 244–250; *Census of Population: 1950*, vol. 2, *Characteristics of the Population*, pt. 5, *California*, 350–351; *Census of Population, 1960*, vol. 1, *Characteristics of the Population*, pt. 6, *California*, 705–707.

104. U.S. Department of Labor, Office of Policy Planning and Research, *The Negro Family: The Case for National Action* (Washington, D.C.: GPO, 1965), 30–36. On responses to the Moynihan report, see Lee Rainwater and William L. Yancey, *The Moynihan Report and the Politics of Controversy* (Cambridge: MIT Press, 1967).

105. California CIO Council, *Proceedings: Eighth Annual Convention*, 156.

106. Los Angeles County Chamber of Commerce, *Our Manpower Problems in the Postwar Years: A Survey and Analysis Showing Where War Industry Employees Want to Live and Work in the Postwar Period* (Los Angeles: Chamber of Commerce, 1944), 1–2.

107. Ruth Milkman, *Gender at Work: The Dynamics of Job Segregation by Sex During World War II* (Urbana: University of Illinois Press, 1987), 126.

108. Author's calculations based on the following documents from the U.S. Bureau of the Census: *Sixteenth Census of the United States: 1940, Population*, vol. 3, *The Labor Force*, pt. 2, *Alabama-Indiana*, 244–250; *Census of Population: 1950*, vol. 2, *Characteristics of the Population*, pt. 5, *California*, 350–351; *Census of Population, 1960*, vol. 1, *Characteristics of the Population*, pt. 6, *California*, 705–707.

109. Arvella Grigsby, interview by author, Los Angeles, 3 June 1998.

110. *Los Angeles Sentinel*, 11 March 1948.

111. Northrup, *The Negro in the Aerospace Industry*, 18.

112. Sherna Berger Gluck, *Rosie the Riveter Revisited: Women, the War, and Social Change* (Boston: Twayne, 1987), 41–42.

113. Mary Cuthbertson, interview by author, Los Angeles, 20 July 1998.

114. Author's calculations based on the following documents from the U.S. Bureau of the Census: *Sixteenth Census of the United States: 1940, Population*, vol. 3, *The Labor Force*, pt. 2, *Alabama-Indiana*, 244–250; *Census of Population: 1950*, vol. 2, *Characteristics of the Population*, pt. 5, *California*, 350–351; *Census of Population, 1960*, vol. 1, *Characteristics of the Population*, pt. 6, *California*, 705–707.

115. Ibid.; U.S. Bureau of the Census, *Census of Population, 1970*, vol. 1, *Characteristics of the Population*, pt. 6, *California* (Washington, D.C.: GPO, 1971), 1579–1581.

116. Paul Bullock, "Negro and Mexican American Experiences in the Labor Market in Los Angeles: A Comparison," statement to Fair Employment Practices Commission, Los Angeles, 17 March 1966.

117. *California Eagle*, 2 August 1929.

118. Greer, "Participation of Ethnic Minorities," 61.

119. Grigsby, interview.

120. U.S. Bureau of the Census, *Census of Population: 1950*, vol. 2, *Characteristics of the Population*, pt. 5, *California*, 126–127; U.S. Bureau of the Census, *Census of Population, 1960*, vol. 1, *Characteristics of the Population*, pt. 6, *California*, 365.

121. U.S. Equal Employment Opportunity Commission, *Job Patterns for Minorities and Women*, D133-D134.

Chapter 4. Race and Housing in Postwar Los Angeles

1. Security-First National Bank of Los Angeles, *Monthly Summary of Business Conditions in Southern California*, 12 January 1949, 10 January 1950, 14 December 1950; U.S. Bureau of the Census, *Census of Housing: 1950*, vol. 1, *General Characteristics*, pt. 2, *Alabama-Georgia* (Washington, D.C.: GPO, 1951), 40, 44.

2. U.S. Commission on Civil Rights, *Hearings Held in Los Angeles and San Francisco, January 25–28, 1960* (Washington, D.C.: GPO, 1960), 203.

3. Here and throughout, the term "South Central" describes a broad area of Los Angeles that became increasingly black between the 1940s and the 1970s. The approximate boundaries of this area were Exposition/Jefferson on the north, Alameda on the east, Rosecrans Boulevard on the south, and Crenshaw on the west. Within this large area were the black neighborhoods of Avalon, South Vermont, and Watts and the unincorporated black communities of Florence, Westmont, and Willowbrook. Unless otherwise stated, neighborhood data in this chapter are drawn from the following U.S. Bureau of the Census sources: *Sixteenth Census of the United States: 1940, Population and Housing, Statistics for Census Tracts, Los Angeles–Long Beach, California* (Washington, D.C.: GPO, 1942); *Census of Population: 1950, Census Tract Statistics, Los Angeles, California, and Adjacent Area, Selected Population and Housing Characteristics* (Washington, D.C.: GPO, 1952); *U.S. Censuses of Population and Housing, 1960,*

Census Tracts, Los Angeles–Long Beach, California, Standard Metropolitan Statistical Area (Washington, D.C.: U.S. Bureau of the Census, 1962) (cited hereafter as *1940 Census Tracts, 1950 Census Tracts,* or *1960 Census Tracts*).

4. See, for example, Douglas S. Massey and Nancy A. Denton, *American Apartheid: Segregation and the Making of the Underclass* (Cambridge: Harvard University Press, 1993); Arnold R. Hirsch, *Making the Second Ghetto: Race and Housing in Chicago, 1940–1960* (Chicago: University of Chicago Press, 1998); Michael B. Katz, ed., *The "Underclass" Debate: Views from History* (Princeton: Princeton University Press, 1993).

5. According to *Ebony* magazine, Little Tokyo in 1946 was a model of interracial harmony; see "The Race War That Flopped: Little Tokyo and Bronzeville Upset Predictions of Negro-Nisei Battle," *Ebony* 1, July 1946, 3–7. See also Kariann Yokota, "From Little Tokyo to Bronzeville and Back: Ethnic Communities in Transition" (M.A. thesis, University of California, Los Angeles, 1996).

6. See Los Angeles City Planning Commission, "Distribution of Negroes: U.S. Census Data, 1940," and "Distribution of Negroes: U.S. Census Data, 1946," box 104, National Urban League Papers, Library of Congress, Washington, D.C.

7. *California Eagle,* 31 December 1945; Carey McWilliams, "The Evolution of Sugar Hill," *Script,* March 1949, 24–35.

8. McWilliams, "Evolution of Sugar Hill," 24.

9. For information about the age of homes in these areas, see *1950 Census Tracts,* 157–158.

10. *California Eagle,* 6 December 1945.

11. *Daily People's World,* 8 June 1946.

12. Donald Wheeldin, interview by author, Pasadena, California, 3 March 1998.

13. Loren Miller, *The Petitioners: The Story of the Supreme Court of the United States and the Negro* (Cleveland: World Publishers, 1967), 321.

14. McWilliams, "Evolution of Sugar Hill," 30.

15. *Los Angeles Sentinel,* 6 May 1948.

16. Lloyd H. Fisher, *The Problem of Violence: Observations on Race Conflict in Los Angeles* (Washington, D.C.: American Council on Race Relations, 1947), 9.

17. U.S. Commission on Civil Rights, *Hearings,* 158. For more discussion of the Los Angeles County Commission on Human Relations, see chapter 5.

18. U.S. Commission on Civil Rights, *Hearings,* 158–159.

19. *Daily People's World,* 7 September 1951, 4 October 1951.

20. *California Eagle,* 20 March 1952.

21. U.S. Commission on Civil Rights, *Hearings,* 159.

22. Ibid. Incidents were reported in Canoga Park, North Hollywood, Palmdale, San Fernando, and Woodland Hills.

23. Mrs. Marguerite Herrick to County Board of Supervisors, 14 August 1946, box 76, folder ee (11), John Anson Ford Papers, Huntington Library, San Marino, California (hereafter cited as JAF Collection).

24. *1940 Census Tracts,* 4, 45, 100, 122; Welfare Planning Council, Los Angeles Region, *A Profile of Four Communities: Compton, Pacoima, Wilmington, Willowbrook* (Los Angeles: Welfare Planning Council, 1962).

25. *1950 Census Tracts,* 9; *1960 Census Tracts,* 36.

26. *California Eagle,* 12 March 1953; *Los Angeles Times,* 21 March 1995.

27. U.S. Commission on Civil Rights, *Hearings,* 230–231.

28. Becky M. Nicolaides, *My Blue Heaven: Life and Politics in the Working-Class Suburbs of Los Angeles, 1920–1965* (Chicago: University of Chicago Press, 2002), 253–255.

29. Mr. Miller to Earl Warren, 9 November 1943, folder 364:3677, Earl Warren Papers, California State Archives, Sacramento (hereafter cited as EW Papers).

30. J. M. Whitley to John Anson Ford, 22 October 1946, box 76, folder ee (11), JAF Collection.

31. William C. Ardery to Earl Warren, 17 July 1946, folder 364:3677, EW Papers.

32. "Memo to the Executive Committee Re: Eagle Rock Chamber of Commerce," 11 September 1948, box 72, folder cc (3), JAF Collection.

33. Glen Jeansonne, *Gerald L. K. Smith, Minister of Hate* (New Haven, Conn.: Yale University Press, 1988), 99.

34. National Association of Real Estate Boards, Committee on Professional Standards, *Interpretations of the Code of Ethics* (Chicago: National Association of Real Estate Boards, 1964), 43.

35. U.S. Commission on Civil Rights, *Hearings,* 160.

36. Miller, *Petitioners,* 326.

37. U.S. Commission on Civil Rights, *Hearings,* 160.

38. *Los Angeles Sentinel,* 16 March 1947.

39. U.S. Commission on Civil Rights, *Hearings,* 217.

40. Ibid., 230.

41. Ibid., 258.

42. John McGovern to Joseph Cassidy, 24 August 1948, box 76, folder ee (13), JAF Collection.

43. See William Warren, "Asian Populations in Los Angeles County" (Ph.D. diss., University of California, Los Angeles, 1985), 14; Leonard Bloom and Ruth Riemer, *Removal and Return: The Socio-Economic Effects of the War on Japanese Americans* (Berkeley: University of California Press, 1949), 67.

44. For an overview of this process, see Karen Brodkin, *How Jews Became White Folks and What That Says About Race in America* (New Brunswick, N.J.: Rutgers University Press, 1998).

45. South Central Area Welfare Planning Council, *Watts Area Study, 1959: A Report* (Los Angeles: South Central Area Welfare Planning Council, 1959), 4.

46. *1940 Census Tracts,* 4–6; *1960 Census Tracts,* 25–161. The Avalon neighborhood was bounded by Main on the west, Jefferson on the north, Alameda on the east, and Slauson on the south.

47. Fisher, *The Problem of Violence,* 11.

48. Duane Robinson, *Chance to Belong: Story of the Los Angeles Youth Project, 1943–1949* (New York: Woman's Press, 1949), 38.

49. See George J. Sánchez, *Becoming Mexican American: Ethnicity, Culture, and Identity in Chicano Los Angeles, 1900–1945* (New York: Oxford University Press, 1993), 74–78.

50. On comparisons between black neighborhoods and East Los Angeles, see Community Redevelopment Agency of the City of Los Angeles, *Los Angeles Community Analysis Program: Socio-Economic Diagnostic Findings for East Los Angeles and Firestone-Willowbrook* (Los Angeles: CRA, 1969). On postwar conditions in East Los Angeles, see Rodolfo F. Acuña, *A Community Under Siege: A Chronicle of Chicanos East of the Los Angeles River, 1945–1975* (Los Angeles: Chicano Studies Research Center, University of California, Los Angeles, 1984).

51. *1960 Census Tracts*, 25–26.

52. On the ratio of Mexicans to blacks in the general population, see note 70 in chapter 3. The disparity between the levels of segregation experienced by Mexicans and blacks in Los Angeles was not unique to that city; see Douglas S. Massey, "Residential Segregation of Spanish Americans in U.S. Urbanized Areas," *Demography* 16 (November 1979): 553–563. Massey also found that socioeconomic factors played a much more important role in determining where Mexicans lived than they did for blacks, whose segregation was based more on race; see Massey, "Effects of Socioeconomic Factors on the Residential Segregation of Blacks and Spanish Americans in U.S. Urbanized Areas," *American Sociological Review* 44 (December 1979): 1015–1022. For an excellent comparison of black and Mexican "exposure" to white neighbors between 1940 and 2000, see Philip J. Ethington, William H. Frey, and Dowell Myers, "The Racial Resegregation of Los Angeles County, 1940–2000," *Race Contours 2000 Study*, Public Research Report no. 2001–04, 12 May 2001, School of Policy, Planning, and Development, University of Southern California, Los Angeles.

53. Alphonso Pinkney, "Prejudice Toward Mexican and Negro Americans: A Comparison," *Phylon* 24 (Winter 1963): 253–259.

54. The nine remaining were against "others," probably Jews; see U.S. Commission on Civil Rights, *Hearings*, 158–159.

55. Charles Gonzalez to Edward Roybal, 15 May 1953, box 10, folder "discrimination #1," Edward Roybal Papers, Department of Special Collections, Young Research Library, University of California, Los Angeles.

56. Anthony Perez to Edward Roybal, 17 August 1950, box 10, folder "discrimination #1," Roybal Papers. The concerns of Gonzalez and Perez were facets of a larger question within the Mexican community and particularly within the Mexican American civil rights movement. As David Gutiérrez suggests, one of the central dilemmas of Mexican ethnic politics has been the extent to which Mexican Americans include Mexican immigrants in their campaigns for equality, a dilemma demonstrated most clearly in the paradoxical policies of the League of United Latin American Citizens; see David G. Gutiérrez, *Walls and Mirrors: Mexican Americans, Mexican Immigrants, and the Politics of Ethnicity* (Berkeley: University of California Press, 1995), 74–87.

57. "Testimony of Mrs. Freita Shaw Johnson," in Governor's Commission on the Los Angeles Riots, *Transcripts, Depositions, Consultants' Reports, and*

Selected Documents of the Governor's Commission on the Los Angeles Riots (Los Angeles, 1966), 9:12.

58. See, for example, U.S. Commission on Civil Rights, *The Mexican American* (Washington, D.C.: GPO, 1968); and U.S. Commission on Civil Rights, *Mexican Americans and the Administration of Justice in the Southwest* (Washington, D.C.: GPO, 1970).

59. *1940 Census Tracts*, 4–6; *1950 Census Tracts*, 9–53; *1960 Census Tracts*, 25–161.

60. Welfare Planning Council, *Profile of Four Communities*, 12.

61. *1960 Census Tracts*, 599, 873.

62. *Los Angeles Sentinel*, 6 March 1947.

63. Ibid., 27 October 1947.

64. Ibid., 23 September 1948, 16 September 1948.

65. Ibid., 18 March 1948.

66. Community Redevelopment Agency, *Los Angeles Community Analysis Program*.

67. Ibid.

68. U.S. Commission on Civil Rights, *Hearings*, 261.

69. Ibid., 60–80.

70. O'Neil Cannon, interview by author, Los Angeles, 10 March 1998.

71. Home Owners' Loan Corporation, "Confidential Report on United States Housing Authority and Federal Housing Administration in Metropolitan Los Angeles," 1939, Federal Home Loan Bank Board Records, RG 195, box 102, National Archives II, College Park, Md.

72. Los Angeles County Housing Authority, *Real Property Inventory and Low Income Housing Area Survey of a Portion of Los Angeles County, California, 1939–1940* (Los Angeles, 1939).

73. Housing Authority of the City of Los Angeles, *Handbook of General Information* (Los Angeles, 1953), 1–35; Housing Authority of the City of Los Angeles, "The Housing Authority of the City of Los Angeles Presents a Solution" (Los Angeles, 1943), 2–3.

74. Hirsch, *Making the Second Ghetto*, 10–11; John F. Bauman, *Public Housing, Race, and Renewal: Urban Planning in Philadelphia, 1920–1974* (Philadelphia: Temple University Press, 1987); Albert S. Broussard, *Black San Francisco: The Struggle for Racial Equality in the West, 1900–1954* (Lawrence: University Press of Kansas, 1993), 176–177; Thomas J. Sugrue, *The Origins of the Urban Crisis: Race and Inequality in Postwar Detroit* (Princeton: Princeton University Press, 1996), esp. chap. 3.

75. Sugrue, *Origins of the Urban Crisis*, 58.

76. Hirsch, *Making the Second Ghetto*, 225.

77. I owe a debt of gratitude to Don Parson, who helped me fill in many important gaps in my understanding of public housing in Los Angeles. See his book, *Making a Better World: Public Housing and the Direction of Modern Los Angeles* (University of Minnesota Press, forthcoming).

78. National Committee Against Discrimination in Housing, *In These Ten*

Cities (Washington, D.C.: National Committee Against Discrimination in Housing, 1951), 7–9.

79. Los Angeles County Commission on Human Relations, "Housing Authority of the City of Los Angeles," December 1947, box 72, folder cc (2), JAF Collection.

80. Karen E. Hudson, *Paul R. Williams, Architect: A Legacy of Style* (New York: Rizzoli, 1993), 25.

81. Andrew Murray and Chester Murray, interview by author, Los Angeles, 22 October 1997.

82. U.S. Commission on Civil Rights, *Hearings,* 23.

83. Ibid.

84. See Mary Randolph to Governor Earl Warren, 7 January 1944, folder 3640:3677, EW Papers; Governor's Commission on the Los Angeles Riots, *Transcripts,* 10:9–10.

85. *Los Angeles Times,* 27 May 1953.

86. Frank Wilkinson, "And Now the Bill Comes Due," *Frontier,* October 1965, 1.

87. South Central Area Welfare Planning Council, *Watts Area Study, 1959,* 7–8.

88. Ivan J. Houston, "Black Leadership in Los Angeles," interview by Ranford B. Hopkins, oral history transcript, 1989, Oral History Program, Department of Special Collections, Young Research Library, University of California, Los Angeles, 181.

89. Ibid., 181–182.

90. "Testimony of Edward Warren," in Governor's Commission on the Los Angeles Riots, *Transcripts,* 14:8.

91. Here, West Adams is defined as the neighborhood bounded by Crenshaw and Western on the west and east, and Washington and Exposition on the north and south.

92. J. Max Bond, "The Negro in Los Angeles" (Ph.D. diss., University of Southern California, 1936), 137.

93. In 1955, African American sociologist E. Franklin Frazier, in his essay "The New Negro Middle Class," identified a trend in the black press to exaggerate the splendor of the middle class: "Although the vast majority of Negroes of middle class status are in reality white collar workers who derive their incomes from salaries, the Negro press represents them as a wealthy group" (*On Race Relations: Selected Writings,* ed. G. Franklin Edwards [Chicago: University of Chicago Press, 1968], 289, 256–266).

94. *1960 Census Tracts,* 576, 585–587.

95. Here, the Leimert Park/Crenshaw area is defined as that area bounded by Crenshaw and Arlington on the west and east, and Exposition and Sixty-Seventh on the north and south.

96. *1960 Census Tracts,* 576, 585–587, 590–591.

97. Rosa Lee Mitchell to the National Association for the Advancement of Colored People, 2 August 1950, branch files, Los Angeles, box c15, National As-

sociation for the Advancement of Colored People, Records, Library of Congress, Washington, D.C.

98. *California Eagle,* 18 February 1954.

99. *Daily People's World,* 16 September 1955.

100. *California Eagle,* 18 February 1954, 25 February 1954, 27 May 1954.

101. Ersey O'Brien, interview by author, Los Angeles, 22 April 1998.

102. Governor's Commission on the Los Angeles Riots, *Transcripts,* 10:9–10.

103. See box 83, folder 19, "Compton 1929–1976," Don Meadows Collection, Special Collections, University of California, Irvine.

104. Sylvester Gibbs, interview by author, Los Angeles, 2 June 1998.

105. Welfare Planning Council, *Compton: A Community in Transition—A Needs and Resources Study of the Compton Area* (Los Angeles: Welfare Planning Council, 1962), 36.

106. *1960 Census Tracts,* 850.

107. *California Eagle,* 13 February 1953.

108. Ibid., 7 May 1953.

109. Ibid., 14 May 1953. For a discussion of similar black militancy prior to the 1960s, see Timothy B. Tyson, "Robert F. Williams, 'Black Power,' and the Roots of the African American Freedom Struggle," *Journal of American History* 85 (September 1998):540–570.

110. *California Eagle,* 23 July 1953.

111. Richard Elman, *Ill-At-Ease in Compton* (New York: Pantheon, 1967), 22.

112. Ibid., 24.

113. Ibid.

114. *1960 Census Tracts,* 577.

115. Mary Cuthbertson, interview by author, Los Angeles, 20 July 1998.

116. Welfare Planning Council, *Compton,* 82.

117. *California Eagle,* 18 June 1953.

118. *New York Times,* 8 June 1969.

119. Gibbs, interview.

120. Karl E. Taeuber and Alma Taeuber, *Negroes in Cities: Residential Segregation and Neighborhood Change* (Chicago: Aldine, 1965), 32–33.

121. *Mirror News,* 2 May 1956.

Chapter 5. Building the Civil Rights Movement in Los Angeles

1. See, for example, Timothy B. Tyson, "Robert F. Williams, 'Black Power,' and the Roots of the African American Freedom Struggle," *Journal of American History* 85 (September 1998):540–570.

2. Donald C. Wheeldin, interview by author, Pasadena, California, 3 March 1998.

3. Andrew Murray and Chester Murray, interview by author, Los Angeles, 22 October 1997.

4. Wheeldin, interview.

5. *Los Angeles Tribune,* 9 August 1955.

6. Los Angeles County Committee on Human Relations, "Report of Executive Secretary, 1949," box 72, folder cc (4); Los Angeles County Committee on Human Relations, "Points and Authorities Relevant to Race Discrimination in Public Housing," ca. 1949, box 72, folder cc (4); both found in the John Anson Ford Papers, Huntington Library, San Marino, California. John Buggs, who served on the committee from 1954 to 1967, went on to direct the U.S. Commission on Civil Rights in 1971, serving under Presidents Nixon, Ford, and Carter. See the obituary for John Allen Buggs, *Los Angeles Times,* 11 March 1995.

7. Lawrence B. de Graaf and Quintard Taylor, "Introduction: African Americans in California History, California in African American History," in *Seeking El Dorado: African Americans in California,* ed. Lawrence B. de Graaf, Kevin Mulroy, and Quintard Taylor (Seattle: University of Washington Press, 2001), 36.

8. The magazine description is cited in Spencer Crump, *Black Riot in Los Angeles: The Story of the Watts Tragedy* (Los Angeles: Trans-Anglo Books, 1966), 27.

9. U.S. Commission on Civil Rights, *Hearings Held in Los Angeles and San Francisco, January 25–28, 1960* (Washington, D.C.: GPO, 1960), 326.

10. Ibid., 326.

11. Ibid., 325.

12. Murray and Murray, interview.

13. *Los Angeles Sentinel,* 15 August 1946.

14. U.S. Commission on Civil Rights, *Hearings,* 296–297.

15. Roberta Washington to Earl Warren, 21 August 1946, folder 3640:3677, Earl Warren Papers, California State Archives, Sacramento.

16. "Questionnaire Regarding Abuse of Police Power: Watts, California," ca. 1950, box 5, file 9, Civil Rights Congress, Los Angeles Chapter Collection, Southern California Library for Social Studies and Research, Los Angeles (hereafter cited as CRC Los Angeles).

17. U.S. Commission on Civil Rights, *Hearings,* 330.

18. J. Gregory Payne and Scott C. Ratzan, *Tom Bradley: The Impossible Dream* (Santa Monica, Calif.: Roundtable Publishing, 1986), 34.

19. U.S. Commission on Civil Rights, *Hearings,* 333.

20. "Statement by Mrs. Laura Burns, Mother of Herman Burns, in her own wards *[sic]*," ca. August 1948, box 1, file "Herman Burns," CRC Los Angeles.

21. "Inquest Held on the Body of Herman M. Burns, Room 102, Hall of Justice," 13 September 1948, box 1, file "Herman Burns," CRC Los Angeles.

22. "Mrs. Velicia Woods, interviewed by Helen Danforth," 22 November 1948; "Anita Callier, interviewed by Helen Danforth," 20 November 1948; both found in box 1, file "Herman Burns," CRC Los Angeles.

23. *California Eagle,* 26 August 1948.

24. *Los Angeles Sentinel,* 16 September 1948.

25. "Statement by Mrs. Laura Burns," CRC Los Angeles.

26. "Justice for Burns Citizens Committee: For Immediate Release," ca. September 1948, box 1, folder 11, CRC Los Angeles.

27. *California Eagle,* 18 August 1949. I can find no evidence that the district attorney ever responded to the request for a grand jury investigation. Because independent commissions such as the Independent Commission on the Los Angeles Police Department, which investigated the LAPD's role in the Rodney King arrest, did not exist at the time, such tragedies were not uncommon.

28. "Los Angeles NAACP News Releases," September 1946, branch files, box c15, National Association for the Advancement of Colored People, Records, Library of Congress, Washington, D.C. (hereafter cited as NAACP Papers).

29. See Maceo Smith to Roy Wilkins, 27 July 1949; Leon Steward to NAACP Board, 16 July 1947; George Thomas to Roy Wilkins, 11 January 1949; all found in branch files, box c15, NAACP Papers.

30. Maceo Smith to Roy Wilkins, 27 July 1949, branch files, box c15, NAACP Papers.

31. *California Eagle,* 30 March 1950.

32. National Association for the Advancement of Colored People, *West Coast Regional Conference, 1947, Report of the Resolutions Committee, San Francisco, March 7–8* (San Francisco: NAACP, 1947).

33. Mary Alton Cutler to Gloster Current, 11 November 1948; cited in Kevin Allen Leonard, "Years of Hope, Days of Fear: The Impact of World War II on Race Relations in Los Angeles" (Ph.D. diss., University of California, Davis, 1992), 340–341.

34. Ibid.

35. "Memorandum to the Committee on Branches from Gloster Current, 8 December 1948," branch files, box c379, NAACP Papers.

36. Dorothy Healey, telephone interview by author, 22 February 1998.

37. See, for example, Harold Cruse, *The Crisis of the Negro Intellectual* (New York: William Morrow, 1967); and Wilson Record, *The Negro and the Communist Party* (1951; reprint, Westport, Conn.: Greenwood Press, 1980).

38. Dorothy Ray Healey and Maurice Isserman, *California Red: A Life in the Communist Party* (Urbana: University of Illinois Press, 1993), 125–126.

39. Ibid., 101.

40. O'Neil Cannon, interview by author, Los Angeles, 10 March 1998.

41. *Daily People's World,* 25 January 1947; *Los Angeles Sentinel,* 23 January 1947.

42. *Daily People's World,* 6 September 1949.

43. Bernard White to Marguerite Robinson, 11 April 1951, box 1, folder 7, CRC Los Angeles. (White changed his name to Brocks after leaving Alabama.)

44. Wheeldin, interview.

45. *California Eagle,* 2 May 1946.

46. Wheeldin, interview.

47. Cannon, interview.

48. Ibid.

49. California State Legislature, Joint Fact-Finding Committee on Un-American Activities in California, *Communist Front Organizations: Fourth Report of the Senate Fact Finding Committee On Un-American Activities, 1948* (Sacramento, 1948), 27, 47, 122.

50. Roger Baldwin to A. A. Heist, 4 April 1946, box 40, folder 5, American Civil Liberties Union of Southern California, Records, Department of Special Collections, Young Research Library, University of California, Los Angeles.

51. *The Crisis,* March 1949, 72.

52. Robert M. Fogelson, *The Fragmented Metropolis: Los Angeles, 1850–1930* (1967; reprint, with new preface and foreword, Berkeley: University of California Press, 1993), 200.

53. U.S. Bureau of the Census, *Census of Population: 1950,* vol. 2, *Characteristics of the Population,* pt. 5, *California* (Washington, D.C.: GPO, 1952), 416.

54. *Daily People's World,* 21 June 1948.

55. Noah Griffin to Clarence Mitchell, 5 May 1948, branch files, box c21, NAACP Papers.

56. *California Eagle,* 10 December 1953.

57. Ibid., 30 December 1954.

58. Ibid., 14 January 1954.

59. Ibid., 15 December 1955.

60. U.S. Bureau of the Census, *Census of Population, 1960,* vol. 1, *Characteristics of the Population,* pt. 6, *California* (Washington, D.C.: GPO, 1963), 706; U.S. Bureau of the Census, *Census of Population, 1970,* vol. 1, *Characteristics of the Population,* pt. 6, *California* (Washington, D.C.: GPO, 1971), 1579–1581.

61. *California Eagle,* 9 December 1954.

62. See, for example, Gary T. Marx, *Protest and Prejudice: A Study of Belief in the Black Community* (New York: Harper and Row, 1967), 94–105.

63. "Los Angeles NAACP Newsletter," March 1956, box 29, NAACP West Coast Region Papers, Bancroft Library, University of California, Berkeley.

64. *California Eagle,* 5 December 1957.

65. Ibid., 16 January 1958.

66. On comparisons of black politics in Los Angeles to politics in other cities, see James Q. Wilson, *Negro Politics: The Search for Leadership* (Glencoe, Ill.: Free Press, 1960); and James Q. Wilson, *The Amateur Democrat: Club Politics in Three Cities* (Chicago: University of Chicago Press, 1962).

67. See "Newsclippings," box 392, Kenneth Hahn Papers, Huntington Library, San Marino, California.

68. Quoted in Katherine Underwood, "Pioneering Minority Representation: Edward Roybal and the Los Angeles City Council, 1949–1962," *Pacific Historical Review* 66 (August 1997):399.

69. *California Eagle,* 24 December 1953.

70. Wilson, *Amateur Democrat,* 283.

71. Wendell Green, "Join the Fight for Our New Frontiers: Two Negro Congressmen, Four Negro Assemblymen: A Position Paper Given to the Interim Committee on Elections and Reapportionment," 17 December 1960, NAACP West Coast Region Papers.

72. *California Eagle,* 25 October 1956.

73. Ibid., 10 November 1960.

74. Ibid., 4 April 1957.

75. Raphael J. Sonenshein, *Politics in Black and White: Race and Power in Los Angeles* (Princeton: Princeton University Press, 1993), 39.

76. Jackson K. Putnam, *Modern California Politics: 1917–1980* (San Francisco: Boyd and Fraser, 1980), 45–58.

77. Mervyn M. Dymally, interview by Elston L. Carr, oral history transcript, 1996–1997, California State Government Oral History Program, Regional Oral History Office, University of California, Berkeley, 145.

78. Ibid., 63–66.

79. Ibid., 53.

80. *Los Angeles Times,* 19 June 1961.

81. *New York Times,* 8 June 1969.

82. See California State Fair Employment Practice Commission, *Annual Report* (Sacramento) for the years 1960 to 1976. For an overview of racial policy during the Pat Brown administration, see Martin Schiesl, "The Struggle for Equality: Racial Reform and Party Politics in California, 1950–1966," *California Politics and Policy* (Los Angeles: Edmund G. "Pat" Brown Institute of Public Affairs, 1997), 55–65.

83. Dymally, interview, 146.

84. Los Angeles City Council Files, Records 114289, 114288, 114290, 114394, Los Angeles City Records Management Division.

85. Michael J. Klarman, "How *Brown* Changed Race Relations: The Backlash Thesis," *Journal of American History* 81 (June 1994):81–118.

86. John Caughey and LaRee Caughey, *To Kill a Child's Spirit: The Tragedy of School Segregation in Los Angeles* (Itasca, Ill.: Peacock, 1973), 2.

87. *Congressional Record,* 92nd Cong., 2d sess., 1972, vol. 118, pt. 1: 564–566.

88. U.S. Commission on Civil Rights, *Hearings,* 77.

89. Ibid., 78.

90. *California Eagle,* 10 December 1953.

91. Ibid., 19 November 1953.

92. Ibid., 24 June 1954.

93. *Jackson v. Pasadena City School District,* 59 Cal. 2d, 876.

94. *California Eagle,* 20 September 1962.

95. Becky M. Nicolaides, *My Blue Heaven: Life and Politics in the Working-Class Suburbs of Los Angeles, 1920–1965* (Chicago: University of Chicago Press, 2002), 288.

96. *California Eagle,* 13 September 1963, 17 September 1963.

97. Built in 1925 in South Central at Forty-Second and Avalon, Wrigley Field was home to the Los Angeles Angels from 1925 through 1961 and the Hollywood Stars from 1926 through 1935. Named after chewing-gum impresario William Wrigley Jr., who owned the Chicago Cubs and the Los Angeles Angels, Los Angeles's Wrigley Field was actually the first ballpark to bear his name. Chicago's Cubs Park was not renamed Wrigley Field until 1926. Los Angeles's Wrigley Field was demolished in 1966. See Lawrence S. Ritter, *Lost Ballparks: A Celebration of Baseball's Legendary Fields* (New York: Viking, 1992), 197–202.

98. Marnesba Tackett, "Black Leadership in Los Angeles," interview by

Michael S. Balter, oral history transcript, 1982 and 1984, Oral History Program, Department of Special Collections, Young Research Library, University of California, Los Angeles, 77.

99. Ibid., 98.

100. *Los Angeles Times,* 31 May 1963.

101. Ibid., 24 June 1963.

102. Tackett, interview, 99.

103. *Los Angeles Times,* 25 June 1963.

104. Ibid., 24 June 1963.

105. *California Eagle,* 8 August 1963.

106. *Los Angeles Times,* 26 June 1963.

107. Ibid., 3 November 1964.

Chapter 6. Black Community Transformation in the 1960s and 1970s

1. John C. Bollens and Grant B. Geyer, *Yorty: Politics of a Constant Candidate* (Pacific Palisades, Calif.: Palisades Publishers, 1973), 149.

2. Governor's Commission on the Los Angeles Riots, *Violence in the City— An End or a Beginning? A Report* (Los Angeles, 1965), 3.

3. Governor's Commission on the Los Angeles Riots, *Transcripts, Depositions, Consultants' Reports, and Selected Documents of the Governor's Commission on the Los Angeles Riots* (Los Angeles, 1966), 1:9–10.

4. *Los Angeles Times,* 31 May 1961, 1 June 1961.

5. *California Eagle,* 11 January 1962.

6. A 1967 Watts survey found that a majority of black residents had an unfavorable evaluation of the black Muslims; see David O. Sears, *Los Angeles Riot Study: Political Attitudes of Los Angeles Negroes* (Los Angeles: Institute of Government and Public Affairs, University of California, Los Angeles, 1967), 18–19.

7. *Los Angeles Times,* 3 September 1961.

8. Frederick Knight, "Justifiable Homicide, Police Brutality, or Governmental Repression?" *Journal of Negro History* 79 (Spring 1994), 186.

9. Hakim A. Jamal, *From the Dead Level: Malcolm X and Me* (London: Andre Deutsch, 1971), 194.

10. Ibid., 197.

11. For detailed accounts of the Watts Riot, see Paul Bullock, ed., *Watts: The Aftermath—An Inside View of the Ghetto by the People of Watts* (New York: Grove Press, 1969); Jerry Cohen and William S. Murray, *Burn, Baby, Burn! The Los Angeles Race Riot, August, 1965* (New York: E. P. Dutton, 1966); Robert Conot, *Rivers of Blood, Years of Darkness: The Unforgettable Classic Account of the Watts Riot* (New York: William Morrow, 1968); Spencer Crump, *Black Riot in Los Angeles: The Story of the Watts Tragedy* (Los Angeles: Trans-Anglo Books, 1966); Gerald Horne, *Fire This Time: The Watts Uprising and the 1960s* (Charlottesville: University Press of Virginia, 1995); David O. Sears and John B.

McConahay, *The Politics of Violence: The New Urban Blacks and the Watts Riot* (Boston: Houghton Mifflin, 1973).

12. Governor's Commission on the Los Angeles Riots, *Violence in the City*, 2.

13. Sears and McConahay, *Politics of Violence*, 28.

14. Governor's Commission on the Los Angeles Riots, *Transcripts*, 12:193.

15. *Long Beach Independent*, 7 December 1965; cited in Horne, *Fire This Time*, 119.

16. See Judith Stein, *Running Steel, Running America: Race, Economic Policy, and the Decline of Liberalism* (Chapel Hill: University of North Carolina Press, 1998); Thomas J. Sugrue, *The Origins of the Urban Crisis: Race and Inequality in Postwar Detroit* (Princeton: Princeton University Press, 1996); William Julius Wilson, *When Work Disappears: The World of the New Urban Poor* (New York: Knopf, 1996).

17. Edward Soja, Rebecca Morales, and Goetz Wolff, "Urban Restructuring: An Analysis of Social and Spatial Change in Los Angeles," *Economic Geography* 59 (1983):195–230.

18. *Los Angeles Sentinel*, 27 August 1964.

19. Youth Opportunities Board of Greater Los Angeles, "The Los Angeles War on Poverty: A Proposal Submitted for Funding to the Office of Economic Opportunity" (Los Angeles, 1964).

20. U.S. Senate Committee on Labor and Public Welfare, *Expand the War on Poverty: Hearings Before the Select Subcommittee on Poverty of the Committee on Labor and Public Welfare*, 89th Cong., 1st sess., 1965, 78.

21. David Zarefsky, *President Johnson's War on Poverty: Rhetoric and History* (Tuscaloosa: University of Alabama Press, 1986), 123.

22. *Los Angeles Sentinel*, 19 August 1965.

23. Robert Alan Bauman, "Race, Class, and Political Power: The Implementation of the War on Poverty in Los Angeles" (Ph.D. diss., University of California, Santa Barbara, 1998), 178–180.

24. Comptroller General of the United States, *Review of the Community Action Program in the Los Angeles Area Under the Economic Opportunity Act* (Washington, D.C.: GPO, 1968), 15.

25. See Bauman, "Race, Class, and Political Power," 206–215.

26. U.S. Department of Labor, Office of Policy Planning and Research, *The Negro Family: The Case for National Action* (Washington, D.C.: GPO, 1965), 19–21, 48.

27. The boundary for the study area from which these figures are drawn also includes parts of East Los Angeles, which my definition of South Central does not. See Joel D. Leidner, "Major Factors in Industrial Location, July 1964," in *Hard-Core Unemployment and Poverty in Los Angeles*, by Institute of Industrial Relations, University of California, Los Angeles (Washington, D.C.: GPO, 1965).

28. Robert Singleton, "Unemployment and Public Transportation in Los Angeles," in Institute of Industrial Relations, *Hard-Core Unemployment and Poverty*.

29. See Barry Bluestone and Bennett Harrison, *The Deindustrialization of America: Plant Closings, Community Abandonment, and the Dismantling of Basic Industry* (New York: Basic Books, 1982); Lloyd Rodwin and Hidehiko Sazanami, eds., *Deindustrialization and Regional Economic Transformation: The Experience of the United States* (Boston: Unwin Hyman, 1989).

30. Myrna Donahoe, "Workers' Response to Plant Closures: The Cases of Steel and Auto in Southeast Los Angeles, 1935–1986" (Ph.D. diss., University of California, Irvine, 1987), 98.

31. Soja, Morales, and Wolff, "Urban Restructuring," 217.

32. Donahoe, "Workers' Response to Plant Closures," 286.

33. Arvella Grigsby, interview by author, Los Angeles, 3 June 1998.

34. California Senate, Committee on Industrial Relations, *In the Matter of Senate Bill 1494, Plant Closures* (Sacramento, 1980), 124–126.

35. Ibid., 214.

36. See, for example, E. Franklin Frazier, *Negro Youth at the Crossways: Their Personality Development in the Middle States* (1940; reprint, New York: Schocken, 1967), 290–292; St. Clair Drake and Horace R. Cayton, *Black Metropolis: A Study of Negro Life in a Northern City* (1945; rev. ed., Chicago: University of Chicago Press, 1993) 202–204; Wilson, *When Work Disappears,* xvii, 51–86.

37. U.S. Bureau of the Census, *1970 Census of Population and Housing: Census Tracts, Los Angeles–Long Beach, Calif., Standard Metropolitan Statistical Area* (Washington, D.C.: GPO, 1972), 569 (hereafter cited as *1970 Census Tracts*).

38. Ibid.

39. *New York Times,* 8 June 1969, 19 January 1972.

40. See Economic and Youth Opportunities Agency, *Distribution of Poor Youths in Los Angeles County by Census Tract and Community Action Agency Area* (Los Angeles, 1967).

41. California Senate, Committee on Industrial Relations, *Senate Bill 1494, Plant Closures,* 212.

42. *Charles H. Bratton, et al v. Bethlehem Steel Corporation and Local 1845 United Steel Workers of America,* 649 F. 2d 658.

43. Ibid.

44. Roger Waldinger, "Who Makes the Beds? Who Washes the Dishes? Black/Immigrant Competition Reassessed," in *Immigrants and Immigration Policy: Individual Skills, Family Ties, and Group Identities,* ed. Harriet Orcutt Duleep and Phanindra V. Wunnava (London: JAI Press, 1996), 265–306; Allen J. Scott, "The Manufacturing Economy: Ethnic and Gender Divisions of Labor," in *Ethnic Los Angeles,* ed. Roger Waldinger and Mehdi Bozorgmehr (New York: Russell Sage Foundation, 1996), 215–246.

45. Watts Labor Community Action Committee, *1967 Report* (Los Angeles, 1967), 1. Biographical information comes from the nonnumbered biographical section in the *1967 Report.*

46. Ibid., 9.

47. *Los Angeles Times,* 17 April 1967.

48. All biographical information about Odessa and Ray Cox comes from Odessa Cox, "Challenging the Status Quo: The Twenty Seven Year Campaign for Southwest Junior College," interview by Malca Chall, typescript, 1978, Regional Oral History Office, Bancroft Library, University of California, Berkeley. See also obituaries for Odessa Cox in the *Los Angeles Sentinel,* 1 November 2001, and in the *Los Angeles Times,* 6 November 2001.

49. Cox, interview, 32.

50. U.S. Bureau of the Census, *Census of Population: 1950,* vol. 2, *Characteristics of the Population,* pt. 5, *California* (Washington: GPO, 1952), 350–351; U.S. Bureau of the Census, *Census of Population, 1970,* vol. 1, *Characteristics of the Population,* pt. 6, *California* (Washington: GPO, 1971), 1579–1581.

51. *New York Times,* 19 January 1972.

52. *1970 Census Tracts,* 66, 72, 201, 207.

53. Ibid., 580–585.

54. Ibid., 533, 558.

55. Los Angeles Department of City Planning, *West Adams–Baldwin Hills–Leimert Socio-Economic Analysis* (Los Angeles, 1971), 69–76.

56. Ibid., 114; Singleton, "Unemployment and Public Transportation."

57. Los Angeles Department of City Planning, *West Adams–Baldwin Hills–Leimert,* 2.

58. Ibid., 24, 26.

59. *The Integrator,* Summer 1968. Issues of this magazine can be found at the Southern California Library for Social Studies and Research, Los Angeles.

60. Edna Bonacich and Robert F. Goodman, *Deadlock in School Desegregation: A Case Study of Inglewood, California* (New York: Praeger, 1972), 47–48.

61. U.S. Bureau of the Census, *1980 Census of Population and Housing: Census Tracts, Los Angeles–Long Beach, Calif., Standard Metropolitan Statistical Area* (Washington, D.C.: GPO, 1982), 445, 472–473.

62. *Los Angeles Times,* 16 June 1976.

63. Governor's Commission on the Los Angeles Riots, *Transcripts,* 9:12–13.

64. *Los Angeles Times,* 16 June 1976.

65. See Lawrence B. de Graaf, "African American Suburbanization in California, 1960 Through 1990," in *Seeking El Dorado: African Americans in California,* ed. Lawrence B. de Graaf, Kevin Mulroy, and Quintard Taylor (Seattle: University of Washington Press, 2001), 415

66. Ibid., 409.

67. *1970 Census Tracts,* 541–545.

68. de Graaf, "African American Suburbanization," 422.

69. Raphael J. Sonenshein, *Politics in Black and White: Race and Power in Los Angeles* (Princeton: Princeton University Press, 1993), 139–175, 159–161.

70. Clarence Y. Lo, *Small Property Versus Big Government: The Social Origins of the Tax Revolt* (Berkeley: University of California Press, 1990), 77. Lo also demonstrates the close relation between the nascent tax revolt movement and the anti-busing movement in Los Angeles County.

71. Thomas Byrne Edsall and Mary D. Edsall, *Chain Reaction: The Impact of*

Race, Rights, and Taxes on American Politics (New York: Norton, 1991), 50–52.

72. Ronald Reagan, "California and the Problem of Government Growth" (1967 inaugural speech), in *A Time for Choosing: The Speeches of Ronald Reagan, 1961–1982,* by Ronald Reagan (Chicago: Regnery Gateway, 1983), 69.

73. David O. Sears and Jack Citrin, *Tax Revolt: Something for Nothing in California* (Cambridge: Harvard University Press, 1982), 100, 239.

74. *Congressional Record,* 92nd Cong., 2d sess., 1972, vol. 118, pt. 1: 565.

75. *Los Angeles Times,* 7 September 1978, 13 September 1978, 17 June 1979.

76. Ibid.

77. Los Angeles Unified School District, "Profile of LAUSD Student Enrollment, 1966–1999," in *Los Angeles Unified School District, Ethnic Survey Report, 1999* (Los Angeles, 1999), 1.

Epilogue

Epigraph: The quotation is from *Devil in a Blue Dress,* by Walter Mosley (copyright © 1990 by Walter Mosley; used by permission of W. W. Norton & Company, Inc.).

1. Sylvester Gibbs, interview by author, Los Angeles, 2 June 1998.

2. Unfortunately, I was not able to obtain permission to use this interviewee's name in this book. However, a transcript of her complete interview, conducted on 11 June 1998 in Los Angeles, is available at the Southern California Library for Social Studies and Research in Los Angeles.

3. David M. Grant, Melvin L. Oliver, and Angela D. James, "African Americans: Social and Economic Bifurcation," in *Ethnic Los Angeles,* ed. Roger Waldinger and Mehdi Bozorgmehr (New York: Russell Sage Foundation, 1996), 382, 384.

4. Ibid., 401.

5. See the following reports by Dowell Myers, both published by the Population Dynamics Research Group, School of Policy, Planning, and Development, University of Southern California, Los Angeles: "Special Report: Demographic and Housing Transitions in South Central Los Angeles, 1990 to 2000" (22 April 2002); and "Actual Percentage Growth for Non-Hispanic Blacks by County, 1990–2000" (April 2001). See also *Los Angeles Times,* 30 March 2001.

6. *Los Angeles Times,* 29 June 1993, 11 July 1996, 13 August 1996, 29 August 2000, 8 December 2001. See also Lawrence B. de Graaf, "African American Suburbanization in California, 1960 Through 1990," in *Seeking El Dorado: African Americans in California,* ed. Lawrence B. de Graaf, Kevin Mulroy, and Quintard Taylor (Seattle: University of Washington Press, 2001), 405–449.

7. Grant, Oliver, and James, "African Americans," 384–385.

8. William Julius Wilson, *When Work Disappears: The World of the New Urban Poor* (New York: Knopf, 1996), 52–53.

9. For earlier observations on this phenomenon, see E. Franklin Frazier, *Negro Youth at the Crossways: Their Personality Development in the Middle States*

(1940; reprint, New York: Schocken, 1967), 290–292; St. Clair Drake and Horace R. Cayton, *Black Metropolis: A Study of Negro Life in a Northern City* (1945; rev. ed., Chicago: University of Chicago Press, 1993), 202–204.

10. Mike Davis, *City of Quartz: Excavating the Future in Los Angeles* (New York: Vintage Books, 1992), 267–322.

11. Lawrence B. de Graaf and Quintard Taylor, "Introduction: African Americans in California History, California in African American History," in de Graaf, Mulroy, and Taylor, *Seeking El Dorado,* 48.

12. On conflict between Koreans and blacks, see Molefi Kete Asante and Eungjun Min, eds., *Socio-Cultural Conflict Between African American and Korean American* (Lanham, Md.: University Press of America, 2000); Edward T. Chang, "New Urban Crisis: Korean-Black Conflicts in Los Angeles" (Ph.D. diss., University of California, Berkeley, 1990); Eui-Young Yu, Earl H. Phillips, and Eun Sik Yang, eds., *Koreans in Los Angeles: Prospects and Promises* (Los Angeles: Center for Korean-American and Korean Studies, California State University, Los Angeles, 1982).

13. Myers, "Special Report," i.

14. *Boston Globe,* 17 September 1997.

15. *Los Angeles Times,* 30 October 1999.

16. Ibid., 23 July 2001.

17. Raphael J. Sonenshein, *Politics in Black and White: Race and Power in Los Angeles* (Princeton: Princeton University Press, 1993), 255–256, esp. chap. 15. See also Raphael J. Sonenshein, "Coalition Building in Los Angeles: The Bradley Years and Beyond," in de Graaf, Mulroy, and Taylor, *Seeking El Dorado,* 450–474.

18. *Los Angeles Times,* 22 July 2002.

Bibliography

Manuscript Collections

American Civil Liberties Union of Southern California. Records. Department of Special Collections, Young Research Library, University of California, Los Angeles.

Charlotta Bass Papers. Southern California Library for Social Studies and Research, Los Angeles.

Fletcher Bowron Papers. Huntington Library, San Marino, California.

Charles Bratt Papers. Southern California Library for Social Studies and Research, Los Angeles.

Civil Rights Congress, Los Angeles Chapter Collection. Southern California Library for Social Studies and Research, Los Angeles.

Committee for Congested War Production Areas. Records. National Archives II, College Park, Md.

Selected Documents from the Records of the Committee on Fair Employment Practice. Microfilm. Glen Rock, N.J.: Microfilming Corporation of America, 1971.

Communist Party of California Papers. Southern California Library for Social Studies and Research, Los Angeles.

Philip Connelly and Los Angeles CIO Industrial Union Council Papers. Department of Special Collections, Young Research Library, University of California, Los Angeles.

Cottrell Laurence Dellums Papers. Bancroft Library, University of California, Berkeley.

Federal Home Loan Bank Board. Records. National Archives II, College Park, Md.

Federal Housing Administration. Records. National Archives II, College Park, Md.

John Anson Ford Papers. Huntington Library, San Marino, California.

Golden State Mutual Life Insurance Company Records. Department of Special Collections, Young Research Library, University of California, Los Angeles.

Kenneth Hahn Papers. Huntington Library, San Marino, California.

Augustus Hawkins Papers. Department of Special Collections, Young Research Library, University of California, Los Angeles.

Dorothy Ray Healey Papers. Department of Special Collections, University Library, California State University, Long Beach.

Independent Progressive Party. Records. Department of Special Collections, Young Research Library, University of California, Los Angeles.

International Association of Machinists, District 727 Papers. Urban Archives Center, Oviatt Library, California State University, Northridge.

International Longshoremen's and Warehousemen's Union, Local 13, AFL-CIO, Collection. Urban Archives Center, Oviatt Library, California State University, Northridge.

Los Angeles City Council Files. Los Angeles City Records Management, Los Angeles.

Los Angeles County Federation of Labor Collection. Urban Archives Center, Oviatt Library, California State University, Northridge.

Los Angeles Urban League Papers. Department of Special Collections, Young Research Library, University of California, Los Angeles.

Carey McWilliams Papers. Department of Special Collections, Young Research Library, University of California, Los Angeles.

Don Meadows Collection. Special Collections, University of California, Irvine.

Wyndham Mortimer Papers. San Francisco Labor Archives and Research Center, San Francisco.

National Association for the Advancement of Colored People. Records. Library of Congress, Washington, D.C.

———. West Coast Region Papers. Bancroft Library, Berkeley, California.

Papers of the National Negro Congress. Microfilm. Frederick, Md.: University Publications of America, 1988.

National Urban League Records. Library of Congress, Washington, D.C.

Public Housing Administration. Records. National Archives II, College Park, Md.

Edward Roybal Papers. Department of Special Collections, Young Research Library, University of California, Los Angeles.

United Steelworkers of America, Los Angeles, District 38 Papers. Special Collections Division, Pennsylvania State University, University Park, Penn.

War Manpower Commission. Records. National Archives II, College Park, Md.

Earl Warren Papers. California State Archives, Sacramento.

Periodicals and Newspapers

American Aeronaut

Boilermakers Journal

California Eagle

Calship Log

The Crisis

Daily People's World

Dispatcher

Houston Informer

The Integrator

Labor Herald

Los Angeles Sentinel

Los Angeles Times

New York Times

Oral Histories

NOTE: Transcripts for all interviews conducted by the author are available in the Southern California Library for Social Studies and Research, Los Angeles.

Beavers, George. "In Quest of Full Citizenship." Interview by Ranford B. Hopkins. Oral history transcript, 1987. Oral History Program, Department of Special Collections, Young Research Library, University of California, Los Angeles.

Cannon, O'Neil. Interview by author. Los Angeles. 10 March 1998.

Cox, Odessa. "Challenging the Status Quo: The Twenty Seven Year Campaign for Southwest Junior College." Interview by Malca Chall. Typescript, 1978. Regional Oral History Office, Bancroft Library, University of California, Berkeley.

Cuthbertson, Mary. Interview by author. Los Angeles. 20 July 1998.

Dymally, Meryvn M. Interview by Elston L. Carr. Oral history transcript, 1996–1997. State Government Oral History Program, Regional Oral History Office, University of California, Berkeley.

Freed, Emil. Self-conducted interview, ca. 1982. Southern California Library for Social Studies and Research, Los Angeles.

Gibbs, Sylvester. Interview by author. Los Angeles. 2 June 1998.

Grigsby, Arvella. Interview by author. Los Angeles. 3 June 1998.

Hawkins, Augustus F. "Black Leadership in Los Angeles." Interview by Clyde Woods. Oral history transcript, 1995. Oral History Program, Department of Special Collections, Young Research Library, University of California, Los Angeles.

Healey, Dorothy. Telephone interview by author. 22 February 1998.

Hendrix, Evelyn. Interview by author. Los Angeles. 11 June 1998.

Hill, John Lamar. "Black Leadership in Los Angeles." Interview by Ranford B.

Hopkins. Oral history transcript, 1992. Oral History Program, Department of Special Collections, Young Research Library, University of California, Los Angeles.

Houston, Ivan J. "Black Leadership in Los Angeles." Interview by Ranford B. Hopkins. Oral history transcript, 1989. Oral History Program, Department of Special Collections, Young Research Library, University of California, Los Angeles.

King, Celes, III. "Black Leadership in Los Angeles." Interview by Bruce M. Tyler. Oral history transcript, 1988. Oral History Program, Department of Special Collections, Young Research Library, University of California, Los Angeles.

Love, George. "ILWU, Local 13." Interview by Tony Salcido. Oral history transcript, 1989. ILWU Local 13 Oral History Project, Urban Archives Center, California State University, Northridge.

Margolis, Ben. "Law and Social Conscience." Interview by Michael S. Balter. Oral history transcript, 1987. Oral History Program, Department of Special Collections, Young Research Library, University of California, Los Angeles.

McGee, Willie. "ILWU, Local 13." Interview by Tony Salcido. Oral history transcript, 1990. ILWU Local 13 Oral History Project, Urban Archives Center, California State University, Northridge.

Miller, Loren. Interview by Lawrence B. de Graaf. Oral history transcript, 3 March and 29 April 1967. Oral History Program, California State University, Fullerton.

Murray, Andrew, and Chester Murray. Interview by author. Los Angeles. 22 October 1997.

O'Brien, Ersey. Interview by author. Los Angeles. 22 April 1998.

Tackett, Marnesba. "Black Leadership in Los Angeles." Interview by Michael S. Balter. Oral history transcript, 1988. Oral History Program, Department of Special Collections, Young Research Library, University of California, Los Angeles.

Washington, Ruth. "Black Leadership in Los Angeles." Interview by Ranford B. Hopkins. Oral history transcript, 1991. Oral History Program, Department of Special Collections, Young Research Library, University of California, Los Angeles.

Wheeldin, Donald C. Interview by author. Pasadena, Calif. 3 March 1998.

Williams, Walter E. "ILWU, Local 13." Interview by Robert Marshall and Tony Salcido. Oral history transcript, 1990. ILWU Local 13 Oral History Project, Urban Archives Center, California State University, Northridge.

General References

Abbott, Carl. *The Metropolitan Frontier: Cities in the Modern American West.* Tucson: University of Arizona Press, 1993.

Acuña, Rodolfo F. *A Community Under Siege: A Chronicle of Chicanos East of the Los Angeles River, 1945–1975.* Los Angeles: Chicano Studies Research Center, University of California, Los Angeles, 1984.

" . . . And 400 New Angels Every Day." *Life,* 13 July 1953, 23–29.

Anderson, E. Frederick. *The Development of Leadership and Organization Building in the Black Community of Los Angeles from 1900 Through World War II.* Saratoga, Calif.: Century Twenty One Publishing, 1980.

Anderson, Karen Tucker. "Last Hired, First Fired: Black Women Workers During World War II." *Journal of American History* 69 (June 1982): 82–97.

Archibald, Katherine. *Wartime Shipyard: A Study in Disunity.* Berkeley: University of California Press, 1947.

Arnesen, Eric. *Brotherhoods of Color: Black Railroad Workers and the Struggle for Equality.* Cambridge: Harvard University Press, 2001.

———. *Waterfront Workers of New Orleans: Race, Class, and Politics, 1863–1923.* New York: Oxford University Press, 1991.

Arroyo, Luis Leobardo. "Chicano Participation in Organized Labor: The CIO in Los Angeles, 1938–1950. An Extended Research Note." *Aztlan* 6 (1975): 277–299.

Asante, Molefi Kete, and Eungjun Min, eds. *Socio-Cultural Conflict Between African American and Korean American.* Lanham, Md.: University Press of America, 2000.

Auletta, Ken. *The Underclass.* New York: Random House, 1982.

Baruch, Dorothy W. "Sleep Comes Hards." *The Nation,* 27 January 1945, 95–96.

Bass, Charlotta. *Forty Years: Memoirs from the Pages of a Newspaper.* Los Angeles: California Eagle Press, 1960.

Bauman, John F. *Public Housing, Race, and Renewal: Urban Planning in Philadelphia, 1920–1974.* Philadelphia: Temple University Press, 1987.

Bauman, Robert Alan. "Race, Class, and Political Power: The Implementation of the War on Poverty in Los Angeles." Ph.D. diss., University of California, Santa Barbara, 1998.

Bean, Frank, and Marta Tienda. *The Hispanic Population of the United States.* New York: Russell Sage Foundation, 1987.

Beasley, Delilah L. *Negro Trail Blazers of California.* New York: Negro Universities Press, 1969.

Beeth, Howard, and Cary D. Wintz, eds. *Black Dixie: Afro-Texan History and Culture in Houston.* College Station: Texas A&M University Press, 1992.

Bernard, Richard M., and Bradley R. Rice, eds. *Sunbelt Cities: Politics and Growth Since World War II.* Austin: University of Texas Press, 1983.

Bernstein, Michael A. *Understanding American Economic Decline.* Cambridge: Cambridge University Press, 1994.

Blackley, Paul R. "Spatial Mismatch in Urban Labor Markets: Evidence from Large US Metropolitan Areas." *Social Science Quarterly* 71 (March 1990): 39–52.

Bloom, Leonard, and Ruth Riemer. *Removal and Return: The Socio-Economic Effects of the War on Japanese Americans.* Berkeley: University of California Press, 1949.

Bluestone, Barry, and Bennett Harrison. *The Deindustrialization of America: Plant Closings, Community Abandonment, and the Dismantling of Basic Industry.* New York: Basic Books, 1982.

Bollens, John C., and Grant B. Geyer. *Yorty: Politics of a Constant Candidate.* Pacific Palisades, Calif.: Palisades Publishers, 1973.

Bonacich, Edna, and Robert F. Goodman. *Deadlock in School Desegregation: A Case Study of Inglewood, California.* New York: Praeger, 1972.

Bond, J. Max. "The Negro in Los Angeles." Ph.D. diss., University of Southern California, 1936.

Bontemps, Arna. *God Sends Sunday.* 1931. Reprint, New York: AMS Press, 1972.

Boyle, Kevin. "The Kiss: Racial and Gender Conflict in a 1950s Automobile Factory." *Journal of American History* 84 (September 1997): 496–523.

Branch, Taylor. *Parting the Waters: America in the King Years, 1954–1963.* New York: Simon and Schuster, 1988.

Brodkin, Karen. *How Jews Became White Folks and What That Says About Race in America.* New Brunswick, N.J.: Rutgers University Press, 1998.

Broome, Homer F., Jr. *LAPD's Black History.* Norwalk, Calif.: Stockton Trade Press, 1977.

Broussard, Albert S. *Black San Francisco: The Struggle for Racial Equality in the West, 1900–1954.* Lawrence: University Press of Kansas, 1993.

Bryant, Clora, et al., eds. *Central Avenue Sounds: Jazz in Los Angeles.* Berkeley: University of California Press, 1998.

Bullock, Paul, ed. *Watts: The Aftermath—An Inside View of the Ghetto by the People of Watts.* New York: Grove Press, 1969.

Bunche, Lonnie G., III. "'The Greatest State for the Negro:' Jefferson L. Edmonds, Black Propagandist of the California Dream." In *Seeking El Dorado: African Americans in California,* edited by Lawrence B. de Graaf, Kevin Mulroy, and Quintard Taylor, 129–148. Seattle: University of Washington Press, 2001.

———. "A Past Not Necessarily Prologue." In *Twentieth Century Los Angeles: Power, Promotion, and Social Conflict,* edited by Norman M. Klein and Martin J. Schiesl, 101–130. Claremont, Calif.: Regina Books, 1990.

Burt, Kenneth C. "Latino Empowerment in Los Angeles: Postwar Dreams and Cold War Fears, 1948–1952." *Labor's Heritage* 8 (Summer 1996): 4–25.

"California Calls." *The Crisis,* May 1942, 153–157.

California CIO Council. *Proceedings: Sixth Annual Convention, October 21–24, 1943, Fresno.* San Francisco: California CIO Council, 1943.

———. *Proceedings: Seventh Annual Convention, August 31–September 3, 1944, Los Angeles.* San Francisco: California CIO Council, 1944.

———. *Proceedings: Eighth Annual Convention, December 5–9, 1945, San Francisco.* San Francisco: California CIO Council, 1945.

California Department of Industrial Relations. *Employment and Earnings in the California Aircraft Industry, 1940–1953.* San Francisco, 1954.

———. *Employment, Hours, and Earnings in the California Apparel Industry, 1949–1953.* San Francisco, 1953.

———. *Employment, Hours, and Earnings in Electrical Machinery, Equipment, and Supplies Manufacturing Industry.* San Francisco, 1955.

California Senate, Committee on Industrial Relations. *In the Matter of Senate Bill 1494, Plant Closures.* Sacramento, 1980.

California State Fair Employment Practice Commission. *Annual Report.* Sacramento, various, 1960–1976.

California State Legislature, Joint Fact-Finding Committee on Un-American Activities in California. *Communist Front Organizations: Fourth Report of the Senate Fact Finding Committee on Un-American Activities, 1948.* Sacramento, 1948.

Cantor, Milton, ed. *Black Labor in America.* Westport, Conn.: Negro Universities Press, 1969.

Carlson, Oliver. "The Negro Moves West," *Fortnight,* 6 October 1954, 22–26.

Caughey, John, and LaRee Caughey. *To Kill a Child's Spirit: The Tragedy of School Segregation in Los Angeles.* Itasca, Ill.: Peacock, 1973.

Chafe, William. *The American Woman: Her Changing Social, Economic, and Political Roles, 1920–1970.* New York: Oxford University Press, 1972.

Chang, Edward T. "New Urban Crisis: Korean-Black Conflicts in Los Angeles." Ph.D. diss., University of California, Berkeley, 1990.

Cohen, Jerry, and William S. Murray. *Burn, Baby, Burn! The Los Angeles Race Riot, August, 1965.* New York: E. P. Dutton, 1966.

Cohen, Lizabeth. *Making a New Deal: Industrial Workers in Chicago, 1919–1939.* New York: Cambridge University Press, 1990.

Cole, Olen, Jr. "Black Youth in the National Youth Administration in California, 1935–1943." *Southern California Quarterly* 73 (1991): 385–402.

Collins, Keith E. *Black Los Angeles: The Maturing of the Ghetto, 1940–1950.* Saratoga, Calif: Century Twenty One Publishing, 1980.

Commission of Immigration and Housing of California. *A Community Survey Made in Los Angeles City.* San Francisco, 1917.

Community Redevelopment Agency of the City of Los Angeles. *Los Angeles Community Analysis Program: Socio-Economic Diagnostic Findings for East Los Angeles and Firestone-Willowbrook.* Los Angeles: CRA, 1969.

Comptroller General of the United States. *Review of the Community Action Program in the Los Angeles Area Under the Economic Opportunity Act.* Washington, D.C.: GPO, 1968.

Congressional Record. 92nd Cong., 2d sess., 1972, vol. 118, pt. 1: 564–566.

Conot, Robert. *Rivers of Blood, Years of Darkness: The Unforgettable Classic Account of the Watts Riot.* New York: William Morrow, 1968.

Cox, Bette Yarbrough. *Central Avenue: Its Rise and Fall, 1890–c. 1955, Including the Musical Renaissance of Black Los Angeles.* Los Angeles: BEEM Publications, 1996.

Crump, Spencer. *Black Riot in Los Angeles: The Story of the Watts Tragedy.* Los Angeles: Trans-Anglo Books, 1966.

Cruse, Harold. *The Crisis of the Negro Intellectual.* New York: William Morrow, 1967.

Dalfiume, Richard M. "The 'Forgotten Years' of the Negro Revolution." *Journal of American History* 55 (June 1968): 90–106.

Daniel, Cletus. *Chicano Workers and the Politics of Fairness: The FEPC in the Southwest, 1941–1945.* Austin: University of Texas Press, 1991.

Daniels, Douglas Henry. *Pioneer Urbanites: A Social and Cultural History of Black San Francisco.* Philadelphia: Temple University Press, 1980.

Davis, Clark. *Company Men: White-Collar Life and Corporate Cultures in Los Angeles, 1892–1941.* Baltimore: Johns Hopkins University Press, 2000.

Davis, Mike. *City of Quartz: Excavating the Future in Los Angeles.* New York: Vintage Books, 1992.

———. "Sunshine and the Open Shop: Ford and Darwin in 1920s Los Angeles." In *Metropolis in the Making: Los Angeles in the 1920s,* edited by Tom Sitton and William Deverell, 96–122. Berkeley: University of California Press, 2001.

de Graaf, Lawrence B. "African American Suburbanization in California, 1960 Through 1990." In *Seeking El Dorado: African Americans in California,* edited by Lawrence B. de Graaf, Kevin Mulroy, and Quintard Taylor, 405–449. Seattle: University of Washington Press, 2001.

———. "The City of Black Angels: Emergence of the Los Angeles Ghetto, 1890–1930." *Pacific Historical Review* 39 (August 1970): 323–352.

———. "Negro Migration to Los Angeles, 1930–1950." Ph.D. diss., University of California, Los Angeles, 1962.

de Graaf, Lawrence B., Kevin Mulroy, and Quintard Taylor. *Seeking El Dorado: African Americans in California.* Seattle: University of Washington Press, 2001.

de Graaf, Lawrence B., and Quintard Taylor. "Introduction: African Americans in California History, California in African American History." In *Seeking El Dorado: African Americans in California,* edited by Lawrence B. de Graaf, Kevin Mulroy, and Quintard Taylor, 3–69. Seattle: University of Washington Press, 2001.

Deverell, William, and Tom Sitton, eds. *California Progressivism Revisited.* Berkeley: University of California Press, 1994.

Dittmer, John. *Local People: The Struggle for Civil Rights in Mississippi.* Urbana: University of Illinois Press, 1994.

DjeDje, Jacqueline Cogdell, and Eddie S. Meadows, eds. *California Soul: Music of African Americans in the West.* Berkeley: University of California Press, 1998.

Donahoe, Myrna Cherkoss. *Resolving Discriminatory Practices Against Minorities and Women in Steel and Auto: Los Angeles, California, 1936–1982.* Los Angeles: Center for Labor Research and Education, Institute of Industrial Relations, University of California, Los Angeles, 1991.

———. "Workers' Response to Plant Closures: The Cases of Steel and Auto in Southeast Los Angeles, 1935–1986." Ph.D. diss., University of California, Irvine, 1987.

Drake, St. Clair, and Horace R. Cayton. *Black Metropolis: A Study of Negro Life in a Northern City.* 1945. Rev. ed., Chicago: University of Chicago Press, 1993.

Duleep, Harriet Orcutt, and Phanindra V. Wunnava, eds. *Immigrants and Immigration Policy: Individual Skills, Family Ties, and Group Identities.* London: JAI Press, 1996.

Economic and Youth Opportunities Agency. *Distribution of Poor Youths in Los Angeles County by Census Tract and Community Action Agency Area.* Los Angeles: EYOA, 1967.

Edsall, Thomas Byrne, and Mary D. Edsall. *Chain Reaction: The Impact of Race, Rights, and Taxes on American Politics.* New York: Norton, 1991.

Elman, Richard. *Ill-At-Ease in Compton.* New York: Pantheon, 1967.

Ervin, James M. "The Participation of the Negro in the Community Life of Los Angeles." M.A. thesis, University of Southern California, 1931.

Ethington, Philip J., William H. Frey, and Dowell Myers. "The Racial Resegregation of Los Angeles County, 1940–2000." *Race Contours 2000 Study,* Public Research Report no. 2001–04, 12 May 2001. School of Policy, Planning, and Development, University of Southern California, Los Angeles.

Ethington, Philip J., Anne Marie Kooistra, and Edward De Young. *Los Angeles County Union Census Tract Data Series, 1940–1990. Version 1.01.* Los Angeles: University of Southern California, 2000.

Fairclough, Adam. *Race and Democracy: The Civil Rights Struggle in Louisiana, 1915–1972.* Athens: University of Georgia Press, 1995.

Federal Home Loan Bank. *The Federal Home Loan Bank System, 1932–1952.* Washington, D.C.: GPO, 1952.

Federal Housing Administration. *Annual Report.* Washington, D.C.: GPO, various, 1934–1958.

First AME Church, Los Angeles. "History of the First AME Church." Typescript, ca. 1992.

Fisher, Lloyd H. *The Problem of Violence: Observations on Race Conflict in Los Angeles.* Washington, D.C.: American Council on Race Relations, 1947.

Flamming, Douglas. "African-Americans and the Politics of Race in Progressive-Era Los Angeles." In *California Progressivism Revisited,* edited by William Deverell and Tom Sitton, 203–228. Berkeley: University of California Press, 1994.

———. "Becoming Democrats: Liberal Politics and the African American Community in Los Angeles, 1930–1965." In *Seeking El Dorado: African Americans in California,* edited by Lawrence B. de Graaf, Kevin Mulroy, and Quintard Taylor, 279–308. Seattle: University of Washington Press, 2001.

Fogelson, Robert M. *The Fragmented Metropolis: Los Angeles, 1850–1930.* 1967. Reprint, with new preface and foreword, Berkeley: University of California Press, 1993.

———. *The Los Angeles Riots.* Salem, N.H.: Ayer, 1969.

Foley, Neil. *The White Scourge: Mexicans, Blacks, and Poor Whites in Texas Cotton Culture.* Berkeley: University of California Press, 1997.

Formisano, Ronald. *Boston Against Busing: Race, Class, and Ethnicity in the 1960s and 1970s.* Chapel Hill: University of North Carolina Press, 1991.

Frazier, E. Franklin. *The Negro Church in America.* New York: Schocken, 1966.

———.*The Negro Family in the United States.* Chicago: University of Chicago Press, 1939.

———. *Negro Youth at the Crossways: Their Personality Development in the Middle States.* 1940. Reprint, New York: Schocken, 1967.

———. *On Race Relations: Selected Writings.* Edited by G. Franklin Edwards. Chicago: University of Chicago Press, 1968.

García, Mario T. "Americans All: The Mexican American Generation and the Politics of Wartime Los Angeles." *Social Science Quarterly* 65 (June 1984): 278–289.

———. *Memories of Chicano History: The Life and Narrative of Bert Corona.* Berkeley: University of California Press, 1994.

Garreau, Joel. *Edge City: Life on the New Urban Frontier.* New York: Anchor Books, 1992.

Glaberman, Martin. "Walter Reuther and the Decline of the American Labor Movement." *International Journal of Politics, Culture, and Society* 11 (Fall 1997): 73–99.

Gluck, Sherna Berger. *Rosie the Riveter Revisited: Women, the War, and Social Change.* Boston: Twayne, 1987.

Goldfield, Michael. *The Color of Politics: Race and the Mainsprings of American Politics.* New York: The New Press, 1997.

Goodman, James. *Stories of Scottsboro.* New York: Vintage Books, 1995.

Gottlieb, Peter. *Making Their Own Way: Southern Blacks' Migration to Pittsburgh, 1916–1930.* Urbana: University of Illinois Press, 1987.

Governor's Commission on the Los Angeles Riots. *Transcripts, Depositions, Consultants' Reports, and Selected Documents of the Governor's Commission on the Los Angeles Riots.* Los Angeles, 1966.

———. *Violence in the City—An End or a Beginning? A Report.* Los Angeles, 1965.

Grant, David M., Melvin L. Oliver, and Angela D. James. "African Americans: Social and Economic Bifurcation." In *Ethnic Los Angeles,* edited by Roger Waldinger and Mehdi Bozorgmehr, 379–408. New York: Russell Sage Foundation, 1996.

Greene, Lorenzo J. "Sidelights on Houston Negroes as Seen by an Associate of Dr. Carter G. Woodson in 1930." In *Black Dixie: Afro-Texan History and Culture in Houston,* edited by Howard Beeth and Cary D. Wintz, 134–154. College Station: Texas A&M University Press, 1992.

Greer, Scott. "The Participation of Ethnic Minorities in the Labor Unions of Los Angeles County." Ph.D. diss., University of California, Los Angeles, 1952.

Grossman, James R. *Land of Hope: Chicago, Black Southerners, and the Great Migration.* Chicago: University of Chicago Press, 1989.

Gutiérrez, David G. *Walls and Mirrors: Mexican Americans, Mexican Immi-*

grants, and the Politics of Ethnicity. Berkeley: University of California Press, 1995.

"Half a Million Workers." *Fortune* 23, March 1941.

Halpern, Rick. *Down on the Killing Floor: Black and White Workers in Chicago's Packinghouses, 1904–1954.* Urbana: University of Illinois Press, 1997.

Halpern, Rick, and Roger Horowitz. *Meatpackers: An Oral History of Black Packinghouse Workers and Their Struggle for Racial and Economic Equality.* New York: Twayne, 1996.

Hayashi, Brian Masaru. *"For the Sake of Our Japanese Brethren": Assimilation, Nationalism, and Protestantism Among the Japanese of Los Angeles, 1895–1942.* Stanford: Stanford University Press, 1995.

Healey, Dorothy Ray, and Maurice Isserman. *California Red: A Life in the American Communist Party.* Urbana: University of Illinois Press, 1993.

Hiestand, Dale L. *Economic Growth and Employment Opportunities for Minorities.* New York: Columbia University Press, 1964.

Hill, Herbert. *Black Labor and the American Legal System: Race, Work, and the Law.* 1977. Reprint, Madison: University of Wisconsin Press, 1985.

———. "Race, Ethnicity, and Organized Labor: The Opposition to Affirmative Action." *New Politics* 1 (1987): 31–82.

———. "Racism Within Organized Labor: A Report of Five Years of the AFL-CIO, 1955–1960." *Journal of Negro Education* 30 (Spring 1961): 109–118.

Himes, Chester. *If He Hollers, Let Him Go.* Garden City, N.Y.: Doubleday, Doran, 1945.

———. *Lonely Crusade.* 1947. Reprint, New York: Thunder's Mouth Press, 1975.

———. *The Quality of Hurt: The Early Years.* Vol. 1 of *The Autobiography of Chester Himes.* 1972. Reprint, New York: Paragon House, 1990.

———. "Zoot Riots Are Race Riots." *The Crisis,* July 1943, 200–201.

Hine, Leland D. *Baptists in Southern California.* Valley Forge, Penn.: Judson Press, 1966.

Hirsch, Arnold R. *Making the Second Ghetto: Race and Housing in Chicago, 1940–1960.* Chicago: University of Chicago Press, 1998.

Hise, Greg. "Home Building and Industrial Decentralization in Los Angeles: The Roots of the Postwar Urban Region." *Journal of Urban History* 19 (February 1993): 95–125.

———. "Industry and Imaginative Geographies." In *Metropolis in the Making: Los Angeles in the 1920s,* edited by Tom Sitton and William Deverell, 13–44. Berkeley: University of California Press, 2001.

———. *Magnetic Los Angeles: Planning the Twentieth-Century Metropolis.* Baltimore: Johns Hopkins University Press, 1997.

Hofsommer, Don L. *The Southern Pacific, 1901–1985.* College Station: Texas A&M University Press, 1986.

Honey, Michael K. *Southern Labor and Black Civil Rights: Organizing Memphis Workers.* Urbana: University of Illinois Press, 1993.

Horne, Gerald. *Fire This Time: The Watts Uprising and the 1960s.* Charlottesville: University Press of Virginia, 1995.

Housing Authority of the City of Los Angeles. *Handbook of General Information*. Los Angeles, 1953.

———. "The Housing Authority of the City of Los Angeles Presents a Solution." Los Angeles, 1943.

Hudson, Karen E. *Paul R. Williams, Architect: A Legacy of Style*. New York: Rizzoli, 1993.

Institute of Industrial Relations at the University of California, Los Angeles. *Hard-Core Unemployment and Poverty in Los Angeles*. Washington, D.C.: GPO, 1965.

Jamal, Hakim A. *From the Dead Level: Malcolm X and Me*. London: Andre Deutsch, 1971.

Jeansonne, Glen. *Gerald L. K. Smith, Minister of Hate*. New Haven, Conn.: Yale University Press, 1988.

Jencks, Christopher, and Paul E. Peterson, eds. *The Urban Underclass*. Washington, D.C.: Brookings Institution, 1991.

Johnson, Charles. "Industrial Survey of the Negro Population of Los Angeles, California, Made by the Department of Research and Investigations of the National Urban League." Los Angeles: Urban League, 1926.

———. "Negro Workers in Los Angeles Industries." *Opportunity*, August 1928, 234–240.

———. *Source Material for Patterns of Segregation, Houston, TX*. New York: International Microfilm Press.

Johnson, James H., Jr., and Curtis C. Roseman. "Increasing Black Outmigration from Los Angeles: The Role of Household Dynamics and Kinship Systems." *Annals of the Association of American Geographers* 80 (June 1990): 205–222.

Johnson, Marilynn S. *The Second Gold Rush: Oakland and the East Bay in World War II*. Berkeley: University of California Press, 1993.

Jones, Marcus E. *Black Migration in the United States with Emphasis on Selected Central Cities*. Saratoga, Calif.: Century Twenty One Publishing, 1980.

Kasarda, John D. "The Jobs-Skills Mismatch." *New Perspectives Quarterly* 7 (Fall 1990): 34–37.

———. "Urban Change and Minority Opportunities." In *The New Urban Reality*, edited by Paul E. Peterson, 33–67. Washington, D.C.: Brookings Institution, 1985.

Katz, Michael B., ed. *The "Underclass" Debate: Views from History*. Princeton: Princeton University Press, 1993.

Katzman, David M. *Before the Ghetto: Black Detroit in the Nineteenth Century*. Urbana: University of Illinois Press, 1973.

Kelley, Robin D. G. *Hammer and Hoe: Alabama Communists During the Great Depression*. Chapel Hill: University of North Carolina Press, 1990.

———. *Race Rebels: Culture, Politics, and the Black Working Class*. New York: Free Press, 1994.

———. "'We Are Not What We Seem': Rethinking Black Working-Class Opposition in the Jim Crow South." *Journal of American History* 80 (June 1993): 75–112.

Kilgore, Thomas, and Jini Kilgore Ross. *A Servant's Journey: The Life and Work of Thomas Kilgore*. Valley Forge, Penn.: Judson Press, 1998.

Klarman, Michael J. "How *Brown* Changed Race Relations: The Backlash Thesis." *Journal of American History* 81 (June 1994): 81–118.

Klein, Norman M., and Martin J. Schiesl. *Twentieth Century Los Angeles: Power, Promotion, and Social Conflict*. Claremont, Calif.: Regina Books, 1990.

Kling, Rob, Spencer Olin, and Mark Poster, eds. *Postsuburban California: The Transformation of Orange County Since World War II*. Berkeley: University of California Press, 1991.

Knight, Frederick. "Justifiable Homicide, Police Brutality, or Governmental Repression?" *Journal of Negro History* (Spring 1994): 182–197.

Korstad, Robert, and Nelson Lichtenstein. "Opportunities Found and Lost: Labor, Radicals, and the Early Civil Rights Movement." *Journal of American History* 75 (December 1988): 786–811.

Kusmer, Kenneth L. "African Americans in the City Since World War II: From the Industrial to the Post-Industrial Era." *Journal of Urban History* 21 (May 1995): 458–504.

———. *A Ghetto Takes Shape: Black Cleveland, 1870–1930*. Urbana: University of Illinois Press, 1976.

Lansing, John B. *Automobile Ownership and Residential Density*. Ann Arbor: Survey Research Center, Institute for Social Research, 1967.

Laslett, John H. M., and Mary Tyler. *The ILGWU in Los Angeles, 1907–1988*. Inglewood, Calif.: Ten Star Press, 1989.

Leader, Leonard. *Los Angeles and the Great Depression*. New York: Garland, 1991.

Lemann, Nicholas. *The Promised Land: The Great Black Migration and How It Changed America*. New York: Knopf, 1991.

Lemke-Santangelo, Gretchen. *Abiding Courage: African American Migrant Women and the East Bay Community*. Chapel Hill: University of North Carolina Press, 1996.

Leonard, Kevin Allen. "Federal Power and Racial Politics in Los Angeles During World War II." In *Power and Place in the North American West*, edited by Richard White and John M. Findlay, 87–116. Seattle: University of Washington Press, 1999.

———. "'In the Interests of All Races': African Americans and Interracial Cooperation in Los Angeles During and After World War II." In *Seeking El Dorado: African Americans in California*, edited by Lawrence B. de Graaf, Kevin Mulroy, and Quintard Taylor, 309–342. Seattle: University of Washington Press, 2001.

———. "Years of Hope, Days of Fear: The Impact of World War II on Race Relations in Los Angeles." Ph.D. diss., University of California, Davis, 1992.

Levenstein, Harvey A. *Communism, Anti-Communism, and the CIO*. Westport, Conn.: Greenwood Press, 1981.

Lewis, David Levering. *W. E. B. Du Bois, A Biography of a Race: 1868–1919*. New York: Henry Holt, 1993.

Lichtenstein, Nelson. *Labor's War at Home: The CIO in World War II*. Cambridge: Cambridge University Press, 1982.

Lipsitz, George. *Rainbow at Midnight: Labor and Culture in the 1940s*. Urbana: University of Illinois Press, 1994.

Lo, Clarence Y. *Small Property Versus Big Government: The Social Origins of the Tax Revolt*. Berkeley: University of California Press, 1990.

Long, Herman H., and Charles Johnson. *People vs. Property? The Restrictive Covenant in Housing*. Nashville: Fisk University Press, 1947.

Los Angeles Board of Education. *Chronology of Los Angeles City Schools*. Los Angeles, 1961.

Los Angeles Board of Harbor Commissioners. *Annual Report of the Board of Harbor Commissioners of the City of Los Angeles, California, Fiscal Year July 1, 1946, to June 30, 1947*. Los Angeles, 1947.

Los Angeles County Board of Supervisors. *Iron and Steel Industry of Los Angeles County*. Los Angeles, 1945.

Los Angeles County Chamber of Commerce. *Facts About Industrial Los Angeles: Nature's Workshop*. Los Angeles: Chamber of Commerce, 1927.

———. *General Industrial Report of Los Angeles County: Advantages of Los Angeles*. Los Angeles: Chamber of Commerce, 1927.

———. *Industrial Establishments in Los Angeles County Employing 25 or More Persons*. Los Angeles: Chamber of Commerce, 1952.

———. *Industrial Survey: Los Angeles–Long Beach Harbor District*. Los Angeles: Chamber of Commerce, 1936.

———. *Notes on Business Trends Within Southern California*. Los Angeles: Chamber of Commerce, March 1963.

———. *Our Manpower Problems in the Postwar Years: A Survey and Analysis Showing Where War Industry Employees Want to Live and Work in the Postwar Period*. Los Angeles: Chamber of Commerce, 1944.

———. *Statistical Record of Los Angeles County Industrial Development: Summary on an Annual Basis for Years 1929–1944*. Los Angeles: Chamber of Commerce, 1945.

Los Angeles County Housing Authority. *Real Property Inventory and Low Income Housing Area Survey of a Portion of Los Angeles County, California, 1939–1940*. Los Angeles, 1939.

Los Angeles Department of City Planning. *West Adams–Baldwin Hills–Leimert Socio-Economic Analysis*. Los Angeles, 1971.

Los Angeles Unified School District. "Profile of LAUSD Student Enrollment, 1966–1999." In *Los Angeles Unified School District, Ethnic Survey Report, 1999*. Los Angeles, 1999.

Lotchin, Roger W. *Fortress California, 1910–1961: From Warfare to Welfare*. New York: Oxford University Press, 1992.

Marx, Gary T. *Protest and Prejudice: A Study of Belief in the Black Community*. New York: Harper and Row, 1967.

Massey, Douglas S. "Effects of Socioeconomic Factors on the Residential Segregation of Blacks and Spanish Americans in U.S. Urbanized Areas." *American Sociological Review* 44 (December 1979): 1015–1022.

———. "Residential Segregation of Spanish Americans in U.S. Urbanized Areas." *Demography* 16 (November 1979): 553–563.

Massey, Douglas S., and Nancy A. Denton. *American Apartheid: Segregation and the Making of the Underclass.* Cambridge: Harvard University Press, 1993.

Mazon, Mauricio. *The Zoot-Suit Riots: The Psychology of Symbolic Annihilation.* Austin: University of Texas Press, 1984.

McGovney, D. O. "Racial Residential Segregation by State Court Enforcement of Restrictive Agreement, Covenants, or Conditions in Deeds Is Unconstitutional." *California Law Review* 33 (1945): 7–11.

McKinnon, Jesse. *The Black Population, 2000.* Washington, D.C.: GPO, 2001.

McWilliams, Carey. "The Evolution of Sugar Hill." *Script,* March 1949, 24–35.

———. *Southern California: An Island on the Land.* 1946. Reprint, Santa Barbara, Calif.: Peregrine Smith, 1973.

Meier, August, and Elliot Rudwick. *Black Detroit and the Rise of the UAW.* New York: Oxford University Press, 1979.

Milkman, Ruth. *Gender at Work: The Dynamics of Job Segregation by Sex During World War II.* Urbana: University of Illinois Press, 1987.

Miller, Loren. *The Petitioners: The Story of the Supreme Court of the United States and the Negro.* Cleveland: World Publishers, 1967.

Miller, Sally M., and Daniel A. Cornford, eds. *American Labor in the Era of World War II.* Westport, Conn.: Greenwood Press, 1995.

Mingus, Charles. *Beneath the Underdog: His World as Composed by Mingus.* 1971. Reprint, New York: Penguin Books, 1982.

Modell, John. *The Economics and Politics of Racial Accommodation: The Japanese of Los Angeles, 1900–1942.* Urbana: University of Illinois Press, 1977.

Mohl, Raymond. "Miami: The Ethnic Cauldron." In *Sunbelt Cities: Politics and Growth Since World War II,* edited by Richard M. Bernard and Bradley R. Rice, 58–91. Austin: University of Texas Press, 1983.

Monroy, Douglas. *Rebirth: Mexican Los Angeles from the Great Migration to the Great Depression.* Berkeley: University of California Press, 1999.

———. *Thrown Among Strangers: From Indians to Mexicans on the Landscape of Southern California, 1769–1900.* Berkeley: University of California Press, 1990.

Moore, Shirley Ann Wilson. *To Place Our Deeds: The African American Community in Richmond, California, 1910–1963.* Berkeley: University of California Press, 2000.

Mortimer, Wyndham. *Organize! My Life as a Union Man.* Edited by Leo Fenster. Boston: Beacon Press, 1971.

Myers, Dowell. "Actual Percentage Growth for Non-Hispanic Blacks by County, 1990–2000." Population Dynamics Research Group, School of Policy, Planning, and Development, University of Southern California, Los Angeles, 22 April 2002.

————. "Special Report: Demographic and Housing Transitions in South Central Los Angeles, 1990 to 2000." Population Dynamics Research Group, School of Policy, Planning, and Development, University of Southern California, Los Angeles, April 2001.

Myrdal, Gunnar. *An American Dilemma: The Negro Problem and Modern Democracy.* New York: Harper and Brothers, 1944.

Nash, Gerald D. *The American West in the Twentieth Century: A Short History of an Urban Oasis.* Englewood Cliffs, N.J.: Prentice-Hall, 1973.

————. *The American West Transformed: The Impact of the Second World War.* Bloomington: Indiana University Press, 1985.

National Association for the Advancement of Colored People. *West Coast Regional Conference, 1947, Report of the Resolutions Committee, San Francisco, March 7–8.* San Francisco: NAACP, 1947.

National Association of Real Estate Boards, Committee on Professional Standards. *Interpretations of the Code of Ethics.* Chicago: National Association of Real Estate Boards, 1964.

National Committee Against Discrimination in Housing. *In These Ten Cities.* Washington, D.C.: National Committee Against Discrimination in Housing, 1951.

National Negro Congress, Los Angeles Council. *Jim Crow in National Defense.* Los Angeles: National Negro Congress, 1940.

Nelson, Bruce. "Class and Race in the Crescent City: The ILWU, from San Francisco to New Orleans." In *The CIO's Left-Led Unions,* edited by Steve Rosswurm, 19–45. New Brunswick, N.J.: Rutgers University Press, 1992.

————. "The 'Lords of the Docks' Reconsidered: Race Relations Among West Coast Longshoremen, 1933–1961." In *Waterfront Workers: New Perspectives on Race and Class,* edited by Calvin Winslow, 155–192. Urbana: University of Illinois Press, 1998.

————. "Organized Labor and the Struggle for Black Equality in Mobile During World War II." *Journal of American History* 80 (December 1993): 952–988.

————. *Workers on the Waterfront: Seamen, Longshoremen, and Unionism in the 1930s.* Urbana: University of Illinois Press, 1988.

Nicolaides, Becky M. *My Blue Heaven: Life and Politics in the Working-Class Suburbs of Los Angeles, 1920–1965.* Chicago: University of Chicago Press, 2002.

Norrell, Robert J. "Caste in Steel: Jim Crow Careers in Birmingham, Alabama." *Journal of American History* 73 (December 1986): 669–694.

Northrup, Herbert. *The Negro in the Aerospace Industry.* Racial Policies of American Industry, Report no. 2, Wharton School of Finance and Commerce. Philadelphia: University of Pennsylvania Press, 1968.

————. *The Negro in the Automobile Industry.* Racial Policies of American Industry, Report no. 1, Wharton School of Finance and Commerce. Philadelphia: University of Pennsylvania Press, 1968.

————. *The Negro in the Rubber Tire Industry.* Racial Policies of American Industry, Report no. 6, Wharton School of Finance and Commerce. Philadelphia: University of Pennsylvania Press, 1969.

Oliver, Melvin L., and Thomas M. Shapiro. *Black Wealth/White Wealth: A New Perspective on Racial Inequality.* New York: Routledge, 1995.

Orfield, Gary. "Ghettoization and Its Alternatives." In *The New Urban Reality,* edited by Paul E. Peterson, 161–193. Washington, D.C.: Brookings Institution, 1985.

Osofsky, Gilbert. *Harlem: The Making of a Ghetto—Negro New York, 1890–1930.* New York: Harper and Row, 1968.

Otis, Johnny. *Upside Your Head! Rhythm and Blues on Central Avenue.* Hanover, N.H.: University Press of New England, 1993.

Parson, Don. "The Development of Redevelopment: Public Housing and Urban Renewal in Los Angeles." *International Journal of Urban and Regional Research* 6 (1982): 393–419.

———. *Making a Better World: Public Housing and the Direction of Modern Los Angeles.* University of Minnesota Press, forthcoming.

Pascoe, Peggy. "Miscegenation Law, Court Cases, and Ideologies of 'Race' in Twentieth-Century America." *Journal of American History* 83 (June 1996): 44–69.

Patterson, William, ed. *We Charge Genocide: The Crime of Government Against the Negro People.* New York: Civil Rights Congress, 1951.

Payne, J. Gregory, and Scott C. Ratzan. *Tom Bradley: The Impossible Dream.* Santa Monica, Calif.: Roundtable Publishing, 1986.

Perry, Louis B., and Richard S. Perry. *A History of the Los Angeles Labor Movement, 1911–1941.* Berkeley: University of California Press, 1963.

Perry, Pettis. *Negro Representation: A Step Towards Negro Freedom.* New York: New Century, 1952.

———. *Pettis Perry . . . Speaks to the Court: Opening Statement to the Court and Jury in the Case of the Sixteen Smith Act Victims in the Trial at Foley Square, New York.* New York: New Century, 1952.

Peterson, Paul E., ed. *The New Urban Reality.* Washington, D.C.: Brookings Institution, 1985.

Philpott, Thomas L. *The Slum and the Ghetto: Neighborhood Deterioration and Middle-Class Reform, Chicago, 1880–1930.* New York: Oxford University Press, 1978.

Pinkney, Alphonso. "Prejudice Toward Mexican and Negro Americans: A Comparison." *Phylon* 24 (Winter 1963): 253–259.

Pitt, Leonard. *The Decline of the Californios: A Social History of the Spanish Speaking Californians, 1846–1890.* Berkeley: University of California Press, 1966.

President's Committee on Civil Rights. *To Secure These Rights: The Report of the President's Committee on Civil Rights.* Washington, D.C.: GPO, 1947.

Putnam, Jackson K. *Modern California Politics: 1917–1980.* San Francisco: Boyd and Fraser, 1980.

Quam-Wickham, Nancy L. "Who Controls the Hiring Hall? The Struggle for Job Control in the ILWU During World War II." In *The CIO's Left-Led*

Unions, edited by Steve Rosswurm, 47–67. New Brunswick, N.J.: Rutgers University Press, 1992.

"The Race Problem at Swimming Pools." *American City* 47 (August 1932): 76–77.

"The Race War That Flopped: Little Tokyo and Bronzeville Upset Predictions of Negro-Nisei Battle," *Ebony* 1, July 1946, 3–7.

Raftery, Judith Rosenberg. *Land of Fair Promise: Politics and Reform in Los Angeles Schools, 1885–1941.* Stanford: Stanford University Press, 1992.

Rainwater, Lee, and William L. Yancey. *The Moynihan Report and the Politics of Controversy.* Cambridge: MIT Press, 1967.

Reagan, Ronald. "California and the Problem of Government Growth." In *A Time for Choosing: The Speeches of Ronald Reagan, 1961–1982,* by Ronald Reagan. Chicago: Regnery Gateway, 1983.

Record, Wilson. *The Negro and the Communist Party.* 1951. Reprint, Westport, Conn.: Greenwood Press, 1980.

Reed, Merl. "The FEPC, the Black Worker, and the Southern Shipyards." *South Atlantic Quarterly* 74 (Autumn 1975): 446–467.

———. *Seedtime for the Modern Civil Rights Movement: The President's Committee on Fair Employment Practice, 1941–1946.* Baton Rouge: Louisiana State University Press, 1991.

Report of the National Advisory Commission on Civil Disorders, 1968. New York: Bantam Books, 1968.

"Resolution Defining Policy with Regard to Colored Members." *Boilermakers Journal* 56 (March 1944): 73, 76, 79.

Rieder, Jonathan. *Canarsie: The Jews and Italians of Brooklyn Against Liberalism.* Cambridge: Harvard University Press, 1985.

Ritter, Lawrence S. *Lost Ballparks: A Celebration of Baseball's Legendary Fields.* New York: Viking, 1992.

Robinson, Duane. *Chance to Belong: Story of the Los Angeles Youth Project, 1943–1949.* New York: Woman's Press, 1949.

Rodwin, Lloyd, and Hidehiko Sazanami, eds. *Deindustrialization and Regional Economic Transformation: The Experience of the United States.* Boston: Unwin Hyman, 1989.

Roseman, Curtis C., and Seong Woo Lee. "Linked and Independent African American Migration from Los Angeles." *Professional Geographer* 50 (May 1998): 204–214.

Rosswurm, Steve, ed. *The CIO's Left-Led Unions.* New Brunswick, N.J.: Rutgers University Press, 1992.

Rowan, Richard L. *The Negro in the Steel Industry.* Racial Policies of American Industry, Report no. 3, Wharton School of Finance and Commerce. Philadelphia: University of Pennsylvania Press, 1968.

Rubin, Lester. *The Negro in the Longshore Industry.* Racial Policies of American Industry, Report no. 29, Wharton School of Finance and Commerce. Philadelphia: University of Pennsylvania Press, 1974.

———. *The Negro in the Shipbuilding Industry.* Racial Policies of American Industry, Report no. 17, Wharton School of Finance and Commerce. Philadelphia: University of Pennsylvania Press, 1970.

Ruggles, Steven, Matthew Sobek, et. al. *Integrated Public Use Microdata Series: Version 2.0.* Minneapolis: Historical Census Projects, University of Minnesota, 1997.

Sánchez, George J. *Becoming Mexican American: Ethnicity, Culture, and Identity in Chicano Los Angeles, 1900–1945.* New York: Oxford University Press, 1993.

Schiesl, Martin. "The Struggle for Equality: Racial Reform and Party Politics in California, 1950–1966." *California Politics and Policy,* 55–65. Los Angeles: Edmund G. "Pat" Brown Institute of Public Affairs, 1997.

Schwartz, Harvey, ed. "A Long Struggle for Equality: The Mexican American Longshoremen of Local 13, 1934–1975." *Dispatcher,* April 1999, 7.

———. "Violence, Struggle, and Victory: San Pedro in '34." *Dispatcher,* December 1994, 6.

———. "Walter Williams: The Fight for Black Equality on the L.A. Waterfront, Longshore Local 13, 1943–1970." *Dispatcher,* February 1999, 6–7.

Scott, Allen J. "The Manufacturing Economy: Ethnic and Gender Divisions of Labor." In *Ethnic Los Angeles,* edited by Roger Waldinger and Mehdi Bozorgmehr, 215–246. New York: Russell Sage Foundation, 1996.

Sears, David O. *Los Angeles Riot Study: Political Attitudes of Los Angeles Negroes.* Los Angeles: Institute of Government and Public Affairs, University of California, Los Angeles, 1967.

Sears, David O., and Jack Citrin. *Tax Revolt: Something for Nothing in California.* Cambridge: Harvard University Press, 1982.

Sears, David O., and John B. McConahay. *The Politics of Violence: The New Urban Blacks and the Watts Riot.* Boston: Houghton Mifflin, 1973.

Security-First National Bank of Los Angeles. *Monthly Summary of Business Conditions in Southern California.* 1949–1959.

Sitton, Tom, and William Deverell, eds. *Metropolis in the Making: Los Angeles in the 1920s.* Berkeley: University of California Press, 2001.

Sleeper, Jim. *The Closest of Strangers: Liberalism and the Politics of Race in New York.* New York: Norton, 1990.

Soja, Edward W. *Postmodern Geographies: The Reassertion of Space in Critical Social Theory.* London: Verso, 1989.

Soja, Edward, Rebecca Morales, and Goetz Wolff. "Urban Restructuring: An Analysis of Social and Spatial Change in Los Angeles." *Economic Geography* 59 (1983): 195–230.

Soja, Edward W., and Allen J. Scott. *The City: Los Angeles and Urban Theory at the End of the Twentieth Century.* Berkeley: University of California Press, 1996.

Sonenshein, Raphael J. "Coalition Building in Los Angeles: The Bradley Years and Beyond." In *Seeking El Dorado: African Americans in California,* edited by Lawrence B. de Graaf, Kevin Mulroy, and Quintard Taylor, 450–474. Seattle: University of Washington Press, 2001.

————. *Politics in Black and White: Race and Power in Los Angeles*. Princeton: Princeton University Press, 1993.

South Central Area Welfare Planning Council. *Watts Area Study, 1959: A Report*. Los Angeles: South Central Area Welfare Planning Council, 1959.

Southern California Research Council. *Help Wanted: Manpower Outlook for the Los Angeles Area in the 1960s*. Los Angeles: SCRC, 1957.

————. *The Next Fifteen Years, 1955–1970: The Los Angeles Metropolitan Area*. Los Angeles: SCRC, 1955.

Spero, Sterling D., and Abraham L. Harris. *The Black Worker: The Negro and the Labor Movement*. New York: Columbia University Press, 1931.

Squires, Gregory D., et al. *Chicago: Race, Class, and the Response to Urban Decline*. Philadelphia: Temple University Press, 1987.

Stack, Carol. *Call to Home: African Americans Reclaim the Rural South*. New York: Basic Books, 1996.

Stein, Judith. "Opening and Closing Doors." *Labor History* 39 (February 1998): 52–57.

————. *Running Steel, Running America: Race, Economic Policy, and the Decline of Liberalism*. Chapel Hill: University of North Carolina Press, 1998.

Stimson, Grace Heilman. *Rise of the Labor Movement in Los Angeles*. Berkeley: University of California Press, 1955.

Sugrue, Thomas J. *The Origins of the Urban Crisis: Race and Inequality in Postwar Detroit*. Princeton: Princeton University Press, 1996.

Taeuber, Karl E., and Alma Taeuber. *Negroes in Cities: Residential Segregation and Neighborhood Change*. Chicago: Aldine, 1965.

Taylor, Quintard. *The Forging of a Black Community: Seattle's Central District, From 1870 Through the Civil Rights Era*. Seattle: University of Washington Press, 1994.

————. *In Search of the Racial Frontier: African Americans in the American West, 1528–1990*. New York: Norton, 1998.

Thomson, Bailey, and Patricia L. Meador. *Shreveport: A Photographic Remembrance, 1873–1949*. Baton Rouge: Louisiana State University Press, 1987.

Trotter, Joe William, Jr. *Black Milwaukee: The Making of an Industrial Proletariat, 1915–1945*. Urbana: University of Illinois Press, 1985.

————, ed. *The Great Migration in Historical Perspective: New Dimensions of Race, Class, and Gender*. Bloomington: Indiana University Press, 1991.

Tuttle, William M., Jr. *Race Riot: Chicago in the Red Summer of 1919*. New York: Atheneum, 1984.

Tyson, Timothy B. "Robert F. Williams, 'Black Power,' and the Roots of the African American Freedom Struggle." *Journal of American History* 85 (September 1998): 540–570.

Underwood, Katherine. "Pioneering Minority Representation: Edward Roybal and the Los Angeles City Council, 1949–1962." *Pacific Historical Review* 66 (August 1997): 399–425.

U.S. Bureau of the Census. *Fifteenth Census of the United States: 1930. Population*, vol. 4. Washington, D.C.: GPO, 1933.

———. *Sixteenth Census of the United States: 1940. Population,* vol. 2, *Characteristics of the Population.* Washington, D.C.: GPO, 1943.

———. *Sixteenth Census of the United States: 1940. Population,* vol. 3, *The Labor Force.* Washington, D.C.: GPO, 1943.

———. *Sixteenth Census of the United States: 1940. Population and Housing: Statistics for Census Tracts.* Washington, D.C.: GPO, 1942.

———. *Census of Housing: 1950.* Vol. 1, *General Characteristics.* Washington, D.C.: GPO, 1951.

———. *Census of Population: 1950.* Vol. 2, *Characteristics of the Population.* Washington, D.C.: GPO, 1952.

———. *Census of Population: 1950.* Vol. 4, *Special Reports.* Washington, D.C.: GPO. 1956.

———. *Census of Population: 1950. Census Tract Statistics.* Washington, D.C.: GPO, 1952.

———. *U.S. Census of Population: 1950. Special Reports: Population Mobility—Farm-Nonfarm Movers: 1949 Residence of the Population by Age, Marital Status, Education, Employment Status, Occupation, Family Income, Etc.* Washington, D.C.: GPO, 1957.

———. *Census of Population, 1960.* Vol. 1, *Characteristics of the Population.* Washington, D.C.: GPO, 1963.

———. *U.S. Censuses of Population and Housing: 1960. Census Tracts.* Washington, D.C.: U.S. Bureau of the Census, 1962.

———. *Census of Population, 1970.* Vol. 1, *Characteristics of the Population.* Washington, D.C.: GPO, 1971.

———. *1970 Census of Population and Housing: Census Tracts, Los Angeles–Long Beach, California, Standard Metropolitan Statistical Area.* Washington, D.C.: GPO, 1972.

———. *1980 Census of Population.* Vol. 1, *Characteristics of the Population.* Washington, D.C.: GPO, 1983.

———. *1980 Census of Population and Housing: Census Tracts, Los Angeles–Long Beach, California, Standard Metropolitan Statistical Area.* Washington, D.C.: GPO, 1982.

———. *County and City Data Book Consolidated File, County Data, 1947–1977.* Ann Arbor, Mich.: Inter-University Consortium for Political and Social Research, 1980.

———. *Historical Statistics of the United States, Colonial Times to 1970.* 2 vols. Washington, D.C.: GPO, 1975.

———. *Negroes in the United States, 1920–1932.* Washington, D.C.: GPO, 1935.

———. *Negro Population in the United States, 1790–1915.* New York: Arno Press, 1968.

———. *Special Census of Los Angeles, California.* Washington, D.C.: GPO, 1946.

U.S. Commission on Civil Rights. *Hearings Held in Los Angeles and San Francisco, 25–28 January 1960.* Washington, D.C.: GPO, 1960.

———. *The Mexican American.* Washington, D.C.: GPO, 1968.

————. *Mexican Americans and the Administration of Justice in the Southwest.* Washington, D.C.: GPO, 1970.

U.S. Committee for Congested Production Areas. *Final Report: December, 1944.* Washington, D.C.: GPO, 1944.

————. *Observations on the Sample Census in the Congested Production Areas, 1944.* Series CA-2, no. 1–10. Washington, D.C.: GPO, 1944.

U.S. Congress. *Proceedings and Debates of the 92nd Congress.* Vol. 18, pt. 1. Washington, D.C.: GPO, 1972.

U.S. Department of Justice, Federal Bureau of Investigation. *Uniform Crime Reports.* Washington, D.C.: GPO, 1943–1950.

U.S. Department of Labor, Office of Policy Planning and Research. *The Negro Family: The Case for National Action.* Washington, D.C.: GPO, 1965.

U.S. Equal Employment Opportunity Commission. *Job Patterns for Minorities and Women in Private Industry, 1966.* Equal Employment Opportunity Report no. 1. Washington, D.C.: GPO, 1966.

U.S. Senate Committee on Labor and Public Welfare. *Expand the War on Poverty: Hearings Before the Select Subcommittee on Poverty of the Committee on Labor and Public Welfare.* 89th Cong., 1st sess., 1965.

Viehe, Fred W. "Black Gold Suburbs: The Influence of the Extractive Industry on the Suburbanization of Los Angeles, 1890–1930." *Journal of Urban History* 8 (November 1981): 3–26.

Vorspan, Max, and Lloyd P. Gartner. *History of the Jews in Los Angeles.* San Marino, Calif.: Huntington Library, 1970.

Waldinger, Roger. "Who Makes the Beds? Who Washes the Dishes? Black/Immigrant Competition Reassessed." In *Immigrants and Immigration Policy: Individual Skills, Family Ties, and Group Identities,* edited by Harriet Orcutt Duleep and Phanindra V. Wunnava, 265–306. London: JAI Press, 1996.

Waldinger, Roger, and Mehdi Bozorgmehr, eds. *Ethnic Los Angeles.* New York: Russell Sage Foundation, 1996.

Warren, William. "Asian Populations in Los Angeles County." Ph.D. diss., University of California, Los Angeles, 1985.

Watts Labor Community Action Committee. *1967 Report.* Los Angeles: WLCAC, 1967.

Watts Writers' Workshop. *From the Ashes: Voices of Watts.* Edited and with an introduction by Budd Schulberg. New York: New American Library, 1967.

Welfare Planning Council. *Compton: A Community in Transition—A Needs and Resources Study of the Compton Area.* Los Angeles: Welfare Planning Council, 1962.

————, Los Angeles Region. *A Profile of Four Communities: Compton, Pacoima, Wilmington, Willowbrook.* Los Angeles: Welfare Planning Council, 1962.

Wilburn, James. "Social and Economic Aspects of the Aircraft Industry in Metropolitan Los Angeles During World War II." Ph.D. diss., University of California, Los Angeles, 1971.

Wild, Mark H. "A Rumored Congregation: Cross-Cultural Interaction in the Immigrant Neighborhoods of Early Twentieth Century Los Angeles." Ph.D. diss., University of California, San Diego, 2001.

Wilkinson, Frank. "And Now the Bill Comes Due." *Frontier,* October 1965, 1–2.

Williamson, Joel. *A Rage for Order: Black-White Relations in the American South Since Emancipation.* New York: Oxford University Press, 1986.

Wilson, Don J. "An Historical Analysis of the Black Administrator in the Los Angeles Unified School District." Ph.D. diss., University of California, Los Angeles, 1972.

Wilson, James Q. *The Amateur Democrat: Club Politics in Three Cities.* Chicago: University of Chicago Press, 1962.

———. *Negro Politics: The Search for Leadership.* Glencoe, Ill.: Free Press, 1960.

Wilson, William Julius. *The Declining Significance of Race: Blacks and Changing American Institutions.* Chicago: University of Chicago Press, 1978.

———. *The Truly Disadvantaged: The Inner City, the Underclass, and Public Policy.* Chicago: University of Chicago Press, 1987.

———. "The Urban Underclass in Advanced Industrial Society." In *The New Urban Reality,* edited by Paul E. Peterson, 129–160. Washington, D.C.: Brookings Institution, 1985.

———. *When Work Disappears: The World of the New Urban Poor.* New York: Knopf, 1996.

Winslow, Calvin, ed. *Waterfront Workers: New Perspectives on Race and Class.* Urbana: University of Illinois Press, 1998.

Wollenberg, Charles. "*James vs. Marinship:* Trouble on the New Black Frontier." *California History* 60, no. 3 (Spring 1981): 262–279.

———. "Working on El Traque: The Pacific Electric Strike of 1903." *Pacific Historical Review* 42 (August 1973): 358–369.

Yokota, Kariann. "From Little Tokyo to Bronzeville and Back: Ethnic Communities in Transition." M.A. thesis, University of California, Los Angeles, 1996.

Youth Opportunities Board of Greater Los Angeles. "The Los Angeles War on Poverty: A Proposal Submitted for Funding to the Office of Economic Opportunity." Los Angeles, 1964.

Yu, Eui-Young, Earl H. Phillips, and Eun Sik Yang, eds. *Koreans in Los Angeles: Prospects and Promises.* Los Angeles: Center for Korean-American and Korean Studies, California State University, Los Angeles, 1982.

Zarefsky, David. *President Johnson's War on Poverty: Rhetoric and History.* Tuscaloosa: University of Alabama Press, 1986.

Index

Text:	10/13 Galliard
Display:	Galliard
Compositor:	G&S Typesetters, Inc.
Printer and binder:	Thomson-Shore, Inc.